THE
ADONIS
COMPLEX

How to Identify, Treat, and Prevent Body Obsession in Men and Boys

HARRISON G. POPE, JR., M.D.

KATHARINE A. PHILLIPS, M.D.

ROBERTO OLIVARDIA, PH.D.

A Touchstone Book
Published by Simon & Schuster
NEW YORK   LONDON   TORONTO   SYDNEY   SINGAPORE

TOUCHSTONE
Rockefeller Center
1230 Avenue of the Americas
New York, NY 10020

First Touchstone Edition 2002
TOUCHSTONE and colophon are registered trademarks
of Simon & Schuster, Inc.
For information about special discounts for bulk purchases,
please contact Simon & Schuster Special Sales:
1-800-456-6798 or business@simonandschuster.com

Designed by Robert Bull Design

Manufactured in the United States of America

1   3   5   7   9   10   8   6   4   2

The Library of Congress has cataloged the Free Press edition as follows:

Pope, Harrison.
The Adonis complex : the secret crisis of male body obsession / Harrison G. Pope, Jr.,
Katharine A. Phillips, Roberto Olivardia.
p.   cm.
Includes bibliographical references and index.
1. Body image in men.   2. Self-esteem in men.   I. Phillips, Katharine A.   II. Olivardia,
Roberto, 1972–   III. Title.

BF697.5.B635   2000   00-025243
155.3'32—dc21

ISBN: 978-0-684-86911-7
ISBN: 0-684-86911-X (Pbk)
Page 287 constitutes an extension of the copyright page.

This page constitutes an extension of the copyright page.

PERMISSION ACKNOWLEDGMENTS

Tables on page 28 adapted from data presented in *Psychology Today* magazine; reprinted with permission from *Psychology Today* magazine, copyright © 1997 Sussex Publishers, Inc.

Figures on pages 64, 65, and 66 adapted with permission from Dr. Timothy S. Olds, International Society for the Advancement of Kinanthropometry.

Table on page 184 adapted with permission from S. J. Paxton et al., "Body Image Satisfaction, Dieting Beliefs, and Weight Loss Behaviors in Adolescent Girls and Boys," *Journal of Youth and Adolescence* 20 (1991):361–379; Plenum Press.

Diagnostic criteria in Appendix II for Anorexia Nervosa, Binge Eating Disorder, and Body Dysmorphic Disorder reprinted with permission from the Diagnostic and Statistical Manual of Mental Disorders, Fourth Edition. Copyright 1994 American Psychiatric Association.

PHOTO CREDITS

Venus and Adonis by Titian. Prado Museum, Madrid, Spain.
Used by permission of Scala/Art Resource, NY.
The photographs on pages 37, 38, 39 (lower right), 41, 42, 43, 44, and 45
used by permission of Captured Moments dba
Photo Quick, Waltham, Massachusetts.
Photograph of Steve Reeves, taken by Tony Lanza in 1947.
Chicago–Mr. America Contest. Used by permission of Steve Reeves.
Photograph on page 39 (lower left) used by permission of Doris
Barrilleaux, Riverview, Florida.
Playgirl magazine centerfold photographs furnished by
Playgirl magazine. Copyright © Playgirl, Inc.
"The Men of Chippendales" used by permission
of Photofest, Inc., New York.
"Fake it" advertisement provided by The Body Shop.

Note to the Reader

Throughout this book, we have taken care to preserve the confidentiality of patients and research subjects. Therefore, all persons referred to by their first names in this book have been disguised in terms of identifying characteristics, or represent composites of more than one individual. Similarly, the Olympic Gym in Chapter 1 is not the real name of an actual facility; instead, it is a fictitious name of a facility that is intended to represent many such facilities throughout the country.

Also in this book, we discuss research findings indicating to us that there is a limit to the degree of muscularity that men can attain without the use of anabolic steroids or other performance-enhancing drugs. On the basis of this research, we believe that most men who exceed this limit probably have used such drugs, and we have stated this opinion at many points in the book. Nevertheless, we do not intend to assert by these statements that any specific individual has used anabolic steroids or other drugs, since the possibility exists that some exceptional men may exceed these limits of muscularity even without drug use.

Contents

Acknowledgments

The ingenuity, skill, and dedication of many scientific researchers, from college undergraduates to senior professors, contributed to the studies that form the core of this book. In our work on muscle dysmorphia, we are particularly indebted to Dr. Amanda Gruber for her many insights and her pivotal role in designing the computerized Body Image Test. Drs. James Hudson and Precilla Choi also contributed greatly both to this work and to much of our research on anabolic steroids. For the steroid research, we also thank many other collaborators, especially Dr. Elena Kouri, Dr. David Katz, and Paul Oliva. Two of our students, Richard Leit and Geoffrey Cohane, provided key ideas and hours of hard work on several projects. Jay Borowiecki, our research assistant, has worked steadily at our side throughout the last two years, especially in our field studies of the computerized Body Image Test and the Adonis Complex Questionnaire.

In Austria, Dr. Barbara Mangweth has collaborated with us since the early 1990s on studies of eating disorders in men and on subsequent studies comparing body image in Europe and the United States. Professor Wilfried Biebl, Dr. Armand Hausmann, and Dr. Christine deCol have also contributed to our work in Austria. Professor Roland Jouvent, Dr. Jean-Paul Mialet, and Benjamin Bureau made possible our studies of body image in Paris.

For our work on body dysmorphic disorder, we are indebted to many people who have worked with us over the years, including Drs. Ralph Albertini, Susan McElroy, Steven Rasmussen, Paul Keck, Lawrence Price, Andrew Nierenberg, Raymond Dufresne, Katherine Atala, Eric Hollander, Gopinath Mallya, Michael Jenike, Craig Gunderson, Richard O'Sullivan, Jane Eisen, and Jon Grant.

Even though they did not collaborate with us directly, countless other scientists have offered us guidance and consultation at all stages of our work. Among many such individuals, we particularly thank Drs. Kirk Brower, Don Catlin, Robert Klitzman, William Pollack, Jack Mendelson, and Martin Keller.

We are indebted to Mr. Colin Angle for his expertise with the programming of our computerized Body Image Test. We also thank the many nonscientists who helped us, especially Mr. Steve Reeves, who kindly provided his photograph for our book; Ms. Aimee Szparaga, chief editor of *Playgirl* magazine, who offered the pictures of the *Playgirl* centerfold men; and Mr. Patrick Keogan, who gave us invaluable insights about the nutritional supplement business.

We thank the institutions and organizations that have provided funding and facilities for our work. These include the National Institute of Mental Health, the National Institute on Drug Abuse, the National Alliance for Research on Schizophrenia and Depression, Butler Hospital and Brown University School of Medicine (Providence, R.I.), McLean Hospital (Belmont, Mass.), and Harvard Medical School. We also acknowledge the pharmaceutical companies that have contributed funding to our work on treatment of eating disorders, body dysmorphic disorder, and associated psychiatric conditions. Finally, we also thank the private donors whose gifts over the years to our research fund have made possible many of our initial studies of body image problems.

We also thank those who offered comments and support during our drafting of this book, including Dr. Ralph Albertini, Harry Phillips, William Phillips, Carol Phillips Ewin, Dr. H. Graham Pope, Mary Pope, Kimberly Pope, Hilary Pope, Sharon Olivardia, Jorge Olivardia, and Adi Olivardia. We also particularly thank Courtney Pope, who inspired the research on action toys.

We especially appreciate the advice of Todd Shuster, our literary agent, and Philip Rappaport, our editor. Both helped us to steadily refine and clarify our message as we attempted to translate a mass of scientific research and years of clinical impressions into a form that would be interesting and accessible to a wide variety of readers.

Most of all, we thank the thousands of boys and men who have volunteered as participants in our many research studies over the last fifteen years. The requirements of confidentiality preclude our listing their names, but our gratitude goes out to all of them. In addition, we thank our many clinical patients; they have given us the privilege of learning about their lives and have taught us much about the psychological and social forces that we describe in this book. We also thank the many women—mothers, wives, and girlfriends—who have deepened our insight about the effects of the Adonis Complex on the boys and men they love. Finally, we thank the countless boys and men, especially friends from the gym, who have provided so many of the anecdotes in these pages. They, too, must remain anonymous—but we hope that they will enjoy seeing in print some of the colorful stories they have shared with us throughout the years.

Preface

There's a widespread crisis among today's boys and men—a crisis that few people have noticed. Men of all ages, in unprecedented numbers, are preoccupied with the appearance of their bodies. They almost never talk openly about this problem, because in our society, men have been taught that they aren't supposed to be hung up about how they look. But beneath the tranquil surface, we see signs of this crisis everywhere. Millions of men are sacrificing important things in their lives to exercise compulsively at the gym, hoping for a bigger chest or a flatter stomach. Men and young boys alike are buying billions of dollars worth of "muscle-building" food supplements and diet aids. As many as three million men have taken anabolic steroids or other dangerous black-market drugs to buff up their bodies. An equally large, even more secret group of men has developed eating disorders—compulsive binge eating, dieting, and exercise rituals—that even their girlfriends or wives may not know about. Another million or more men have developed "body dysmorphic disorder," an excessive preoccupation with perceived flaws in their appearance. They worry, for example, that their hair is thinning, their breasts are fat, or their penis is too small. Each year, hundreds of thousands of men seek out cosmetic surgery, from hair replacement to liposuction. They've spent billions of dollars on products to smooth their skin or otherwise improve their appearance. Unlike healthy men and boys, they have an unrealistic view of how they should look—and so they may abuse drugs, exercise excessively, and spend billions on products that are often worthless.

These many different body obsessions are all forms of what we call the "Adonis Complex." It's a problem that affects even teenagers and young boys. Recent studies have shown that as early as elementary school, many boys are already dissatisfied with their bodies, and as a result may suffer loss of self-esteem or depression. Some go on in adolescence to take anabolic steroids, develop eating disorders, or experience other psychiatric conditions involving body image. Parents, teachers, and coaches are usually unaware of these problems because boys, like adult men, don't spontaneously talk about their appearance concerns. In our society, "real boys" aren't supposed to worry about such things. Parents don't ask, and boys don't tell.

Why are boys' and men's body-appearance disorders so underrecognized? One answer is that both scientific researchers and the popular press have assumed for decades that body image problems and eating disorders were women's illnesses. Men have been overlooked. Another answer is that men with body image preoccupations often don't reveal their problems for fear that they will be considered "effeminate" or "gay." Yet another reason is that much of the male body image crisis is new. It's just in the last twenty years or so that we've seen a huge rise in compulsive exercising, soaring rates of anabolic steroid use, exploding sales of nutritional supplements, proliferating cosmetic treatments for men, and the birth of dozens of magazines and other publications devoted to male "fitness" and "health." In this book, we'll discuss how and why these dramatic changes have come about.

For a long time, even we as scientists didn't recognize the extent of this new obsession with appearance. Our awareness emerged gradually as we did research studies and saw patients who suffered with these kinds of concerns. At first, none of the three of us planned to focus our studies on men's body image. For years we had studied eating disorders—but this work initially focused on women. We did many studies on the abuse of anabolic steroids but at first did not realize how closely this form of drug use was linked to body image concerns. We also published many papers on body dysmorphic disorder, bringing this disorder to the attention of professionals and the public. One of us (Dr. Phillips) wrote the only book on this topic, *The Broken Mirror: Understanding and Treating Body Dysmorphic Disorder.* Gradually, in our research work and our clinical practices at Harvard and Brown Medical Schools, we began to recognize how much these problems affected not only women but also men—men with workout addictions, men with binge-eating and sometimes even self-induced vomiting, men whose lives had become dominated by preoccupations with their hair, skin, or other body areas. We saw men, and even teenagers as young as 14 or 15, who had used large doses of anabolic steroids and other body-shaping drugs. As we talked to these men and boys and began to learn about their lives, the pieces came together. The common thread in their stories was an excessive, yet secretive, concern with body image. Realizing how these problems in men had gone largely unnoticed, each of us began to focus more of our work on men. In addition, recognizing how complementary our research was, we began to collaborate on interview studies of men with various types of body image problems. One was muscle dysmorphia, a new syndrome in which boys and men believe that they aren't muscular enough. They have no idea of how they really look. When these men look in the mirror they think that they look small and frail, even though they're actually big—a sort of "anorexia nervosa in reverse."

The popular press began to take notice. When, for example, we wrote about "muscle dysmorphia," to our amazement scores of journalists sought us out to interview us about this syndrome. Our research on other aspects of the Adonis Complex evoked a similar response. We had hit a nerve. The public—and we along with them—had finally awakened to a serious threat to the health of men and boys, a threat as dangerous as anorexia and bulimia for women and girls.

And so, we decided to step out of the laboratory and put our knowledge together into a popular book. We want to tell these men and the people who love them—women, parents of growing boys, and partners of gay men—that they no longer need to suffer alone, that the Adonis Complex—this secret crisis of male body obsession—afflicts millions in our society and around the world. This problem, we believe, is created by biological and psychological forces that combine with modern society's and the media's powerful and unrealistic messages emphasizing an ever-more-muscular, ever-more-fit, and often-unattainable male body ideal.

We're not questioning that it's good for boys and men to work out, eat a healthy diet, pay attention to grooming, and want to look their best. But the need to push beyond what's healthy and reasonable can have a devastating impact on emotional and physical development in the young, and on well-being for men of all ages. With this book, we hope to alert everyone to these consequences of the Adonis Complex before it's too late.

In this book's initial chapters, we discuss the surprisingly broad scope of the crisis and its roots. We provide two new body image tests that readers can take to determine whether they have the Adonis Complex. We describe different types of body image problems, in both their milder and more severe forms, telling the stories of many men with these concerns. We then focus on aspects of the Adonis Complex of special interest to parents, to women, and to gay men. We end the book with suggestions on how to cope with the Adonis Complex and the preoccupations, low self-esteem, and shame that it can cause. With these approaches, the burden of the Adonis Complex can often be lifted from men's shoulders.

CHAPTER ONE

Secrets of the Men
at the Olympic Gym

It is 6 P.M. on a warm spring evening in a small city ten miles west of Boston. In an industrial park near the highway, the two-storied, white-brick Olympic Gym is surrounded by nearly half an acre of parking, but the lot is overflowing with cars. Some are old Fords and Chevys belonging to students at the nearby college; others are the pickups and delivery trucks of tradesmen and service men who've stopped to lift weights after work. There are also pristine Corvettes and Porsches, a Mercedes or two, and half a dozen BMWs. Every social class in America has come here to work out.

Inside, the frenetic beat of "Get Ready for This" is punctuated by the occasional clanging of a weight stack on a machine, or a 45-pound plate being loaded onto a bar. Although the gym has half an acre of floor space, it still seems crowded. Groups of weightlifters cluster around the cables and the squat racks; others wait to use the lat pull-down machine or the Roman chair. A blond-haired twenty-six-year-old trainer instructs a prominent Boston attorney on the fine points of abdominal exercises. The gym's owner is out on the floor, giving a tour of the facilities to two young high school students who want to sign up. Wide-eyed and slightly frail-looking, they glance furtively at two big bodybuilders doing shoulder presses at the dumbbell rack nearby. Dozens of treadmills, Stair-Masters, stationary bicycles, and ergometers hum and whir on the balcony overhead. At the front counter, a handsome, highly muscular staff member, still in his teens, smiles brightly and mixes protein shakes in a blender as groups of clients joke together, read magazines, and search for their car keys among the hundreds of key rings hanging on the big pegboard on the wall. And this is only the evening crowd. At five-thirty tomorrow morning, twenty or thirty people will line up at the door, waiting eagerly for the gym to open. A hundred more will show up over the next couple of hours to lift weights before work. They will be followed by dozens of lunchtime regulars, with many stragglers in between.

The Olympic Gym has 2,400 members, and it is only one of several gyms in this small city of 60,000. All over the United States, in small towns, suburbs, and cities, big gyms like this one have their own large and faithful followings. In greater Boston alone, the major gyms collectively count well over 100,000 members—and some metropolitan areas have far more. As recently as twenty or thirty years ago, you would hardly ever see a crowd like this at any gym, with the possible exception of a few hard-core bodybuilding establishments in Southern California. But over the last two decades, gym memberships have exploded across America.

More than two-thirds of the people working out at the Olympic Gym tonight are men. Some wear old T-shirts and dirty cutoff shorts; others are carefully dressed in striped workout pants and Olympic Gym sweatshirts; a few wear deep-cut tank tops and tight spandex shorts, carefully chosen to show off their musculature. But the "muscleheads" are only a small minority of the gym community. Most of the members are ordinary-looking guys: they're a slice of America, ranging from squeaky-voiced boys of twelve or thirteen to gray-haired elders in their seventies.

You would think that the men at the Olympic Gym, or any gym, would be happy with their bodies. After all, they're here getting in shape rather than vegetating on the couch watching TV after work. But surprisingly, many aren't content at all. Many, in fact, harbor nagging anxieties about how they look. They don't talk about it publicly—and they may not even admit it to themselves—but they suffer silently from chronic shame and low self-esteem about their bodies and themselves. And many are obsessed with trying to change how they look. Beneath the seemingly benign exterior of this scene at Olympic, and among millions of other men around the country, a crisis is brewing.

If we begin to look carefully around the gym, we see hints of this crisis everywhere. John and Mark, both twenty-four-year-old graduate students at a nearby university, are at the counter debating what kinds of protein supplements to buy from the bewildering display of boxes that crowd the wall. Many of the boxes boast "supermale" images: photographs of smiling bodybuilders with massive shoulders, rock-hard pectorals, and impossibly sculptured and chiseled abdominal muscles. All of the supermales exude health, power, and sexuality. Not even the biggest bodybuilder at the Olympic Gym resembles these images, and John and Mark don't come close—even though they've been lifting weights for years and have spent thousands of dollars on nutritional supplements they hoped would thin their waists, stomachs, and buttocks, while swelling their chests, arms, and thighs. Privately, John and Mark are slightly embarrassed that they don't even begin to look like the guys in the pictures. But they've never admitted these concerns to anyone.

Supermale images appear not only on the boxes of protein powder, but throughout the gym. They're on magazine covers in the waiting area, on posters on the walls, and on a clothes advertisement posted on the bulletin board. John examines a magazine showing amazing "before" and "after" pictures of a middle-aged man who appears to have transformed in three months from a couch potato into a muscle-bound hunk, allegedly with the help of the food supplement advertised. John has tried a lot of food supplements himself, and he wonders why he still hasn't achieved the same Herculean image. All of these displays convey the same message to men: *If you're a real man, you should look bigger and better than you do.*

While John may feel as though he's the only guy at the gym who's so worried about his appearance and size, in reality he's surrounded by many others with similar secret feelings. But lost in his own thoughts of insecurity, John doesn't seem to notice all the other men who are covertly checking out their reflections in the big mirrors that line the walls. When they're sure that nobody is looking, some flex their arms, puff out their chests, or suck in their stomachs, almost as a reflex gesture. They don't say anything, of course. But many, like John, can't stop thinking about the discrepancy between the image in the mirror and the one they desperately want.

Alan, a math teacher from nearby Cambridge, notices, for the tenth or the twentieth time that day, the stubborn ring of fat that has accumulated around his abdomen in the years since college. Bob, a truckdriver, wears a baseball cap with the visor turned back, even though he's thirty-eight years old and the baseball-cap look is usually reserved for teenagers. But he'd rather wear the cap than expose his "prematurely" receding hairline. Meanwhile, John himself wears three layers of shirts— a T-shirt, then a regular shirt on top, and then a sweatshirt on top of that. He's sweating inside all of those layers, but they make him look bigger, and he's ashamed of how small he'd look without them. Bertrand, an attorney in his fifties who arrived a few minutes earlier in an immaculate, six-foot-high sport utility vehicle, despondently eyes his unappealing reflection in the mirror next to the drinking fountain. Above the drinking fountain, a poster of a famous bodybuilder twice his size, majestically posing on a rocky summit in the desert, stares back at him.

These are men who have achieved success in their careers; some are leaders in their community. They come from different classes, races, and sociological backgrounds. But they are all victims of a relentless message: *You don't look good enough.* Most of the time, men are unable to talk to each other about this message and the inferiority it makes them feel. So the message gets louder, the problem becomes bigger, and the isolation grows deeper.

Three college students arrive and head into the locker room. They're laughing and joking with each other, exchanging gossip about a party last weekend, while they get ready to go out onto the gym floor. But once they're in the locker room, none of them actually takes off his clothes in front of the others. Although they haven't shared their feelings with one another, one of the young men is terribly ashamed of the acne scars on his back. Another is convinced he's too fat, and he's especially upset at the "female" fat that he thinks has accumulated under his nipples. The third privately worries that his penis is too small. Even though they've been good friends for years, none of these young men has felt comfortable enough to reveal these secret concerns to any other person.

MALE BODY IMAGE OBSESSION:
A TROUBLING DOUBLE BIND

In our research at Harvard and Brown Medical Schools, and in studies collaborating with scientists across the country and overseas, the three of us have met countless otherwise "normal" boys and men who share these same feelings of inadequacy, unattractiveness, and even failure. By interviewing hundreds of men working out at gyms, and compiling our collective clinical experience with the hundreds more who have seen us at our offices, we've learned that men like John, Alan, Bob, Bertrand, and the three college students represent a broad and growing group who feel insecure and anxious—even paralyzed—by how they look. Society is telling them now, more than ever before, that their bodies define who they are as men. Because they find it impossible to meet this supermale standard, they are turning their anxiety and humiliation inward.

On the surface, most of the boys and men we've talked with, and the millions of other men like them across the country and around the globe, lead what appear to be regular, well-adjusted lives. In fact, the vast majority would never dream of going to see a mental health professional. But behind the smiling, behind the cheerful athletic bravado, many of these men worry about their looks and their masculinity. Some are even clinically depressed, and many are intensely self-critical. Because these men carry a secret that they're uncomfortable sharing even with their closest loved ones, their self-doubts can become almost toxic, insidiously eating away at their self-esteem and self-confidence as men.

Indeed, many of these men, we believe, are caught in a double bind they can neither understand nor escape. On the one hand, they're increasingly surrounded with media images of masculine perfection—not just here in the gym, but in advertisements, on television, in the movies. And if this alone weren't enough to make them feel inadequate about their bodies, they're also bombarded with messages from burgeoning multibillion-dollar industries that capitalize upon their body insecurities. These "male body image industries"—purveyors of food supplements, diet aids, fitness programs, hair-growth remedies, and countless other products—now prey increasingly on men's worries, just as analogous industries have preyed for decades on the appearance-related insecurities of women.

But the problem gets compounded further. Women, over the years, have gradually learned—at least to some extent—how to confront society's and the media's impossible ideals of beauty. Many women can now recognize and voice their appearance concerns, speaking openly about their reactions to these ideals, rather than letting them fester inside. But men still labor under a societal taboo against expressing such feelings. Real men aren't supposed to whine about their looks; they're not even supposed to worry about such things. And so this "feeling and talking taboo" adds insult to injury: to a degree unprecedented in history, men are being made to feel more and more inadequate about how they look—while simultaneously being prohibited from talking about it or even admitting it to themselves.

And so, trapped between impossible ideals on the one side and taboos against feeling and talking on the other, millions of boys and men are suffering. For some, body image concerns have grown into outright psychiatric disorders, ruining their own lives and often the lives of those who care about and love them. And for every boy or man with a full-scale body image disorder, there are many more with milder cases of the same body obsessions—not disabling in any way, but still enough to hurt.

THE ADONIS COMPLEX:
MEN UNHAPPY WITH THEIR BODIES

We call this syndrome the "Adonis Complex." In Greek mythology, Adonis was half man and half god—the ultimate in masculine beauty. So beautiful was his body that he won the love of Aphrodite, queen of the gods. But Persephone, who had raised Adonis, refused to give him up to Aphrodite. So Zeus, the king of the gods, brokered a deal: Adonis would spend four months out of every year in the underworld with Persephone, four months with Aphrodite, and four months on his own. It is said that he chose to spend his own personal four months with Aphrodite as well.

Throughout the centuries, many a great artist has attempted to depict the physical perfection of Adonis. Most famously, the Renaissance painter Titian shows him about to go hunting with his dogs, with Aphrodite clutching his body in her arms. The body of Adonis presumably represents the ultimate male physique imaginable to a sixteenth-century artist—but Titian's Adonis looks fat and out of shape in comparison to the men pictured on the boxes of protein powder at the Olympic Gym.

We should note that "Adonis Complex" isn't an official medical term, and it doesn't describe any one body image problem of men. We use it in this book to refer to an array of usually secret, but surpris-

Venus and Adonis *by Tiziano Vecellio di Gregorio (Titian).*

ingly common, body image concerns of boys and men. These concerns range from minor annoyances to devastating and sometimes even life-threatening obsessions—from manageable dissatisfaction to full-blown psychiatric body image disorders. In one form or another, the Adonis Complex touches millions of boys and men—and inevitably, the women in their lives.

Nowadays, it seems, increasing numbers of boys and men, including some of those lifting weights tonight at the Olympic Gym, have become fixated on achieving a perfect, Adonis-like body. Take Scott, for example. He's a twenty-six-year-old personal trainer at the gym. Right now, he isn't training anybody because it's his own time to lift. He's just started his leg routine—three sets of squats, two sets of leg presses, two or three sets of leg extensions on a Nautilus machine, three sets of leg curls on another machine, and then on to some hack squats, leg abductions, and side leg raises. The whole routine will take him an hour and a half, and then he still has to do his calves for another half hour after that. He's working out alone, because he doesn't like any distractions to come between him and the weights.

To a casual observer, Scott seems like a perfect picture of fitness and health. Five feet nine inches tall, with shortly cropped dark brown hair and handsome facial features, Scott weighs 180 pounds and has only 7 percent body fat, making him leaner than at least 98 percent of American men his age. Beneath his worn gray sweatpants and sweatshirt, he has the proportions of a Greek statue. He has a 31-inch waist, a "six-pack" of sculptured abdominal muscles, a 46-inch chest, and shoulders as big as grapefruits. But surprisingly, and unknown to even many of his closest friends, Scott constantly fears that he isn't big enough.

As a result, Scott has surprisingly low self-esteem. He puts all his hopes and dreams into his workouts and not into his daily life. This makes him withdraw from others and hold himself back from social situations he would otherwise enjoy. Although women are enormously attracted to Scott, he secretly thinks he isn't really big enough or masculine enough to appeal to them. In fact, he doesn't have a girlfriend right now, partly because his self-image is so poor and his confidence about dating so crippled.

Scott came to see us at our research laboratory in response to a notice we put on the bulletin board at the Olympic Gym, looking for bodybuilders who weren't satisfied with their physiques. In this study, we were comparing male bodybuilders who were insecure about their appearance with those who felt comfortable with how they looked. The study involved an office visit in which we measured each man's height, weight, and body fat, had him fill out some questionnaires, and then interviewed him about his body image and other psychological issues. When Scott arrived for his interview, he was ill at ease, almost embarrassed to be coming to see us for such a study. "You've really had a lot of guys who've called about your ad?" he asked. He was surprised when we told him that we'd already seen many men like himself.

Scott took a chair, seeming a little relieved. He wore loose cotton pants with a drawstring at the waist, and an oversized blue sweatshirt with a bodybuilding logo on the back. The words TAKE NO PRISONERS were emblazoned under a figure of a muscled bodybuilder wearing combat fatigues.

Scott soon grew relaxed and told us his story in a warm, soft-spoken, almost self-effacing manner. An honors graduate of a prestigious New England college and holder of a business degree, Scott was highly educated. But his heart, it turned out, had never been in business.

"I started going to the gym fairly regularly when I was in college," he said. "But I don't think it was until I started business school that it became an obsession. I remember, one day when I was in business school, looking at myself in the mirror and hating how I looked. I started wondering how I'd ever tolerated what I looked like when I was back in college. Gradually, I got more and more fixated on getting my time in the gym each day, and I got more and more impatient with all of the demands at school. The other guys were all talking about companies that they wanted to work for, and how much money they were going to make, but I could never seem to get into it."

By the time Scott graduated from business school, his body obsession dominated his life. "I had several good job offers," he continued, "but I just couldn't picture myself working in an office. I was afraid that if I was forced to sit behind a desk all day, I'd turn into a fat slob. In fact, even at school, I couldn't sit in front of a computer screen for more than about fifteen minutes before I started worrying that I wasn't getting any exercise."

During his graduate studies, Scott worked as a personal trainer at a local health club. After business school, it became his full-time job. "This probably sounds strange," he said, "but it was the only job I could think of that gave me enough time to do my own training."

He paused and studied our faces for several seconds, seeming to fear we would have a negative reaction to what he had said. Instead, we asked questions to hear more about and understand his concerns.

"Did people criticize you for not going on to a business career?" we asked.

"Everybody," he said with resignation. "Especially my mother, and also my girlfriend at that time. They just couldn't understand why I'd throw away my years of education to work at a gym. I guess it does seem a little weird. But I couldn't imagine going back to a business job now. I guess I've just become too wrapped up with working out."

As the interview progressed, Scott began to reveal the full extent of his preoccupations. "If you could see what I was thinking about during the day, ninety percent of the time it would have something to do with either my weightlifting, my diet, or the way I look. I can't go past a mirror without posing just for a minute to check out my body—as long as I'm sure nobody's watching. I even check myself out when I see my reflection in a store window or car window." He laughed nervously. "Sometimes when I'm in a restaurant, I even study my reflection in the back of a spoon."

Most of the time, Scott explained, he sees his reflection as small and puny, even though he's actually massively built. "I know it sounds silly," he said, "but there are times that even on hot summer days, after getting a bad shot of myself in the mirror, I'll put on heavy sweatshirts to cover up my body because I think I don't look big enough." For the same reason, he explained that he almost always wears heavy sweats when working out at the gym. He sometimes even turns down invitations to go to a swimming pool or the beach, for fear that when he takes his shirt off, people will notice him and think he's too small.

"How would you feel if you were forced to miss working out for a day?" we asked.

He looked shocked. "I'd probably go bananas and start breaking things. In fact, one day last winter there was a blizzard and I couldn't get out of my house to go to the gym. I felt trapped. I got so frustrated from not being able to work out that I put on my weight belt and started bench-pressing the furniture in my living room. My girlfriend thought I was crazy."

"Has your relationship with your girlfriend been affected by your weightlifting preoccupations?"

Scott fell silent, and for a brief moment, tears seemed to form in his eyes. "Actually, my girlfriend broke up with me because of my weightlifting. It got to be too much for her. Sarah could never really understand why I needed to go to the gym or why it mattered so much to me what I looked like. I'd ask several times a day whether she thought I looked big enough or muscular enough. I guess she got pretty tired of my asking her. She also complained a lot because she said I was too inflexible. She'd want to go out and do something, and I'd say that I couldn't because I needed to go to the gym and train. But I'd warned her that I was that way. I told her that when we first started living together: the gym comes first, my diet second, and she was third. I guess she couldn't take being in third place anymore. And I don't really blame her.

"It's weird," he continued. "I think the truth is that I actually thought Sarah would break up with me if I didn't work out enough. I actually thought she'd leave me for some bigger guy. But the real reason she left me was because I was so caught up in working out that I didn't do anything or go anyplace with her. She told me that I was screwed up and that our relationship was getting 'lost.' When I think about it, I guess maybe she was right."

"Why do you think you have such intense feelings about your body and about working out?" we asked.

"I don't know. I guess I've really never stopped to think about just how much this muscle thing has affected my life. At first, it was a healthy thing, wanting to pursue a healthy lifestyle and be in shape. But now, it's gotten out of control. It's a trap. I can't get out of it."

"Have you ever considered some type of therapy to look at your feelings about your body?"

"Yeah, I've thought about it sometimes, but it would never work. Someone who doesn't lift weights himself would never understand." As he spoke, Scott flexed his arm unconsciously.

Over the last several years, we've interviewed many men with Scott's condition. We call it "muscle dysmorphia"—an excessive preoccupation with body size and muscularity. Many of these men, like Scott, revealed that this preoccupation had spiraled out of control and profoundly affected their lives—causing them to change their careers, or destroying relationships with people they loved. But practically none of them had sought treatment for their condition—usually because they doubted that any type of professional would actually understand or be able to help them.

MUSCLE DYSMORPHIA: "PUNINESS" IN THE MIND

The body image distortions of men with "muscle dysmorphia" are strikingly analogous to those of women (and some men) with anorexia nervosa. In fact, some people have colloquially referred to muscle dysmorphia as "bigorexia nervosa" or "reverse anorexia." People with anorexia nervosa see themselves as fat when they're actually too thin; people with muscle dysmorphia feel ashamed of looking too small when they're actually big. A recent study of ours illustrates these parallels. In this study, we compared interview and questionnaire responses from twenty-four young men with muscle dysmorphia, recruited from gymnasiums in the Boston area; thirty young men without muscle dysmorphia, recruited from the same gymnasiums; twenty-five college men with eating disorders such as anorexia nervosa and bulimia nervosa (binge eating and vomiting); and twenty-five ordinary college men without eating disorders. On question after question, the men with muscle dysmorphia showed levels of pathology similar to the college men with eating disorders. In particular, the men from these two groups shared a need to exercise every day, shame about their body image, feelings of being too fat, dislike of their bodies, and often, lifetime histories of anxiety and depression. By contrast, the group of weightlifters without muscle dysmorphia closely resembled the ordinary college men on all of these same indices. In other words, men with muscle dysmorphia report that they are suffering just as badly as men with anorexia nervosa.

Also like people with anorexia nervosa, men with muscle dysmorphia often risk physical self-destruction. Frequently, they persist in compulsive exercising despite pain and injuries, or continue on ultra low-fat, high-protein diets even when they are desperately hungry. Many take potentially dangerous anabolic steroids and other drugs to bulk up, all because they think they don't look good enough.

But these men's nagging worries are rarely relieved by increasing their bodybuilding. In psychological terms, we call such persistent worries "obsessions." And in response to these obsessions, people are driven to repetitive behaviors—in Scott's case, constant weightlifting—which, in turn, we call "compulsions." Though people may realize, on one level, that their obsessive beliefs are irrational and their compulsive behaviors futile, they still cannot "shut off" their endless and often self-destructive behaviors. Scott is a case in point. Although his feelings of self-criticism were utterly irrational, Scott was so convinced of his deficiencies that, at the end of the day, he chose catering to his muscle obsession over maintaining his relationship with Sarah.

The sources of Scott's muscle obsessions and weightlifting compulsions are not known with absolute certainty, but most likely are threefold. First, there's almost certainly a genetic, biologically based component. In other words, some people like Scott inherit a chemical predisposition to developing obsessive-compulsive symptoms. But genetics do not act alone. The second likely component is psychological—obsessive and compulsive behavior stems, in part at least, from one's experiences growing up, such as being teased. Scott still remembers being called "dorky" and "wimpy" in school, and these memories still fuel his muscle obsession and his compulsion to work out. And finally, we believe that society plays a powerful and increasing role, by constantly broadcasting messages that "real men" have big muscles—just like the bodybuilders in the pictures on the walls of the Olympic Gym. Men like Scott have been exposed to these images ever since they were small boys, thus laying the groundwork for muscle dysmorphia and other forms of the Adonis Complex in adulthood.

BODY-DISSATISFIED MEN: A SILENT EPIDEMIC

Cases as severe as Scott's may be uncommon. But for every man with severe muscle dysmorphia, dozens of others experience at least some distress about their muscularity. For example, a 1997 study found that an amazing 45 percent of American men were dissatisfied with their muscle tone—almost double the percentage found in the same survey in 1972. Thus, we can calculate that there are presently well over 50 million muscle-dissatisfied men in our country. And these millions of men are surrounded by many millions of very perplexed family members, friends, and loved ones, who probably can't quite understand what this anxiety about bigness and muscles is all about.

Why is muscle dissatisfaction, together with other body-appearance preoccupations, becoming so common among modern men? Our grandfathers didn't seem to worry about how muscular they looked. They didn't do bench presses or abdominal exercises three days a week, or go to the gym to work out on the StairMaster, or worry about their percentage of body fat. Why has the Adonis Complex infected so many men over the last thirty years or so?

One reason is that our grandfathers were rarely, if ever, exposed to the "supermale" images—aside from Charles Atlas on an occasional matchbox cover—that Scott and his friends see every day. In modern society, these images aren't confined to pictures in the gym—they're everywhere. Look at television over the last several decades. The hard-bodied lifeguards in *Baywatch* are viewed by over 1 billion viewers in 142 countries—figures unmatched by any previous television series. Or look at the movies. Hollywood's most masculine men of the 1930s, 1940s, and 1950s—John Wayne, Clark Gable, Gregory Peck—look like wimps in comparison to modern cinema's muscular action heroes—Arnold Schwarzenegger, Sylvester Stallone, or Jean-Claude van Damme. Today, while growing up, a young man is subjected to thousands and thousands of these supermale images. Each image links appearance to success—social, financial, and sexual. But these images have steadily grown leaner and more muscular, and thus more and more remote from what any ordinary man can actually attain. And so society and the media preach a disturbing double message: a man's self-esteem should be based heavily on his appearance, yet by the standards of modern supermale images, practically no man measures up.

It becomes understandable, then, that millions of modern American men are unhappy with how they look. And it isn't surprising that among these millions, we are seeing increasing numbers of serious casualties—men like Scott, whose lives have been damaged by these trends. Growing up in the 1970s and '80s, Scott steadily absorbed the stream of supermale images from the modern media. In fact, he described to us how he watched Rambo movies and Schwarzenegger action thrillers and, even as a child, fantasized that he would someday look like those heroes. Gradually, body appearance became the dominant basis—and ultimately the only basis—for his self-esteem. To lose even a little of that muscle, or to gain even a little body fat, brought him instant shame and humiliation. For Scott, a muscled body became more important, much more important, than being a successful businessman. It became so important that it brought him nearly complete social isolation and even cost him his relationship with the woman he loved.

BILL AND STACY: FALLOUT FROM FAT

Back at the Olympic Gym, another man is suffering from a very different form of the Adonis Complex. Bill is tall, thin, and in his early thirties. He's drenched with sweat after thirty-five minutes of running on the treadmill at seven minutes per mile. He's wondering, at this moment, whether he's run long enough or fast enough, whether he's burned off enough calories to compensate for the food he ate earlier in the day, and whether he still looks a little too fat. And he's already beginning to feel guilty about the eating binge that he knows will happen after he gets home tonight.

On his way home from the gym, Bill will purchase two large Italian submarine sandwiches, two large bags of Doritos, two cans of onion dip, and a quart of chocolate-chip cookie-dough ice cream. After shut-

ting off the ringer on his phone, he'll begin to eat as fast as he can—
sometimes even using both hands to feed himself, grabbing food with his
left while eating from his right. Before he even has a chance to think
about it, nothing will be left but a bunch of empty bags, containers, and
wrappers.

Bill told us about his secret eating binges when he came to see us
for one of our research studies of men with eating disorders. Even
though he knew that we were familiar with this type of problem, it still
took him a long while to let down his guard and tell us the full story.

"As soon as I've finished the last potato chip or the last gulp of ice
cream," he said, "I feel totally guilty and disgusted with myself. I just
can't believe that I've done it again, that I've lost control. When I was
younger, I even tried to make myself vomit in the bathroom after the eating binges. But I wasn't very good at it. Now, I just try to diet in between
the binges. Or I'll go and run some extra miles to try to burn off the
food. Sometimes, I've even gone running at three o'clock in the morning.
No one in the world knows that I do this. For years, I even kept it a secret from my wife. When I didn't show much interest in sex, she kept
thinking I was having an affair. Actually, I was just too caught up in the
binge eating and my weight. I hated the way I looked."

He grew visibly uncomfortable. "It probably sounds ridiculous,
but my food problem ruined my marriage. Early on, we had a really
close relationship—we'd been high school sweethearts and best friends.
I really loved Stacy and felt I was the luckiest guy in the world to be married to her. But when my food problem started, I began to retreat. I re-
treated into this little world where food was really all that mattered,
where I spent my entire day planning my meals and thinking about my
weight. I gradually shut her out even though I really didn't want to. I just
lost control."

Stacy eventually divorced Bill. She never found out that Bill's real
problem was an eating disorder. In fact, she'd thought she was to
blame—that something was wrong with her. Bill had tried to reassure
her that it wasn't her problem, but he was still unable to reveal to her
that the real problem was his chronic feeling of worthlessness. Despite
all of the love he and Stacy shared, Bill felt he wasn't good at anything.
He felt fat, mediocre, and unattractive.

Bill's self-hatred crept up on him insidiously. First, he began to
withdraw from Stacy, his sex drive waning daily. Next he started going
to the gym excessively in an attempt to convert his body into a mass of
muscle. And then he became obsessed with food, so obsessed that it de-
stroyed the most important relationship of his life.

"I loved Stacy so much. I still really love her. I wish I could have her back," he said plaintively. "She was my soul mate. I could tell her a lot of things—except this."

Bill's condition is called "binge-eating disorder." Only recently has this condition been recognized by professionals as an actual psychiatric problem. In fact, Bill told us that for many years he hadn't even known that his peculiar eating pattern had a name. And when he found out, at last, that he wasn't alone with his illness, he refused to see a therapist, or even tell his family doctor.

"I guess I never really wanted to admit that I had a serious eating problem," he said. "I was really ashamed, because I felt that it was a female thing to have eating problems like that. I'd never heard of a man with an eating disorder. I got more and more worried about being too fat. When I was younger, there was a time when it got to the point where I would weigh myself four or five times in a day. Sometimes if I gained even a pound, I would go to the gym or go running because I thought I was getting fatter. But then, half the time, I'd get hungry again, and then I'd go on another eating binge and be right back where I started. I mean, how many guys struggle with that?" Bill took a deep breath and sighed, "I feel I don't measure up."

"Where do you think those feelings come from?" we asked.

"I guess I've pretty much always felt like a failure," Bill explained. "I came from a family with five older sisters and no brothers at all. When I was born, my parents put all their hopes in me."

"That must have been pretty hard on you, being the only son with your parents' high expectations," we offered.

"Well, especially when you understand what my father was like. He was a well-meaning man, but he was very tough with me. He couldn't understand why I was scared to go to school as a child, and he would yell at me until I cried in the morning when I was forced to get on the school bus. I had a lot of little fears like that while I was growing up, and my father just couldn't figure out why I couldn't just instantly overcome them."

"It sounds as though your father put a lot of pressure on you."

"Yes. A lot of pressure—pressure to play sports, pressure to act tough, pressure to be masculine. But it was also about control. He had a pretty hard childhood himself—his father was a violent alcoholic who would get drunk and beat him—so for my father everything had to do with keeping a stiff upper lip and showing no fear."

"And what happened if you failed to meet his expectations?"

"He would just become a horrible person if you didn't do what he wanted or didn't live up to his expectations. He'd say: 'You're such a disappointment' or 'I'm ashamed to be the father of such a little cry baby' or 'You're a spoiled brat.'"

"How did you handle it back then?"

"I don't know. I just recall feeling totally helpless and hopeless. I felt like the world's biggest loser—shy, stupid, ugly, you name it. My mother was always afraid of my father, so she stood behind whatever he did. I felt like there was nowhere to turn."

"Well, it's little wonder that you don't feel completely good about yourself now, as an adult."

"I don't feel good about myself at all. I still feel like that little kid, terrified to get on the school bus with the other kids. Only now, to make matters worse, I also constantly feel as though I'm fat and overweight."

In fact, Bill wasn't fat at all. His body fat measured only 11 percent—making him far leaner than an average American man of his age.

"But you realize that, in reality, you're not fat all?" we asked.

"Yeah, I know, I know. Everybody says that," he admitted. "I look around at other guys and realize that I'm thinner than they are, but it still doesn't make the feelings go away.

"When I was a teenager, I went on this mission to improve my appearance. I started lifting weights and running every day after school. It made me feel good because I felt like I was proving myself to my father. Also, I figured that if I kept it up, I'd be more confident in social situations, because I'd be more muscular and athletic."

Bill went on to describe an episode of depression he experienced during his senior year of high school. He began to feel hopeless about what he would do after graduating. He started sleeping ten or eleven hours each night, he couldn't concentrate on anything, and he felt guilty and down on himself for no reason. "I felt like shit. I couldn't talk to anyone about it. And no one asked about what was going on even though they must have been able to see something was wrong."

Bill suffered through the blackness of the depression for another year, and gradually discovered that exercise made him feel better. But when he went to college, he injured his ankle while running and was forced to stop exercising for many weeks. The depression returned, more severely. About that time, Bill discovered that binge eating would temporarily alleviate his depression.

"It was a high. It kind of numbed me," he said. "All of those messages inside of my head about being too shy, being stupid, being ugly—

for a moment those voices went quiet and I could feel at peace with myself."

At first, Bill binged only occasionally, but gradually he became drawn into a cycle of binge eating, dieting, working out, and binge eating again. This cycle seemed to keep the depression at bay, but increasingly, he became preoccupied that he was getting too fat. He began to weigh himself and look at himself in the mirror more and more often. Soon the thoughts of food, body weight, exercise, and fat came to consume virtually all of his day.

"But I still couldn't talk about it with anybody. I didn't think any of my friends would understand. In fact, I'm surprised I'm here right now. Guys aren't supposed to get all hung up about their appearance."

And so Bill's preoccupations remained secret for years. Despite all of his physical and emotional problems, despite having been severely depressed, Bill's visit to our research laboratory was the first time he'd ever seen a mental health professional—the first time he had ever reached out for help.

SECRET DIETARY RITUALS

Among men suffering from the Adonis Complex, secrets like Bill's are common. Not only does society forbid men to talk about their feelings of vulnerability and inadequacy, but it also indoctrinates them with the idea that only women are supposed to worry about their looks. Men, according to our society, do not—and should not—worry about their appearance or the shape of their bodies. A man who does focus on his appearance is often seen as vain, narcissistic, or "feminine." For a man like Bill, then, a Catch-22 situation arises when he begins to dwell on his body. If he doesn't talk about his feelings, the pain gets internalized and the problem persists. If he does find the courage to do so, society tells him he's being inappropriate, that he's not acting in a healthy, masculine way. Then, of course, he feels worse: more ashamed, more vulnerable, more troubled. The result of this Catch-22 situation is that most men coping with eating disorders simply keep quiet about their painful feelings. No one, therefore, can calculate exactly how many men suffer from covert eating disorders and chronic body image preoccupations like Bill's. But there's little question that today's professionals are seeing cases like his with increasing frequency. In our own clinical practice, more and more men are telling us about their concerns with eating, their bodies, and their appearance. Of course, this raises the question as to

whether eating disorders are actually more common among men nowadays, or whether we are simply becoming more aware of them. We believe that both of these changes have occurred.

Many people, like Bill, still think that eating disorders are "women's
diseases." But binge-eating disorder seems almost as common among
men as among women, with studies in the United States typically showing a ratio of about 40 percent male to 60 percent female. That translates
into a million or more men in America today with binge-eating disorder.
And then, too, there are hundreds of thousands of others who actually
make themselves vomit, or do other drastic things to lose weight after
binges, like taking large doses of laxatives. This disorder, called "bulimia
nervosa," was first recognized in women about twenty years ago, but is
now increasingly being recognized in men. And we're even seeing more
men with anorexia nervosa—dieting to the point of becoming emaci-
ated—even though this condition has traditionally been assumed to affect women almost exclusively.

Furthermore, for every man who suffers from one of these eating
disorders, many others have developed milder but still dysfunctional eating patterns in response to their appearance concerns. In fact, probably
a third of the men in the Olympic Gym are involved in dietary rituals
that affect their day-to-day lives. Jonas, a blond graduate student running on a treadmill, is constantly thinking about the fat content of his
food. Sometimes he'll decline invitations to eat at restaurants for fear
that he won't be able to order anything sufficiently low in fat. Last night,
he went to an ice-cream shop with his girlfriend, but found to his dismay
that they offered only "low-fat" rather than "nonfat" frozen yogurt. A
serving of the "low-fat" yogurt contained only four grams of fat, but he
wouldn't compromise, and ordered nothing at all, even though he was
hungry.

Charles, a businessman in his early forties and an Olympic Gym
"regular," is simultaneously listening to headphones and reading a magazine to distract himself from the tedium of his workout on a StairMaster. Dozens of times per day, he silently laments his slowly enlarging
stomach and "love handles." At breakfast and lunch, he practices a rig-
orous dietary routine, counting every calorie that he consumes, frequently consulting his pocket "calorie counter" book. But invariably,
sometime in the evening, his resolve collapses and he polishes off several
hundred calories worth of M&M's and Tootsie Rolls. Tomorrow, when
he wakes up, he'll resolve to be good—but inevitably, the pattern will re-
peat itself. The StairMaster workouts don't keep up with his candy
habit; as a result, he's wondering about liposuction.

Steve, a thirtyish plumbing contractor, worries mostly about carbohydrates. He religiously uses sugar substitutes in his coffee, drinks only Diet Cokes, and never eats dessert. But most nights, when he gets home, he makes up for his carbohydrate deficit by drinking beer. After four or five beers, totaling 600 to 750 calories, he has more than erased any of the calorie savings that he achieved through carbohydrate restriction during the day. Strikingly, he worries a lot more about the look of his belly than about his level of alcohol consumption.

Armand, a lanky teenager, also suffers from food preoccupations, but he's worried that he's too thin. In an attempt to bulk up, he's constantly counting the grams of protein in everything that he eats; sometimes, in his own words, he'll "force-feed" himself to ensure that he gets at least 150 grams of protein per day. He spends more than $50 per week—a substantial portion of his income—on protein bars, protein shakes, and various other food supplements that he hopes will make him hard and muscular. It seems strange that he should worry, for in reality, Armand is already a gifted athlete, playing varsity soccer and varsity lacrosse at his high school. But he refuses to be happy with his tall, lean body. No one, not even his closest friends, and certainly not his parents, knows how much he secretly despises his appearance. In a vain attempt to quell his anxieties and overcome his own genetics, he keeps stuffing himself with protein. He's heard that excessive protein might be bad for his kidneys over the long term, but his body obsessions today override any concerns about possible damage to his body in the distant future.

The eating patterns of these men can almost all be traced to the Adonis Complex—overconcern, dissatisfaction, or outright obsessions with body image. Men who have eating disorders, especially the more severe forms, may suffer not only from a distorted image of their bodies, but also from a profoundly distorted image of themselves as men. Tragically, they often think that their preoccupations are rare or unique; they have trouble believing that other men around them in the gym could possibly be victims of similar concerns.

Some of the men with more serious eating disorders, like Bill, may also be clinically depressed. With techniques like brief psychotherapy or an antidepressant medication like Prozac, both the depression and the eating disorder—along with the associated nagging preoccupations about fatness and body image—may vanish. But since most of these men don't reveal their symptoms to anyone, they continue to suffer needlessly.

If only we could get out the message to men with eating problems that they are not alone, much of their suffering might be relieved. In the past twenty years, this approach has greatly benefited women. Since the early 1980s, news stories, magazine articles, and books have educated women about binge eating, compulsive dieting, and obesity. As a result, more and more women dared to voice their eating problems. They joined self-help groups, contacted educational organizations devoted to helping women with eating disorders, and sought therapy from knowledgeable professionals. Within less than a decade, practically every young woman in America had heard about eating disorders, knew that they were common, and knew that help was available. If a similar trend could occur for men, then men like Bill might no longer have to suffer in silence.

BIGGER BODIES THROUGH DRUGS

Elsewhere in the Olympic Gym, the Adonis Complex has bred another type of secret. In the free-weight area of the gym, Jerry, Cliff, and Vince, three high school seniors, are busy doing bench presses. All three boys are hoping to enter a local bodybuilding competition this summer, and they're feverishly working out to bulk up. They're enormously muscular, dressed in Olympic Gym sweatpants and stringy tank tops. Their tank tops are ripped, seemingly worn to shreds from long and heavy use. But actually, the rips don't quite look accidental; they're in just the right places to show off their bulging chests and shoulders.

Jerry, Cliff, and Vince are particularly distinctive because their necks and shoulders look unnaturally big in comparison to the rest of their bodies. And for good reason: they *are* unnatural. Over the last several years, these boys have each taken multiple "cycles" of "juice"—drugs known as anabolic steroids. Anabolic steroids are a family of drugs that includes the male hormone, testosterone, as well as numerous synthetic derivatives of testosterone. Steroids have few legitimate medical uses, and doctors won't prescribe them to athletes simply trying to gain muscle. Unless prescribed for specific medical treatment, steroids are illegal in the United States and many other countries. But these drugs are widely available on the black market through underground dealers in gyms everywhere. Taken in pill form or by injection, steroids can allow boys and men to gain huge amounts of muscle, far beyond the limits of muscularity that any ordinary man could attain without these drugs.

Vince, a good-looking boy of average height with wavy sandy-blond hair and dark brown eyes, is on a cycle of steroids right now.

Every three days, he uses a needle to inject himself with almost a teaspoonful of testosterone cypionate, alternating with occasional shots of Equipoise, another anabolic steroid. Actually, Equipoise is a veterinary preparation intended only for horses—but Vince knows that it also works effectively on people, and it's cheaper on the underground market than human steroids. Vince has also managed to score some bottles of Anavar and Hemogenin pills, which he takes on top of his injectable steroids—a standard practice that steroid users call "stacking." The four steroids for this "stack" cost Vince almost all of his savings—$800—and he's considering dealing some steroids to make a profit so he can buy more for his own use.

Amazingly, these boys' parents aren't aware that their sons are taking steroids. They think their sons' muscles are all the result of hard work, good diet, and protein supplements. Like most parents, they don't realize that it's medically almost impossible to get this big without chemical assistance. Our research indicates that there's a fairly sharp limit to the degree of muscularity that a man can attain without drugs. We believe that most boys and men who exceed this limit, and who claim that they did so without drugs, are lying.

Jerry, Cliff, and Vince can't stay this big without continuing to take steroids periodically over the years. And the longer you take steroids, the greater the danger to your body. Many scientific studies, including those from our own laboratory, have shown that steroids decrease the proportion of "good" cholesterol in the bloodstream (technically known as "HDL cholesterol") relative to the "bad" cholesterol (the "LDL cholesterol"). As a result, atherosclerosis, or "hardening of the arteries," speeds up. For every month that you take large doses of steroids, your arteries may "age" by two or three months or even more—scientists don't know for sure. But it certainly appears possible that long-term use of high-dose steroids could take ten or twenty years off your life expectancy, leading to an early death from a heart attack or clogged arteries in the brain.

Vince and his friends know these risks. Vince even witnessed the ominous change in his own cholesterol numbers when he was on steroids, because we actually measured them while he was taking a "cycle." But he tries not to think about the dangers he might face when he's older. Occasionally, he tells us, the risk crosses his mind—but the prospect of never again taking steroids, and gradually losing his muscle size, frightens him a lot more than the prospect of a stroke or heart attack decades in the future. Vince's fear of getting smaller—of no longer feeling strong, confident, and athletically successful—trumps any fears that he might be slowly killing himself.

And steroids aren't the only drugs in the bodybuilding business. Also available from local underground dealers are human growth hormone, thyroid hormones, human chorionic gonadotropin, amphetamines, gamma-hydroxybutyrate, clenbuterol, Nubain, and an array of other drugs. Some of these drugs are legally available only by prescription; others are not marketed for human consumption at all. Jerry, Cliff, and Vince know the names and uses of every one of these black market substances. They've even tried several of them along with their steroids. Each boy owns copies of underground guides on how to use these drugs to increase muscularity and lose body fat.

We know Vince well because he participated in one of our studies of anabolic steroid users. Although the study has been completed, he calls us every few months to find out if we've published any new papers on the subject, and asks us to send him copies. He reads everything he can find—all of the monthly muscle magazines, reports on bodybuilding foods and supplements, anything that contains information about bodybuilding drugs. He knows more about bodybuilding physiology and anabolic steroids than 99 percent of practicing physicians. But then, that's his business—the gym is his world.

When we first asked Vince what prompted him to take steroids, he had no trouble explaining. "I saw what it did for a couple of my friends, and I said, 'I want that for myself.' I was tired of being a small kid and being picked on at school."

"When you first started out taking steroids, did you realize that we scientists still can't estimate the long-term risks?" we asked.

"Yeah, but you can die getting hit by a truck, too," Vince rationalized. "And steroids have done more for me than any other single thing I've done in my life."

"More for you in what way?"

"In making me feel good about myself. In making me self-confident. In making me more confident with girls."

WHAT DO WOMEN REALLY THINK?

Vince's last remark brings to mind another consequence of the Adonis Complex: the strange and striking disparity between men's and women's views of the ideal male body. Recently, we developed a computerized test to look at this difference between the sexes in body perception. In this test, the computer presents an image of a male body, and then invites the user to make the image more or less muscular and more or less fat by using the mouse to click on "buttons" on the screen. The computer then poses a series of questions about body image, and asks the user to choose the body image that best answers each question. When we give the test to men, one of the questions is, "choose the male body image that you think is the most attractive to women." When we give the same test to women, we rephrase the question to read, "choose the male body image that you feel is the most attractive."

In test after test, the results of this comparison have been dramatic. The body that men *think* women like is typically about *15 to 20 pounds more muscular* than what women *actually* like. We've found this discrepancy in our studies of men and women in both the United States and Europe.

If watermelon-sized muscles aren't appealing to most women, why are so many men attempting to get so big? For some men, it's simply an erroneous belief that massive muscles will improve their sex appeal. But for other men, we believe that there may be another, more surprising explanation: a new emotional problem, unique to modern society, that we call "threatened masculinity."

"Threatened masculinity" arises from the long-standing desire of boys and men to establish their "maleness" within their societal group. Throughout most cultures in history, men who exhibited traditional "male" behaviors and who succeeded at traditional "male" pursuits have received approval and respect. But nowadays, what are these male behaviors and pursuits? What can a modern boy or man do to distinguish himself as being "masculine"?

In professional settings, modern women can do almost anything that men can do. Women can fly jet fighters in combat. They can be police captains or brain surgeons or chief executive officers of multinational corporations. Women have penetrated even the most hallowed of male sanctuaries: venerable all-male military schools now accept female cadets, female journalists are allowed into the locker room to interview professional football players, and the all-male club has become nearly extinct. Of course, there's still more work to be done to give women full equality, but women's gains are impressive. As positive as these advances obviously are, however, perhaps they cause some men to wonder, in effect, "What is there left for me to do to distinguish myself as a man?"

For some men, there may be only one such thing: no matter what the triumphs of feminism, no matter what laws are passed to ensure equality between the sexes, no matter what crowning achievements women accomplish, they will never, ever, be able to bench-press 350 pounds.

In other words, muscles are one of the few areas in which men can still clearly distinguish themselves from women or feel more powerful than other men. But muscles are a tenuous foundation on which to base all of one's sense of masculinity and self-esteem.

LESSONS FROM THE LOCKER ROOM

There are at least a hundred other men in the Olympic Gym tonight, and most aren't as badly afflicted with the Adonis Complex as Scott, Bill, and Vince. But as we move back into the locker room, we continue to catch glimpses of men who, to varying degrees, are feeling embarrassed by their bodies. For example, most of the men don't take showers at the gym. They simply pack up and go home. Is it really more convenient to drive all the way home in their sweaty gym clothes than to take a shower in the locker room? How many, in reality, are simply uncomfortable with having their bodies seen in public? Looking around the locker room, we see that even some of the men who are changing their clothes do so quickly, almost furtively, as if they don't want anyone to see them. Here are big, muscular men who seem worried about exposing their bodies to other men. Curiously, the only men who seem unconcerned about taking off their clothes are forty, fifty, or sixty years old. Why are the older men seemingly more comfortable with their bodies than the younger, fitter ones?

Again, this difference between the age groups may be a symptom of important changes in our society and its attitudes toward men and masculinity. When the older men were growing up, in the times of Elvis and carhops and beatniks in the 1950s, or with the Beatles and the flower children of the 1960s, fitness and muscularity weren't a big deal. There were few media images to suggest that body appearance should be the main basis for a man's self-esteem. Steroid use was confined only to a small circle of elite bodybuilders, mostly in Southern California. Men rarely worried about their body fat. Eating disorders, such as binge eating and vomiting, were almost unheard of among males. Admittedly, the young men of the fifties and sixties had their own repertoire of hangups—but embarrassment about their appearance and muscularity wasn't typically one of them.

And so, perhaps, the older men in the locker room today may never have gotten obsessed with their bodies when they were growing up. As a result, they're not embarrassed to be seen naked by other men.

Of course, if we casually asked the younger men in the locker room, they'd probably protest that they're not really worried about their appearance at all. They'd probably provide quick explanations for why they don't need to change their clothes at the gym, or why they plan to take a shower somewhere else. But consciously or unconsciously, they may be more embarrassed about their bodies than they would like to admit. Many are unwitting victims of one aspect of an insidious masculinity code: men aren't supposed to be bothered by preoccupations with their looks. Only women are supposed to get hung up about such things. To speak of anxieties about their bodies or physical appearance, for most men, is to violate the taboo. Many men would far prefer to disavow their worries—thus internalizing their self-criticism—rather than risk the "loss of face" that would come with disclosure.

BECOMING ADONIS: THE IMPOSSIBLE IDEAL

But behind the denials, body concerns have increasingly infected millions of modern American men. For every severe or dangerous case, such as Scott, Bill, or Vince, there are dozens of less severe cases—men who cope quietly with emotional pain about some aspect of how they look. The suffering affects not only men who go to gyms like Olympic, but millions more who are too embarrassed about their appearance to be seen at a gym in the first place. In extreme cases, men may become so concerned about parts of their bodies—a balding head, a potbelly, a small penis, or some other perceived deficiency—that they do their best to avoid being seen in any public settings at all.

As clinicians and researchers in psychiatry and psychology, we've witnessed this growing male distress more and more in recent years. We've seen how the Adonis Complex can affect the lives of ordinary American men, young and old, producing a crippled masculine identity, chronic depression, compulsive behaviors, and often seriously impaired relationships with family members and loved ones.

What's particularly worrisome is that so many of these men are unaware of the societal forces that are constantly undermining their self-esteem. Boys and men have grown so accustomed to the constant barrage of supermale images in the media, and in advertising by the male body image industries, that they don't stop to question them. Rarely do they realize the extent to which they have accepted these Herculean images as sensible representations of male beauty. Instead, they change their behavior to try to make their own bodies conform to the new standard. Rarely do they consider that no previous generation in history was ever assaulted with comparable images—partly because it was impossible to create many of these modern supermale bodies before the availability of anabolic steroids. Rarely, also, do modern men fully acknowledge, even to themselves, how much their self-esteem and sense of masculinity is linked to their body image concerns. As a result of these feelings, they may become increasingly focused on deficiencies in their bodies, without really understanding why.

The starting place for healing this crisis of male body obsession—a crisis that extends across race, nationality, class, and sexual orientation—is to help men understand that they are not alone with these feelings, that millions of others share the same concerns and tribulations. It is time to help men appreciate the underlying social forces that contribute to their negative feelings about their bodies. Men must learn to acknowledge and talk about these feelings, to overcome the "feeling and talking taboo" that society has long imposed on them. And in our society, it is time to create widespread awareness about body-appearance concerns in men, and allow men to voice these concerns to those who care about and love them. We need to expose the societal and cultural forces that are inculcating new unattainable male body standards, and share the stories and voices of scores of men who have become frustrated and ashamed by their failure to meet these standards. In the pages that follow, we will describe how we, as professionals, have counseled men faced with these painful feelings. We hope to help men achieve the freedom and relief that has been attained by many women with eating disorders and other body image concerns: the ability to acknowledge their problems, seek new ways of perceiving their bodies and themselves, and find new paths toward self-confidence and fulfillment.

CHAPTER TWO

The Rise of the Adonis Complex
Roots of Male Body Obsession

The booming business at the Olympic Gym is a recent phenomenon. Thirty years ago, huge gyms like this, with thousands of members, were almost nonexistent. With rare exceptions, men of the 1950s or 1960s didn't worry about their muscularity; they didn't pour money into gym dues or protein supplements or weight machines for the basement. Similarly, male eating disorders, such as binge eating and vomiting, were almost unknown. Most men hadn't even heard of a body fat measurement, nor did they worry greatly about how much body fat they had. And for all practical purposes, there was no such thing as a "personal trainer."

But over the last three decades, the Adonis Complex has spread dramatically among boys and men, and more and more men are struggling to improve their appearance in one way or another. To get an idea of just how many men are affected by this trend, consider the findings of a landmark national survey of 548 men, published in *Psychology Today* magazine in 1997. An amazing *43 percent—nearly half*—of the men in this survey reported that they were dissatisfied with their overall appearance. More than half were dissatisfied with their abdomen (63 percent) or weight (52 percent). Forty-five percent were dissatisfied with their muscle tone, and 38 percent with their chest.

These numbers have risen sharply from those in earlier surveys. As you can see on the next page, men's dissatisfaction with body appearance has nearly tripled in less than thirty years—from 15 percent in 1972 to 34 percent in 1985 to 43 percent in 1997. And dissatisfaction with nearly every individual body area has risen steadily.

Another surprising finding is that men are catching up to women. In 1997, nearly as many men as women were dissatisfied with their over-

Rates of Body Dissatisfaction Among Men and Women in Three Sequential Surveys by *Psychology Today* Magazine

	1972 Survey %		1985 Survey %		1997 Survey %	
	Women	Men	Women	Men	Women	Men
Overall appearance	25	15	38	34	56	43
Weight	48	35	55	41	66	52
Height	13	13	17	20	16	16
Muscle tone	30	25	45	32	57	45
Breasts/chest	26	18	32	28	34	38
Abdomen	50	36	57	50	71	63
Hips/upper thighs	49	12	50	21	61	29

all appearance. The same is true for most specific body areas. In dissatisfaction with chest and breasts, men even outnumbered women!

You might expect body image dissatisfaction to be more common in men of certain ages—for example, during the awkward teenage years, when physical appearance becomes so important, or perhaps later in life, as men start losing their hair and muscle tone. But this doesn't appear to be the case. The *Psychology Today* survey found that a surprisingly high percentage of men of *all* ages were unhappy with their looks—from eighth-graders to thirty-somethings to men approaching sixty.

Dissatisfaction with Overall Appearance for Men of Different Ages in the 1997 *Psychology Today* Survey

Age	% Dissatisfied
13–19	41
20–29	38
30–39	48
40–49	43
50–59	48

Other findings from this survey strikingly convey just how dissatisfied—even desperate—many boys and men have become about their appearance, and what they'd be willing to do to improve their looks. For example, in response to the question "How many years of your life would you trade to achieve your weight goals?" *17 percent of men said they would give up more than three years of their lives. Eleven percent would sacrifice five years.* These numbers, by the way, closely approach the numbers obtained in women. In addition,

- 30 percent of men said they smoke to control their weight.
- 58 percent of men reported having dieted to lose weight.
- 4 percent of men said they make themselves vomit to control their weight.
- 40 percent of men said that at least half of their workout time is spent exercising to control their weight.

In light of figures like these, it's no wonder so many boys and men are working out at the Olympic Gym. Many want to lose weight; others want to bulk up, and some are so desperate to accomplish these goals that they would give up years of their life in return.

NOT JUST A WOMEN'S PROBLEM

These figures also bring out another important point. Until recently, it's been widely assumed that body image preoccupation, dissatisfaction, and distortion afflict primarily women. But over the past decade it's becoming obvious from many studies that these are big issues for men, too. Men spend a surprisingly large amount of time thinking about their appearance. In a study of undergraduate students, Marci McCaulay and her colleagues found that 52 percent of men reported thinking about their weight or appearance "all the time" or "frequently." Even when the researchers restricted their analysis to men of normal weight, the proportion answering "all the time" or "frequently" was still 46 percent. Similarly, in a nationwide survey published in 1986, examining 2,000 respondents, only 18 percent of men said that they had little concern about their appearance or did little to improve it. In fact, one study found that men are even more likely than women to want to look attractive to the opposite sex. And a recent poll found that body discontent is also surprisingly widespread in other countries: 47 percent of Venezuelan men, for example, said that they constantly think about their looks.

Not only do men spend a lot of time thinking about their appearance, but many are dissatisfied with it and upset about it. We've already mentioned the *Psychology Today* survey results demonstrating this; many other studies show the same. For example, body image experts Marc Mishkind, Judith Rodin, and their colleagues found that *95 percent* of college-age men expressed dissatisfaction with some part of their bodies! Men consistently express the greatest dissatisfaction with their chest, weight, and waist, but they're also often unhappy with other body areas. Older men are particularly dissatisfied with their facial features.

Recent studies have also found that a majority of men would like to change their weight in one direction or the other. When asked what type of physique they would like, the overwhelming majority of men say they would like to be well built and muscular as opposed to either thin or fat. This same preference is also expressed even by boys as young as age five or six. Several studies found that men specifically prefer a highly muscular "muscleman" type of body, characterized by well-developed chest and arm muscles, with wide shoulders tapering down to a narrow waist. Our own research studies, as we'll describe in the next chapter, have strongly confirmed these trends.

Women are often believed to be much more frequently dissatisfied with their looks than men are. But in reality, according to recent research, this perception is wrong: many men are just as unhappy, or almost as unhappy, with their appearance as women. Furthermore, men aren't just preoccupied or dissatisfied with their body image; they may also have a *distorted* body image, perceiving themselves as looking different (and generally worse) than they really do. There's often a vicious circle here: the more a person focuses on his body appearance, the worse he tends to feel about how he looks—obsession breeds discontent. And whether men experience outright distortions of body image or are simply dissatisfied with their bodies, they tend to have lower self-esteem and more depression than body-satisfied men. In fact, some recent studies have indicated that the connection between a bad body image and low self-esteem is even stronger among men than among women.

Why aren't these problems among men better known? We hear a lot about body image problems in women, but we rarely hear stories about men's shame or dissatisfaction with their bodies. As we mentioned in the last chapter, we think the "feeling and talking taboo" is much of the explanation. In our society, boys and men usually keep their body image concerns secret. They don't tell their friends, girlfriends, even their wives. Most men, we suspect, would be mortified to reveal how much they care about, dislike, and try to improve their looks. Instead, they suffer in silence.

THE MALE BODY-APPEARANCE MARKET

Although they say little about their concern with body image, a lot of boys and men are quietly working to do something about it. For example, in McCaulay's survey of college undergraduate men, 39 percent of *normal-weight* men said they did things to increase their body weight or size "all the time" or "frequently." That statistic would be easily supported by a glance around the Olympic Gym: at any time of the day, numerous men from nearby colleges are working out. Most could use their own college gyms for free if they wanted, but they're spending about $400 per year out of their own pockets to buy a membership at Olympic because it has better weightlifting facilities.

These men aren't the only ones spending a lot of money to improve their looks. In the last year alone, American men spent over $2 billion on commercial gym memberships, and another $2 billion–plus on home exercise equipment, including weight machines, treadmills, and other types of equipment—and that doesn't count the money spent on equipment for other conditioning sports. Simultaneously, the market for men's fitness magazines has exploded. The paid circulation of *Men's Health*, for example, climbed more than sixfold in only seven years, from 250,000 in 1990 to more than 1.5 million in 1997. Dozens of other health and exercise magazines for men have arisen in every niche. They range from hard-core bodybuilding publications to magazines aimed at aging baby boomers, gay men, or weekend athletes. Although these magazines may have words like "health" and "fitness" in their titles, they are often heavily focused on male body appearance. Most of these magazines didn't even exist ten or twenty years ago.

And that's still only one piece of the expanding body-appearance market. We have to add another several billion dollars that men are now spending annually for cosmetic procedures. In 1996 alone, men received 690,361 cosmetic procedures, including 217,083 hair transplantations or restorations, 65,861 chemical peels, 54,106 liposuctions, and 28,289 treatments to remove varicose veins, not to mention eyelid surgery, nose reshaping, breast reduction, face-lifts, antiwrinkle injections, calf implants, pectoral (chest) implants, buttock implants, and penis augmentations. Growing numbers of men are even having botulinum toxin injected into their faces to smooth out wrinkles; in larger quantities, botulinum is one of nature's most deadly poisons. Advertising for cosmetic surgery is increasingly targeted at men, and the proportion of men receiving cosmetic surgery procedures has increased steadily over the last decade. The number of men receiving liposuction has at least quadrupled since 1990, and a growing number of men are undergoing a new type of liposuction procedure that defines the abdominal muscles by removing the fat around them.

In 1997, the international market analyst Euromonitor estimated that men in the United States spent a shocking *$3.5 billion* on men's toiletries (hair color, skin moisturizers, tooth whiteners, etc.). And a 1996 survey in *Men's Health* found that approximately 20 percent of American men get manicures or pedicures, 18 percent use skin treatments such as masks or mudpacks, and 10 percent get professional facials. Another survey found that "6% of men nationwide actually use traditionally female products, such as bronzers and foundation to create the illusion of a youthful appearance." One company has even started marketing men's nail polish, with such studly names as Gigolo and Testosterone.

Then we have to add in the billions spent on nutritional supplements that claim to build muscle or burn fat. A huge industry now hawks protein products, amino acids, "fat burners," vitamin combinations, minerals, and other, more exotic substances—many of them worthless and some downright dangerous—to millions of gullible American boys and men who hope to become leaner and more muscular. Thirty years ago, the supplement industry hardly existed.

What has happened? Why are men so much more insecure about their bodies than they were a generation ago?

THE 'ROIDED BODY: MALE HORMONES IN OVERDOSE

Many biological, psychological, and sociocultural forces contribute to men's body image concerns. Some of these forces, such as traditional cultural standards of "masculinity," have long existed throughout many societies. But two recent changes, we would argue, have powerfully altered the forces affecting the present generation of men. The first was the discovery of a chemical that could make men bigger than they had ever been for the last million years.

The story of anabolic steroids begins almost a century ago, when scientists began to hypothesize that some substance, presumably secreted by the testicles, conferred maleness on men and animals. Indeed, as early as the late nineteenth century, a French doctor named Charles-Édouard Brown-Séquard injected himself with an extract from fresh guinea pig and dog testicles, and was convinced that it gave him strength and vitality. It turns out, in retrospect, that there were no active hormones in Brown-Séquard's potion at all, but scientists eventually realized his ideal. By the 1930s, German scientists had discovered testosterone, the primary male hormone, and soon thereafter they began to create synthetic "analogs" of testosterone—drugs that represented small chemical variations from the original testosterone molecule. This family of drugs is known as the "anabolic-androgenic steroids."

It didn't take long to find out what these drugs could do. Even in the early 1940s, it is said, Hitler's troops were given steroids to make them stronger and more aggressive in battle. No written records of this experiment appear to have survived, but we do possess an abundant scientific literature from the same time period: physicians began to give testosterone to middle-aged men, thinking that it might reverse the "male menopause" in men suffering from depression, or lacking energy or sex drive. The drug clearly had antidepressant effects in some of these men. But as more effective antidepressant treatments became available, testosterone lost favor.

It wasn't until the 1950s that the real potential of anabolic steroids—their muscle-building ability—was recognized. It started with the Russians, who appeared at the weightlifting championships in Vienna in 1954 with some of the first steroid-doped athletes. Quickly thereafter, elite athletes all over the world began to jump on the bandwagon—and a number of shrewd businessmen realized that with steroid-using athletes, they could make a lot of money. Steroids rippled through the bodybuilding world and soon found their way into other sports that required size and strength, like football, field events, and many more. By the 1970s, steroids had become entrenched in the bodybuilding world. Our research suggests that, over the years, competition bodybuilders grew bigger and bigger because they steadily upped their doses to stay on top. Increasingly, images of their inflated shoulders and arms proliferated in magazines, television shows, and movies.

The public remained almost completely unaware of this silent revolution. The athletes had no desire to reveal their secret, the promoters even less so. Better to tell the public that the muscles were all a result of hard work, dedication, improved training techniques, and optimal dietary supplements. American boys and men, looking at images of progressively bigger bodies, rarely stopped to think that no human being had ever looked like this throughout history. The most muscular Greek and Roman statues, the most masculine heroes portrayed in centuries of art around the world—none approached the proportions of a modern competition bodybuilder.

Look again at the sixteenth-century painting of Adonis in Chapter 1. The master artist, Titian, no doubt intended to portray the ultimate male body. Yet Titian's Adonis couldn't even win a two-bit bodybuilding contest today. There's good reason for this: prior to the steroid era, no artist had ever seen a man with the muscle size and definition of a modern steroid user. No such man ever existed—until the modern discovery of drugs that could shatter nature's longstanding physiological limits.

At first, the images of a few inflated bodybuilders didn't inflict any major psychological damage on American men. But by the 1980s, the steroid-stoked body had found its way into Hollywood, and young men and boys began to see movies of male heroes with bodies larger than nature. Some of these movie viewers started going to the gym, naively thinking that with enough hard work and dedication they could look the same.

By the late 1980s, the deception and secrecy surrounding steroids began to crack. Ben Johnson got busted for using them in the 1988 Seoul Olympics and forfeited his gold medal. The Berlin Wall fell the next year, and the rampant steroid use of Eastern bloc athletes was exposed. Scientific studies, including some of the early studies from our own laboratory, began to capture the attention of the media. Survey data started to pour in: a 1988 study found that more than 6 percent of high school boys admitted having used steroids at some time before age eighteen. Other studies produced similar numbers—and in many of these studies, a large portion of the boys and men admitted that they used steroids purely to improve their appearance, and not for any athletic purposes at all.

Meanwhile, the "'roided" body began to infiltrate the media. Male models in ads for everything from underwear to sport utility vehicles began to sport washboard abdominal muscles, massive chests, and inflated shoulders. Dozens of new fitness magazines appeared, often featuring bodybuilders on their covers and in their advertisements. Many of these bodybuilder models displayed a combination of muscularity and leanness probably achievable only with drugs. Male actors in TV commercials and soaps, fitness programs and rock videos, began to show up with similar features. Millions of American boys and men saw these images. Often, they didn't know that many of these models secretly relied on drugs. For years, some of them have told us, they wondered why they couldn't look like the men in the pictures, no matter how hard they worked out at the gym. No wonder they felt insecure.

Does this all sound too cynical? Before we go on, let's digress for a moment to provide a little hard data on the difference between a drug-free and a drug-spiked body. You can skip the technical parts of the next section if you want, but you should at least look carefully at the photos on the following pages.

VIOLATING MOTHER NATURE'S LIMITS

We often give talks about our research on steroids and body image. Sometimes, even after the talk is over, someone will look at a picture of a huge bodybuilder and still ask, "But do you think *he* used steroids?"

In response, we're almost tempted to say, "Do you think that World War II actually happened, or was it just made up by the history books?" It's astonishing how little the public has been told about the effects of steroids on body build and muscularity.

Our research has persuaded us that the male body simply cannot exceed a certain level of muscularity without the help of steroids or other chemicals. We have demonstrated this phenomenon using a mathematical formula that we have published. The formula uses a man's height, weight, and approximate percentage of body fat to calculate a number called the "fat-free mass index," or FFMI. For the reader interested in the technical details, we've provided in Appendix I a complete explanation of the formula, showing how to calculate your own or somebody else's FFMI.

The FFMI is simply a number that indicates a man's degree of muscularity. A man with an FFMI of 16 to 17 has a very low level of muscle; he's someone who might be described as "frail" or "flabby." An FFMI of 19 to 20, by contrast, would be typical of an average American or European college student. When we get up to an FFMI of 22 to 23, we're describing a man who would be noticeably muscular. We believe that an FFMI of 25 to 26 represents the upper limit of muscularity attainable without steroids. In our research, dozens of drug-free weightlifters have scored in the high 24s or even the low 25s, but above that there was a sharp cutoff: of the unequivocally drug-free men we've measured, none has scored beyond 26.

By contrast, we've measured countless steroid users who scored well above 26, with many going even into the low 30s. Steroids allow a man to break through his normal biological "ceiling" of muscularity and to soar into a range far beyond what Mother Nature ever intended. And it seems that the more drugs he's prepared to take, the farther beyond that ceiling he can go.

We should add one precaution: all of the above numbers apply to men who have low or moderate body fat. If a man becomes quite fat, then he can get his FFMI above 26 without drugs, because when you add fat to the body, you increase the amount of muscle that can be added as well. Thus, a fat Olympic powerlifter or a Japanese sumo wrestler might come out well above 26 using our formula. But on the basis of our research, we believe that it's impossible to be extremely muscular *and* lean without chemical assistance.

In short, we believe that if a man is fairly lean, has an FFMI greater than about 26, and claims that he has achieved this physical condition without the use of drugs, he is almost certainly lying. If all American men and boys understood this simple fact, they might breathe a huge sigh of relief. They would realize that many of the men in pictures and advertisements—these seemingly fit and athletic role models whom they can never seem to equal—couldn't have gotten that way without drugs.

CLUES THAT A MAN HAS TAKEN STEROIDS

To see what these numbers mean, let's take a look at some pictures. On the next page, we see pictures of two men of identical height (5 feet 7 inches each), similar age (about twenty), and both quite lean (about 4.5 percent body fat for the man on the left and 7 percent for the man on the right—as compared to about 15–20 percent for an average American man of this age). The man on the left in each picture has never taken steroids; he has a fat-free mass index of approximately 23.7, a little below the upper limit of muscularity that we believe can be attained by natural means. On the right is a man who has used massive doses of steroids over several years. His fat-free mass index is approximately 31.7—a figure far beyond the limit that we believe can be attained without drugs. Note that the muscles of his shoulders, chest, and upper arms (shown in the bottom photo) are particularly hypertrophied (enlarged) relative to those of the natural bodybuilder. This effect is characteristic of steroids: the drugs stimulate growth of the upper body musculature, especially the area around the shoulder, more than the rest of the body. When you think about this observation, it isn't surprising. Men have high levels of the natural steroid testosterone as compared to women—and men differ from women particularly in the muscularity of their upper bodies, especially around the shoulder. Taking high doses of steroids, therefore, makes the user look "more male than male." This slightly disproportionate "hypermale" look alerts the eye that there's something unnatural about the figure of the man on the right.

The contrast between these first two bodybuilders is pretty obvious, but on page 38 we see three more subtle examples of steroid use that an untrained observer might not recognize. In fact, the picture could almost be titled "Clues that your son (or your boyfriend or your husband) may be secretly taking steroids." The man in the upper picture has an FFMI of only about 23, and the two men on the bottom each have an FFMI of about 25. In theory, therefore, all three fall into the range of muscularity attainable without drugs. But note that all of the men display a disproportionate amount of muscularity in the shoulders and upper arms—the same "more male than male" look that we noted in the

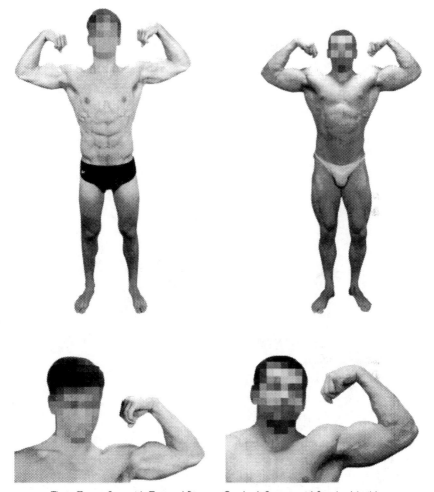

The effects of steroids. Top and Bottom: On the left, a steroid-free bodybuilder; on the right, a steroid user.

steroid user in the previous picture. Contrast the shoulders and upper arms of these men with those of the drug-free weightlifter on the left. The drug-free man is quite muscular, but he's muscular in a more proportional and natural way. By comparing the pictures, you may learn to recognize possible steroid use even in some men with an FFMI of less than 25.

The set of photographs on page 39 shows another, similar comparison. Steve Reeves is one of the greatest (some would say the single great-

Clues that your son or your boyfriend may be secretly taking steroids.

est) bodybuilder of the presteroid era, winner of the Mr. America contest in 1947 and the Mr. Universe contest in 1950. At the time he won the Mr. America title, Steve had a fat-free mass index of approximately 25.7—another good illustration of the upper limit of muscularity that we believe can be attained without drugs. In the bottom two photographs, by comparison, are two 1999 bodybuilding competitors. The effects of drugs are obvious: they're much bigger than Steve, and both have that oddly disproportionate drug-induced look that we mentioned above.

As these pictures illustrate, the discovery of steroids has allowed today's men to violate Mother Nature's longstanding limits. As a result, the 'roided, bigger-than-life male body has infiltrated the media and our societal ideals, completely changing the messages that boys and men receive about their bodies. In fact, as we'll show in the next several photographs, kids start getting these messages in the first years of childhood.

Steve Reeves, Mr. America contest 1947, Chicago.

Two modern steroid-using bodybuilders.

G.I. JOE GOES ON STEROIDS

Many of children's earliest messages about body image come from the dolls they play with. As you may have heard, studies of the popular girls' doll Barbie show that she has become thinner and thinner over the years. In fact, one study found that if Barbie were the height of an actual woman, she'd have only a 16-inch waist! As a result, scientists have speculated, little girls get the message that thin is beautiful, and this message may have contributed to the rise of eating disorders—anorexia nervosa and bulimia nervosa—in modern times.

We began to wonder if there was a male equivalent of this. What about the little plastic soldiers—so-called action toys—that young boys play with? As Barbie has been growing thinner, has G.I. Joe been growing muscles? What has happened to Superman's biceps or Batman's chest over the years? To study this, we contacted many collectors of vintage action toys, and soon became experts on the evolution of these little plastic heroes.

G.I. Joe is undoubtedly the most famous and longest-running of American action toys. He has appeared in two different versions. One version was the large $11\frac{1}{2}$-inch-sized series of figures who came dressed as soldiers, sailors, air force pilots, and marines. These were manufactured starting in 1964, and continued until about 1980, when they were replaced with a new collection of smaller $3\frac{3}{4}$-inch figures that first hit the shelves of toy stores in 1982. The little Joes went through many different series, with new characters added as the years went by—the Cobra Soldier, the Nemesis Enforcer, the Fridge, etc. Then, in 1991, the big $11\frac{1}{2}$-inch Joes were reintroduced, and both sizes are sold today.

No other action toy has had such a long and continuous history as G.I. Joe, but there are lots of both vintage and modern figures of other types on the market: the *Star Wars* and *Star Trek* figures, Superman, Batman, and others. To select among these, we examined the annual sales surveys in *Playthings* magazine, an industry publication in the field, to find out which toys had been among the top-selling product lines over the last two decades. We quickly became avid action toy collectors. Through mail order, we purchased early examples of G.I. Joe and *Star Wars* figures from the sixties and seventies. Then we went off to the local Toys R Us, found the nearest seven-year-old boy, and asked him to tell us which toys would be his top choices for Christmas. He led us down the aisles, pointing out, "This one!" and "That one!" We bought them all for our collection.

Soon, our laboratory began to fill up with an army of plastic men. G.I. Joes from various eras stood at attention in a row on the desk. The little 1978 versions of Luke Skywalker and Han Solo perched on the windowsill, side by side with their much beefier modern counterparts. Batman, the Avenger, and the Wolverine menacingly confronted visitors from their observation post on top of the computer. Men arriving at the laboratory for our studies must have wondered if someone was beginning to go through a second childhood.

The pictures on the next pages document the changes that have taken place over the last thirty years. In the first picture, we see a chronological sequence of the big 11½-inch G.I. Joes. On the left, we have a G.I. Joe Land Adventurer with the original body style introduced in 1964. If he were a man 5 feet ten 10 inches tall, he would have a 32-inch waist, a 44-inch chest, and a 12-inch bicep—a perfectly respectable physique, similar to that of an ordinary man in reasonably good physical shape. In the middle picture, we see the G.I. Joe Land Adventurer

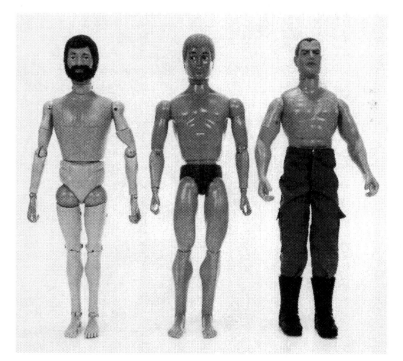

The evolution of G.I. Joe.

with the new body style introduced ten years later in 1974. Unlike his earlier counterpart, this G.I. Joe has been putting in a little time at the gym. His bicep has grown to the equivalent of 15 inches—already 2 or 3 inches bigger than the bicep of an average untrained man. And Joe has been been doing situps, too. His abdominal muscles, hardly visible in his predecessor, are now nicely defined. But both of the earlier Joes are shamed by the contemporary figure on the right, introduced in 1991, known as the Salute to G.I. Joe. His waist has shrunk to only 29 inches, and his biceps are up to 16½ inches—approaching the limits of what a lean man might be able to attain without steroids. Not only that, but Joe now has a six-pack of abdominals that would be the envy of even many bodybuilders. And he even has visible serratus muscles—the comblike muscles that run along the ribs on the sides of his body.

We also have a collection of the smaller series of G.I. Joe figures. As shown below, the evolution here is even more dramatic. On the left, we have the cute little original 1982 G.I. Joe Grunt. His 1992 equivalent, in the middle, is already visibly more muscular. But both of these are dwarfed by the figure on the right, the G.I. Joe Extreme, introduced in the mid-1990s. If G.I. Joe Extreme were full-sized, he would have a 55-inch chest and a 27-inch bicep. His bicep, in other words, is almost as big as his waist—and bigger than that of most competition bodybuilders.

The evolution of G.I. Joe is only one example of the increasing muscularity of action figures over the years. You'll probably recognize two favorite characters from *Star Wars*, Luke Skywalker and Han Solo.

The evolution of G.I. Joe, continued.

Star Wars figures, then and now.

On the left are their original versions, released by the Kenner Toy Company at the time of the original *Star Wars* movie in 1978. On the right are the two new versions from the mid-1990s, at the time when *Star Wars* was rereleased. Both have now acquired the physiques of bodybuilders, with bulging "pecs" (chest muscles) and "delts" (shoulders). Indeed, we remember one toy dealer who told us a story, perhaps apocryphal, about Mark Hamill, who played Luke in the original 1978 movie. Upon picking up the 1995 plastic rendition of himself, Hamill is said to have exclaimed, "Good God, they've put me on steroids!"

If you're still not convinced, the picture on page 44 shows some of the other male action figures that have topped the sales charts recently—the Gold Ranger, Ahmed Johnson, Iron Man, Batman, and the Wolverine. All have physiques suggestive of steroid-using bodybuilders. And some—like the Wolverine—exceed even the outer limits of what drugs can do. If he were 5 feet 10 inches tall, the Wolverine would sport a 32-inch bicep—only an inch smaller than the circumference of his waist.

Finally, on page 45, we show a complete army of plastic action heroes, chosen at random from the toy chest of the four-year-old son of one of our research associates. The picture speaks for itself.

Certainly, these action toys suggest that the ideal male body has

Popular action toys.

evolved in only about thirty years from a normal and reasonably attainable figure, such as that of the Vietnam-era G.I. Joes, to a hugely muscular figure that we believe no man could attain without massive doses of steroids. Boys are exposed to these figures while they are still very young—long before they are old enough to form an independent opinion about what a realistic man's body should look like. Is this message having an effect on American boys as they grow up? It's hard to prove this, but consider just one statistic: each year, the sales of male action toys for American boys exceed *$1 billion.*

MALE SOAP OPERAS: HULK HOGAN
AND OTHER MUSCLE STARS

These messages continue as boys move into adolescence. For example, professional wrestling has grown increasingly popular among boys and teenagers. Starting in the 1980s, the World Wrestling Federation (WWF) began to sell out arenas around the country with supermuscular stars like Hulk Hogan, "Macho Man" Randy Savage, the Ultimate Warrior, Andre the Giant, and Rowdy Roddy Piper. But in early 1990, Vince McMahon, Jr., who owned the business, was indicted on counts that he acted in a conspiracy to dope his wrestlers with anabolic steroids (he was later acquitted and cleared of the charges). His biggest star, Hulk

An army of action toys.

Hogan, admitted that he had taken steroids for thirteen years; he even testified that he picked up his drugs at the WWF headquarters, along with his paycheck and his mail.

But the steroid scandal was only a brief setback for WWF. Now professional wrestling is watched by an estimated half-billion viewers worldwide each week—most of them men and boys—and it has graduated from a simple wrestling show to a veritable male soap opera. Men in their twenties can recall having started to follow wrestling as young teenagers, and they still tune in regularly to watch. Among the many large, muscular, well-chiseled bodies that enter the wrestling ring are characters who suggest that muscularity is closely linked to sexuality: the message is that muscles attract girls. One example is Sexual Chocolate, a 6-foot-11-inch, 400-pound former powerlifter who is known for the "loving" attention he gives the ladies.

Even if they don't watch professional wrestling, American teenagers are exposed to a burgeoning array of fitness and health magazines. Just like the action toys, these magazines contain many images of men with bodies that we believe could not be attained by natural means. Recently, for example, we noticed an array of magazines for sale at the checkout counter of a large department store—one of those big chain stores that sells everything from cheap clothes to household items to auto parts. Among the thirty-five or forty magazine titles, no fewer than seven were devoted to men's fitness or bodybuilding—and five of the seven had a cover picture of a man who we strongly suspected had used steroids. Interestingly, however, three of these five men appeared only "politely 'roided"—in other words, their bodies were still within the range that might theoretically be achieved without drugs—but their combination of leanness and muscularity was a little too impressive for that to seem plausible. Of course, the unspoken implication was that these men had achieved their physiques naturally—by special workout routines, nutritional strategies, and other techniques that the reader could learn, presumably, by buying the magazine.

None of the men in the checkout line, of course, looked even remotely like the models on the magazine covers confronting them. How many times in a week, we wonder, did these men see an image like this, of a man with a body that they themselves could never naturally attain?

Men have been indoctrinated by such images since early childhood—through action toys, comic strips, television, and movies—long before they were old enough to stop and question whether these images were realistic or reasonable goals for a man's body. Remember, no previous generation of men has grown up being exposed to such a plethora of supermuscular images; before the drugs, they hardly existed. What happens when you violate nature's limits, and when you subject men to ideals beyond their reach? What do these constant messages do to men's feelings about their bodies? We're convinced that this phenomenon has fueled the rise of the Adonis Complex over the last several decades.

PLAYGIRL CENTERFOLDS HIT THE GYM

Up to this point, we've spoken of the increasingly muscular male body portrayed to boys and men. But what about the "ideal" male body that the media portrays to women? Has it followed the same trend? In our attempts to study this question, we recalled an earlier study of female body image from a clever group of investigators in Canada: they looked at the dimensions of all of the women in *Playboy* magazine centerfolds from 1959 to 1979, and were able to prove that the models had been growing steadily thinner over the years. The same scientists also found that Miss America Pageant contestants had grown steadily thinner over the same period, and that the winners of the pageant, in turn, were even thinner than the losers. Over the twenty years, the pageant contestants lost about 6 pounds of weight, and the pageant winners managed to shed about 7½ pounds. The results of this study helped to confirm the widely held impression that our society has been preaching an increasingly thin ideal body standard to women—thus perhaps contributing to the rise of eating disorders among girls and women over the last several decades.

After reading the Canadian study, an ingenious young American psychology student named Richard Leit suggested to us the logical male equivalent: why not examine the dimensions of male centerfolds over the last twenty-five years in *Playgirl* magazine? As their female counterparts were growing thinner, had the *Playgirl* men been growing more muscular, as our hypothesis would predict? In other words, could we document that society is preaching an increasingly muscular ideal body standard for men—and possibly fueling an increase in the Adonis Complex?

To test our theory, we went to the Library of Congress, which carried a complete collection of *Playgirl* from its inception in 1973 to the present—carefully housed in the rare book room to secure it against thievery. As the library attendants brought up armloads of bound volumes of *Playgirl*, Richard went through them and selected all of the centerfold models whose heights and weights were quoted by the magazine. Then we estimated their body fat on the basis of their pictures, presented by Richard in random order without giving us any information to reveal which year they came from, to avoid biasing the study results. It took an entire day of grueling work just to estimate the body fat on hundreds of pictures of naked men. By that evening, when we emerged from the library onto the streets of Washington, it was almost shocking to see that all of the men on the street were clothed!

The results were just as we had predicted. The figure on page 48 shows what is known as a "scatterplot," in which each dot represents the measurements of one centerfold man. As you'll see, the average muscularity of the centerfold men, as measured by our FFMI formula described earlier, has gone steadily up—from around 20 in the mid-1970s to over 22 by the late 1990s. Putting this in more specific terms, the average *Playgirl* centerfold man has *shed about 12 pounds of fat, while putting on approximately 27 pounds of muscle* over the last twenty-five years! You can observe this difference for yourself on page 49, in our comparison of a *Playgirl* centerfold man from the 1970s with one from the 1990s.

WOMEN FIGHTER PILOTS
AND THREATENED MASCULINITY

The *Playgirl* study brings us to our second theory about the rise of the Adonis Complex over the last generation. During this period, women have increasingly approached parity with men in many aspects of life,

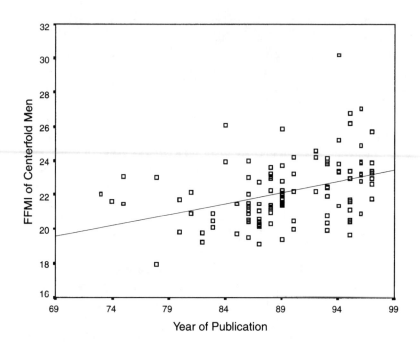

A "scatterplot" showing the increasing muscularity of Playgirl *magazine centerfold men,*
1973–98.

leaving men with primarily their bodies as a defining source of masculinity.

This theory may sound controversial, but it rests on simple observations. First, there's nothing new about the idea that men want to be
physically appealing to women or that men value bodily beauty. For example, in an excellent article, "The Beauty of the Beast," anthropologist
David Gilmore demonstrates that many other eras and cultures focus
on—or are even obsessed with—the male body. Many of these observations, however, are not widely known. Mr. Gilmore writes: "What is
most interesting about all this is how we have managed to overlook consistent evidence that in many cultures, the appearance of the male is as
important as that of the female. . . ."

One striking example comes from Africa. The Wodaabe tribe val-
ues and focuses on male beauty far more than female beauty. Men in this
society are strong warriors and political leaders, but they also "primp
and preen and fret over their imperfections and wrinkles." They carry
pocket mirrors and combs with them at all times. They lavish large
amounts of time perfecting their painted faces and magnificent hairdos.

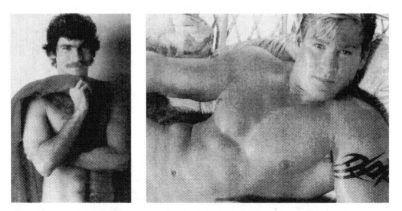

Playgirl centerfolds, then and now. On the left, a model from the 1970s; on the right, a model from the 1990s.

The Wodaabe tribe even stages male beauty contests, with women as judges!

Many other cultures also emphasize male beauty. In some cultures, not looking right is devastating. Gilmore notes that among the Sambia of New Guinea, "a short, plain, or ugly man is an outcast. The Sambia call an ugly or puny man a 'misfit': his unhappy fate is to be rejected by women and scorned by men. The women stigmatize the homely man as a 'rubbish man' not worthy of their attention. He is shunned and humiliated daily because of his unimpressive physique."

Looking back over the centuries, we can also find abundant adoration of the male body in Western European culture. The muscularity of Greek and Roman sculpture is one obvious example. Masculine beauty was also glorified in the Middle Ages, with Christian heroes depicted as physically gorgeous specimens: tall, robust, and handsome. In Elizabethan England, men were very vain about their looks, showing off their legs in tights and wearing bejeweled codpieces—a clothing accessory designed to emphasize the genital bulge.

These preferences for certain male body characteristics, and the age-old importance of the male body in attracting a mate, are partly biologically and evolutionarily based. Considering certain body and facial characteristics to be beautiful appears to a certain extent to be innate— hard-wired into our collective brains over millions of years. Symmetrical features and smooth unblemished skin, for example, are considered universally beautiful; they seem to signify health and reproductive fitness. An example from the animal world comes from male Japanese scorpion flies: those flies with the most symmetrical wings get the most mates.

A large body size may be another example of a collective, biologically based preference. In the animal world, body size confers particular advantages, with the largest animal tending to be most dominant. Similarly, since early human times, having a large body and upper body strength would give a man many advantages, such as being better able to wield ancient weapons. It may also have given men an advantage when protecting their offspring or battling other men for a female. Echoing these earlier evolutionary advantages, a large body and broad chest may still signify survival skill and strength in today's world.

In short, male appearance has been valued in many cultures around the world for millennia. Much of this stems from the desire to dominate other men and appeal to women. But are modern men more insecure about their bodies than their Elizabethan or Roman counterparts?

We think they are, and that the evolutionary perspective is insufficient to explain this change: after all, the biological "givens" have presumably been present since the dawn of man and haven't changed in recent years. This forces us to consider other, sociocultural, explanations. We believe that some of men's more recent body image insecurities may stem from the growing equality between women and men in many aspects of daily life. As we pointed out in the previous chapter, today's women can do practically anything that a man can do: they can fly combat aircraft, work as police chiefs, operate heavy machinery, or become chief executive officers of national corporations. Women can enter formerly all-male military schools, join formerly all-male clubs, and win elective offices once held almost exclusively by men. Women have become less dependent upon men for money, power, and self-esteem. What, then, do men have left to distinguish themselves, to mark their masculinity? One of the few attributes left, one of the few grounds on which women can never match men, is muscularity. Therefore, we hypothesize that the body is growing in relative importance as a defining feature of masculinity.

Of course, it must be acknowledged that women's influence has evolved over a long time—certainly for at least a century. But even looking at the early 1900s, a time when women gained a noticeable increment of power, several authors have noted a threat to masculinity and a corresponding uptick in men's concern about their body appearance. With regard to this era, one commentator pointed out, "Masculine anxiety at the turn of the century was experienced in the accentuation of the physical and assertive side of the male ideal. . . ." This period saw the rise of "the flamboyant strongman and health enthusiast Bernarr Macfadden," who published the magazine *Physical Culture*. Macfadden is said to have "exhorted men to realize that 'it lies with you, whether you shall be a strong virile animal . . . or a miserable little crawling worm.'" But these small tremors at the turn of the century were modest in comparison to the seismic changes of the most recent generation. The interval from the 1960s to the 1990s has seen history's most dramatic advances for women, and in parallel, the most striking changes in cultural attitudes toward men's bodies. Our time line on the next page illustrates a few of the recent milestones achieved by feminism, side by side with events that have suggested a growing societal fixation on men's bodies during the same time period.

Looking at the time line, we acknowledge that parallels in timing do not necessarily prove a causal connection—but the thirty-odd years covered in this table have certainly witnessed some dramatic setbacks for the male ego. As women have advanced, men have gradually lost their traditional identities as breadwinners, fighters, and protectors. Women are no longer so dependent upon men for these services. Accordingly, as the importance of these other identities has declined, the relative importance of the male body appears to have increased, although men may not be consciously aware of these motivating forces.

Muscularity in particular has become increasingly important, because it symbolizes masculinity. As body image researchers Marc Mishkind, Judith Rodin, and their colleagues have stated, "We believe the muscular [body] is the ideal because it is intimately tied to cultural views of masculinity and the male sex role, which prescribes that men be powerful, strong, efficacious—even domineering and destructive. . . . A muscular physique may serve as an embodiment of these personal characteristics." And indeed, research has shown that well-proportioned muscular men and boys are considered more masculine.

Mishkind, Rodin, and other authors, like ourselves, have similarly noted a connection between the recent rise of women and society's increasing focus on the male body. For example, authors James Gillett and Philip White have suggested that "the hypermasculine body symbolizes an attempt by men to restore feelings of masculine self-control and worth." They further hypothesize that the desirability of a "hypermasculine" body and the recent explosion of bodybuilding may be rooted in the growing "threat to male privilege" caused by the ascendancy of women. Aaron Randall and his colleagues, similarly, have written about "the dilemma posed by democratic relationships emphasizing equality between the sexes, leaving men with few sure bases for acting as pro-

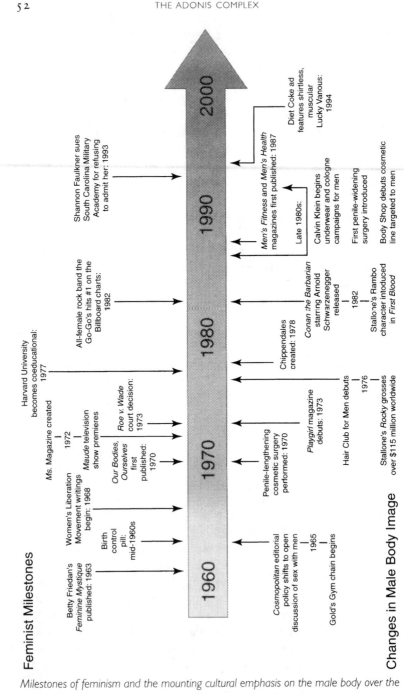

Feminist Milestones

Betty Friedan's *Feminine Mystique* published: 1963

Women's Liberation Movement writings begin: 1968

Ms. Magazine created 1972

Birth control pill: mid-1960s

Maude television show premieres

Our Bodies, Ourselves first published: 1970

Roe v. Wade court decision: 1973

Harvard University becomes coeducational: 1977

All-female rock band the Go-Go's hits #1 on the Billboard charts: 1982

Shannon Faulkner sues South Carolina Military Academy for refusing to admit her: 1993

Changes in Male Body Image

Cosmopolitan editorial policy shifts to open discussion of sex with men 1965

Gold's Gym chain begins

Penile-lengthening cosmetic surgery performed: 1970

Playgirl magazine debuts: 1973

Hair Club for Men debuts 1976

Stallone's *Rocky* grosses over $115 million worldwide

Chippendales created: 1978

Conan the Barbarian starring Arnold Schwarzenegger released

Stallone's Rambo character introduced in *First Blood* 1982

Men's Fitness and *Men's Health* magazines first published: 1987

Late 1980s: Calvin Klein begins underwear and cologne campaigns for men

First penile-widening surgery introduced

Body Shop debuts cosmetic line targeted to men

Diet Coke ad features shirtless, muscular Lucky Vanous: 1994

1960   1970   1980   1990   2000

Milestones of feminism and the mounting cultural emphasis on the male body over the past forty years.

viders and protectors." Becoming strong and muscular is a clear way for men to radiate power and manliness. As Barry Glassner writes, "Muscles are *the* sign of masculinity."

These authors argue that in bodybuilding—the surest way to achieve muscularity—the male body symbolically represents power and strength, and represents men's attempts to reclaim feelings of masculinity. Randall and his colleagues argue that "bodybuilders embody the traditional message that muscles are the sign of masculinity." Gillett and White, similarly, discuss "the erosion of conventional notions of masculine identity." They write that "one way in which men can attempt to reclaim and reassert this conventional patriarchal version of masculinity is through the cultivation of their bodies according to some hypermasculine body image. In focusing on the body in the weight room, men are able to construct a sense of masculinity within a space commonly viewed as male, through the development and display of body images that signify strength, power, authority, and other characteristics associated with a traditional male identity."

Sociologist Michael Kimmel, similarly, has chronicled the ascent of women into traditionally masculine arenas, particularly the workplace. Men are no longer defined by their role as "breadwinners"—a term used since the early 1800s, but now fading from our vocabulary. Kimmel believes the current interest in the male body is a result of "the collapse of the workplace as an arena in which to test and prove masculinity." In another recent book, *Stiffed: The Betrayal of the American Man,* feminist author Susan Faludi has argued, through the use of rich case examples, that masculinity is in crisis as gender lines have blurred in contemporary society. Journalist Michelle Cottle, in an influential recent article, has noted that "with women growing ever more financially independent, aspiring suitors are discovering that they must bring more to the table than a well-endowed wallet if they expect to win (and keep) the fair maiden."

In the elite world of competitive bodybuilding, we may see a particularly graphic demonstration of this attempt by some men to feel more in control, more masculine, more powerful. Alan Klein, an anthropologist, has documented this "search for requisite masculinity" in the subculture of competitive bodybuilders. "If he loses size," Klein writes, "the bodybuilder feels he is less of a man in every way."

THE GROWING MARKET VALUE OF MEN'S BODIES

How can one test the hypothesis that men's bodies matter more today than they did a generation ago? A simple interview study of contemporary men and women would almost certainly generate biased answers. A more quantitative and objective test of this hypothesis would be to track the value of men's bodies in the marketplace.

Consider, for example, the expanding industry of male strippers. In the 1960s, floor shows featuring scantily clad or naked women were commonplace—as they had always been—but similar shows featuring men were rare indeed. To be sure, some gay clubs offered male strip shows, but male strip shows for female audiences were practically unheard of. The lack of male strip shows during this era cannot easily be explained on the grounds of sexual inhibitions in our culture; sexual inhibitions were certainly not a feature of the 1960s. It appears, then, that there simply wasn't much of a market for male strippers at the time. But in the 1970s, business started to pick up, and in 1978 one of the most famous male strip shows, Chippendales, was born. The show started out performing one night a week in a Los Angeles nightclub but soon acquired nightclubs of its own. By the late 1990s, the show had graduated to a major theatrical act, playing to packed houses in dozens of American cities every year and touring many European countries. Chippendales now even has its own line of merchandise and a successful licensing program. The company advertises that it "appeals to women of all ages, single and with families, with middle-class lifestyles."

Another index of the male body's market value is commercial advertising. If men's bodies have grown proportionately more important than their roles as warriors or breadwinners, then advertisements portraying men to women audiences over recent decades would be expected to contain an increasing proportion of undressed men. For convincing evidence of this hypothesis, a study would have to demonstrate that only the proportion of undressed *men* had increased over the last generation, whereas the proportion of undressed *women* in advertisements had remained unchanged. Otherwise, it could be argued that it isn't just men's bodies, but simply all bodies, that have become more important.

To test this possibility, we examined best-selling women's magazines that met the following criteria: (1) they had been published for at least the last thirty years, and (2) they contained a large number of advertisements with male images. *Cosmopolitan* and *Glamour* were the clear first choices. We then counted, at five-year intervals, the number of men and women appearing in advertisements throughout one full year

Chippendales dancers, probably from the early 1980s.

of publication, and the percentage of these men and women portrayed in a state of undress. We defined "undress" as anything too risqué to be seen on a city street. For example, a man with the top three buttons of his shirt open would still be defined as "dressed," whereas a man wearing no shirt at all would meet our "undressed" definition.

Our predictions were confirmed. As can be seen in the two graphs on the next page, the proportion of undressed women in both magazines has remained fairly steady over the last thirty to forty years, oscillating around 20 percent. Meanwhile, the proportion of undressed men has skyrocketed, from as little as 3 percent in the 1950s to as high as 35 percent in the 1990s. What's even more interesting is that there seems to be a noticeable "inflection point": the proportion of undressed men seems to take off in the early 1980s, right in the wake of many of the feminist milestones depicted in the time line on page 52.

Of course, one might think of other hypotheses to explain the sudden surge of undressed men. But remember—any competing hypothesis would have to explain why the proportion of undressed men has gone up, whereas the proportion of undressed women has stayed flat. Note also that these increases can't be explained by the whims of one or two advertisers, since they represent a general trend throughout many different types of advertisements. Also keep in mind that if the advertisements hadn't sold products, they would have quickly disappeared. Advertising lives or dies by its commercial success, and as shown by the hunks on pages 58–59, the undressed men haven't been going away. In the first three pictures, male bodies are at least being used to sell body-related products, such as clothes and tanning lotion. But the remaining three advertisements use male bodies to promote products having nothing to do with bodies at all—from ironing boards to cell phones to liqueurs. And these are just a few examples—half-naked men are being used to sell countless other products, such as upscale hotels, couches, and even bank loans.

Advertisements in women's magazines aren't the only indicator of the mounting dollar value of men's bodies. As journalist Michelle Cottle has noted, a corresponding industry of men's magazines, largely focused on body appearance, has exploded over the last ten or twenty years. The paid circulation of *Men's Health* has risen from 250,000 to more than 1.5 million in less than a decade; its cousins, such as *Men's Journal*, *Details*, and *GQ*, are thriving as well. Many of the readers of these magazines are in their thirties or forties and married. In an earlier era, these readers would have been content to be respected husbands and breadwinners. But as these traditionally masculine roles have eroded, these men are now reading articles about tightening their abs, saving their hair, and fighting fat. The male body image industries that advertise in these magazines, quick to capitalize on these new insecurities, are making a killing.

Glamour **Magazine**

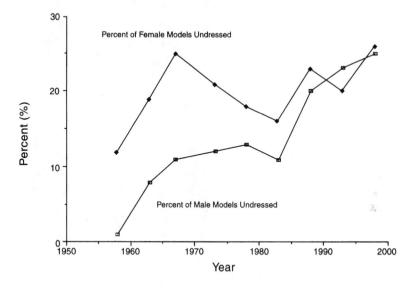

Cosmopolitan **Magazine**

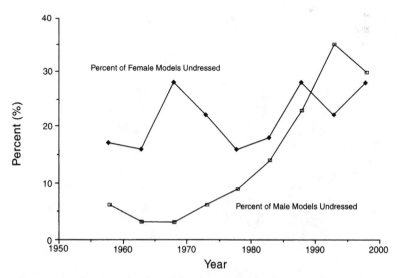

Percentages of undressed male and female models in leading women's magazines,
1958–1998.

Recent magazine advertisements featuring male bodies.

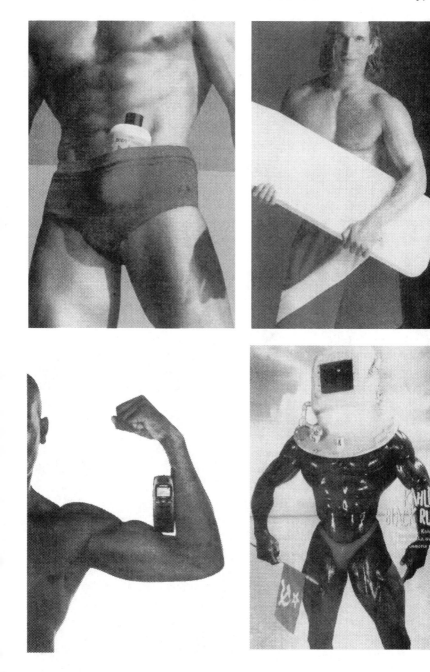

A recent article in the *New York Times* trumpeted the headline THE CHEF AS BEEFCAKE. As the author stated, "the message was as arresting as some of the buff studs pictured, one naked except for a well-placed blender. . . . Today's top chef is a sex kitchen utensil." With messages like these infiltrating men's consciousness, it's no wonder that the Adonis Complex has become epidemic among today's men.

THE MALE BODY IMAGE CRISIS

The origins of the Adonis Complex are complicated, and include biological givens, personal experiences (such as being teased about one's appearance), and other factors. In addition, our discussion above is speculative, because it is difficult to devise experimental tests for our theories. However, research shows that sociocultural influences, such as the media, tend to make women feel worse about their bodies, and preliminary studies of these influences suggest the same is true for men. In addition, there seems little doubt that over the last generation our culture has placed a growing emphasis on male body image—as exemplified in toys, comic books, magazines, newspapers, television, the movies, and advertisements of all types. As one advertising executive stated, the male torso reigns as the decade's most powerful "cross-over image" (appealing to women, gays, and heterosexual men alike). We've presented evidence in this chapter that these unprecedented changes are most likely related to two important sociocultural factors that distinguish the present generation from every generation before it: the availability of anabolic steroids and the increasing parity of women.

Even then, the Adonis Complex could not have grown to its present proportions if men felt more comfortable in talking openly about their deepest thoughts and feelings. Because men aren't supposed to worry or complain about their looks, few would ever admit that they'd secretly like to have a steroid-sized body or that they fret about their inadequacies when examining their bodies in the mirror. Fewer still would acknowledge that their obsessions about body appearance have anything to do with threatened masculinity as a result of the growing empowerment of women. Indeed, few men have stopped to even think about the underlying forces that may be driving them to put in long hours at the gym, contort their diets and eating patterns, splurge on cosmetic procedures, or take dangerous drugs such as steroids.

Women, in contrast, have learned in recent years to be more candid about their body image concerns—and they've grown stronger in their ability to reject societal messages that appearance is all-important. But men lag far behind in this respect; the Adonis Complex, like the forces behind it, remains in the shadows.

To penetrate this secrecy, we've devised two tests, described in the next chapter, and applied them to men of all ages in America and Europe. If you're a man, you can try these tests yourself. If you're a woman, you may want to offer these tests to a man you know. In any event, you'll likely be surprised by our findings—which document both the extent of the Adonis Complex and its mounting list of casualties.

CHAPTER THREE

Do You Have the Adonis Complex?
Two Tests and Their Astonishing Results

D o you—or does some boy or man you know—suffer from the Adonis Complex? How widespread and serious is the Adonis Complex among today's boys and men? To penetrate the "feeling and talking taboo" and get reliable answers to these questions, we've created two new tests to measure men's attitudes about body image. The first test uses a "library" of male body images, stored on a laptop computer. The second is a paper-and-pencil questionnaire. Our initial studies with both tests have already produced striking evidence of the extent of body image problems among boys and men both in America and Europe.

CREATING A NEW, COMPUTERIZED
BODY IMAGE TEST FOR MEN

For our first test, we wanted to use drawings of male bodies of all different sizes, and then assess attitudes toward body image by asking the test-taker to select the body that best answered various questions. This is a standard technique used by many previous researchers studying body image in both men and women. But most of these previous studies simply asked men to select from a row of body drawings of increasing size; the studies made no distinction between increased size due to fat and increased size due to muscularity. It seemed that this approach wouldn't do for many of the men we had encountered. These men wanted to be bigger, but they certainly didn't want to be fatter. To distinguish between muscle and fat, we developed a more scientifically accurate computerized body image test—we believe the first of its kind—that allows a man to choose among body images that vary along two dimensions, one of increasing fatness and another of increasing muscularity. In our scientific papers, we call this computerized test the "somatomorphic matrix." The word "somatomorphic," derived from the Latin, means "body-changing." In this book we will refer to this test simply as the computerized Body Image Test.

We designed the computerized Body Image Test in collaboration with our colleague, Dr. Amanda Gruber, an expert on both body image and computers. First, we needed to develop a "library" of male body images of all levels of fat and muscularity, which we did by recruiting twenty-seven men of various sizes and shapes to go to a local photography studio to pose for a picture. We carefully measured each man's height, weight, and body fat, and used the resulting numbers to calculate his fat-free mass index, or FFMI—the measure of muscularity explained in the previous chapter and described in detail in Appendix I. Each man then had his photograph taken.

We then gave the twenty-seven photographs to a graphic artist. Using them as a guide, he drew one hundred different figures of male bodies, representing a very wide range of ten levels of body fat and ten levels of muscularity—including levels of muscularity that we believe can be attained only with steroids. To give an idea of the range of body sizes portrayed in our "image library," we show on the next page the four images that occupy the extreme corners of the matrix, clockwise from the upper left: the "bodybuilder" (lowest fat, highest muscle), the "sumo wrestler" (highest fat, highest muscle), the "couch potato" (highest fat, lowest muscle), and the "pencil neck" (lowest fat, lowest muscle).

These one hundred images were then imported into a computer database program, set up so that people could "navigate" among them by clicking "buttons" on the computer screen. As shown on page 65, the computer poses a question, such as "please choose the image that represents the body that you ideally would like to have." By clicking on the "buttons" on the screen, the participant can gradually make the image fatter or thinner, and more or less muscular. This process is illustrated on page 66, which shows a sample image and the images a step away from it in each direction. When the test-taker has found the image that he thinks best answers the question, he clicks the button that says SELECT THIS IMAGE. The computer then asks him the next question.

After some trial and error, we settled on four questions that the computer asks each man:

1) Choose the image that best represents your own body.

2) Choose the image that represents the body you ideally would like to have.

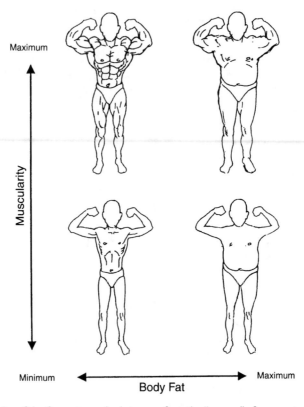

Examples of the four extreme body images from the "corners" of our computerized Body Image Test.

3) Choose the image that represents the body of an average person of your age.

4) Choose the image that represents the body most desired by the opposite sex.

When using the computerized Body Image Test with gay men, we change the last question to read, "Choose the image that represents the body most desired by gay men." In cooperation with our collaborators around the world, we have translated these questions into French, Spanish, German, and Japanese.

We present on pages 68–70 a smaller printed version of our computerized Body Image Test, using twelve selected images from the one

Somatomorphic Matrix

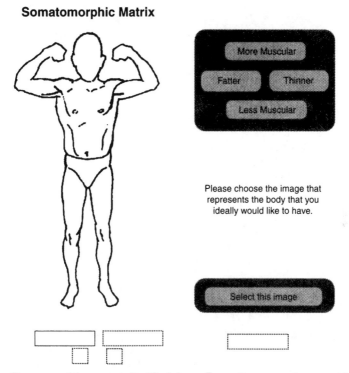

More Muscular

Fatter   Thinner

Less Muscular

Please choose the image that
represents the body that you
ideally would like to have.

Select this image

*The screen of the computerized Body Image Test as it appears to a person
taking the test.*

hundred images that the test contains. If you're a male reader, you might
want to take the test yourself before reading the rest of this chapter,
where we describe the results of our studies. If you're a female reader,
and you have a male friend or family member who wants to take the
test, be sure he tries it before reading the results provided later in this
chapter. Otherwise, there's a risk that his answers might be biased by
knowing how other men have answered the same questions. Also, if
you're a woman, you might want to scan the images and choose the
male body type that appeals most to you. Then, later in this chapter,
you'll find out what most women think is appealing and conversely,
what men *believe* is most appealing to women.

As you look at the images, bear in mind that we had to make some
compromises to keep the number of images manageable. For example,
men vary not only in their amount of body fat and muscularity, but also

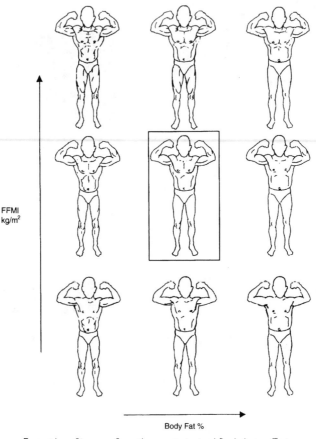

Examples of images from the computerized Body Image Test.

in the way that their bodies are put together, such as the ratio of chest size to waist size, or waist size to hip size. For simplicity, we chose a single body type for our male images, with relatively broad shoulders as compared to the waist or hips. Thus, the images are not ideal for everyone; a man whose upper body is small relative to his lower body (for example, a runner) may find that none of the images corresponds to his own proportions. In cases like this, we ask the participant to do his best, recognizing that the images may not be perfectly reflective of his own body type.

Okay. Now that you've taken the test on pages 68–70 and written down your answers to the four questions, here are the results from other men in the United States and Europe.

WHAT MEN IN THE LOCKER ROOM REALLY THINK

Once we had the computerized Body Image Test up and running on a laptop machine, we took it down to a local gym for a trial run. With permission from the gym's owners, we put an ad at the locker room entrance offering "free body-fat and muscle-mass estimates" for any man who wanted to participate in the study. In two evenings, we netted forty-four men. We carefully measured each man's height and body weight, and then calculated his body fat on the basis of six skinfold measurements that we made with skin calipers. On the basis of these measurements, we calculated each man's FFMI, using the formula described in Chapter 2 and spelled out in Appendix I. Then, we asked each man to take the computerized Body Image Test. The computer asked the four questions listed above, except that in this early version the fourth question was phrased as, "choose the image that you think represents society's ideal."

The average body fat of the forty-four men was approximately 15 percent—about 5 percent less than that of an average American man. On the computer, however, the men in the locker room perceived themselves to be about 3 percent fatter than they actually were. When asked to estimate the fatness of an average man of their age, the respondents estimated just over 20 percent—probably a fairly accurate estimate, on the basis of our experience in measuring hundreds of American men in our studies. So on the fat dimension, there were no major surprises.

But on the muscle dimension, as shown in the bar graph on page 71, the story was very different. The actual FFMI of the forty-four men was impressively high, at 22.7, indicating that they were on average serious weightlifters who would be visibly muscular to even a casual observer. And as shown in the second bar of the graph, their perceived muscle mass corresponded very accurately to their actual muscle mass. But then, when asked to choose the body that they would ideally like to have, the men averaged an astonishing 24.6. In other words, even though these men were already impressively muscular, they still wanted to have another 15 pounds of muscle on top of what they already had!

The next two questions revealed the men's surprisingly low opinion of their bodies. When asked to estimate the muscularity of an average man of their age, they chose images only very slightly less muscular than themselves, with a mean FFMI of 21.9. This means that they overestimated, by about 15 pounds, the actual muscularity of an average American man. Finally, when asked to choose "society's ideal," they again selected an image more than 10 pounds more muscular than themselves. In short, even though they were muscular athletes, these men still

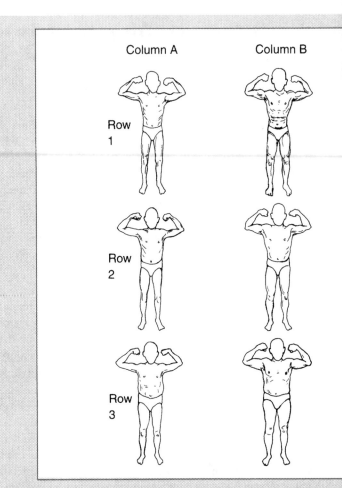

**A self-test using images
from the computerized Body Image Test**

Instructions:

1) To get the most out of this test, it would be helpful to know your own approximate percentage of body fat. If you have had your level of body fat measured at a gym or a clinic, you could use this figure, together with your height and your weight, to calculate your approximate muscularity, using the "fat-free mass index" (FFMI) formula presented in Appendix I.

2) Next, whether or not you have your own measurements of body fat and FFMI, you can still answer the four questions below, using as a reference the twelve images presented on these two pages. If you feel that the best answer to the question is an image that falls in between two of the rows or columns of images, feel free to choose an answer that is halfway between the rows or columns. For example, when asked to choose the image that looks most like

your own body, you may decide that you are slightly fatter than the images in the uppermost row, but slightly thinner than the images in the middle row. In that case, your answer to the question would simply be "halfway between Row 1 and Row 2." It is also possible to answer "halfway above Row 1," or "halfway to the right of Column D," and so forth. Using this method, choose the images that seem to best answer the following four questions:

1) Choose the image that best represents your own body.

2) Choose the image that represents the body you ideally would like to have.

3) Choose the image that represents the body of an average person of your age.

4) Choose the image that represents the body most desired by the opposite sex.

Make sure that you have chosen all four of the images in answer to the questions before turning to the "scoring manual" on the next page.

Self-Test Scoring:

Here are the levels of body fat and and muscularity of the 12 images:

Fat-free Mass Index (FFMI):	Body Fat:
Column A = 16.5	Row 1 = 8%
Column B = 19.5	Row 2 = 20%
Column C = 22.5	Row 3 = 32%
Column D = 25.5	

If you chose an image that falls in between two of the rows or columns, then you must calculate the levels of body fat and/or FFMI accordingly. For example, if you chose an image that fell halfway between Row 1 and Row 2, and also halfway between Column A and Column B, then your image would have a body fat of 14% and an FFMI of 18.0.

Using this method, calculate the body fat and FFMI of each of the four images that you chose in response to the four questions at the beginning of the test. You can then compare your responses with those of other groups of men described in the text.

---

saw themselves as only barely more muscular than an average American, and far short of what they considered society's ideal, much less their own ideal.

Furthermore, these numbers almost certainly underestimate the true levels of body dissatisfaction among the men in the gym as a whole. Since we were performing the study in a public locker room, where men were coming and going throughout the evening, it seems likely that only the men most comfortable with their bodies were willing to participate in the study at all. Those who were more ashamed of their appearance probably didn't sign up, since they didn't want to be measured while other people were watching. In other words, if we had somehow been able to examine a truly random sample of the men in the gym, we probably would have found even higher levels of body dissatisfaction.

BODY IMAGE AMONG COLLEGE MEN IN THREE
DIFFERENT CULTURES: MORE SURPRISING FINDINGS

Could the results of the pilot study be misleading? Maybe men who went to the gym were atypical—unusually dissatisfied with their bodies,

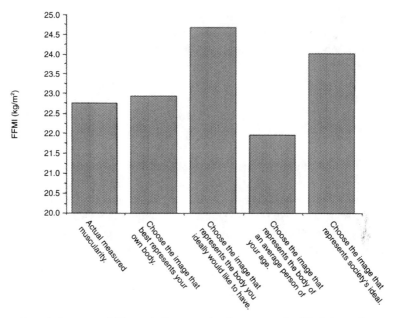

Muscularity scores of 44 men in the gym using the computerized Body Image Test.

or unusually concerned with their physiques. And maybe Americans as a whole were more neurotic about their muscularity than, say, Europeans. To test these possibilities, we decided to give the computerized Body Image Test to ordinary college students in three countries. For this study, we first visited our close associate, Dr. Barbara Mangweth, at the University of Innsbruck in Austria. Innsbruck is an athletic town, a former site of the Winter Olympics, with world-class skiing right at the city outskirts. Even though it is a small city, it has at least three good public gyms—not as many as an American city of the same size, but certainly more than one might expect elsewhere in Europe.

Next, we stopped in Paris and met with our collaborators at the Salpêtrière—a famous hospital and medical research center. Paris is a lot less athletic than Innsbruck, with very few gyms relative to its huge population. There, with the help of another collaborator, Benjamin Bureau, we studied a group of French college students and medical students. Finally, we returned to the United States and recruited a group of college students from a big university in Boston, Massachusetts.

We predicted that the ordinary American college students wouldn't be as dissatisfied with their muscularity as the men in the American gym, since the college students presumably weren't so preoccupied with working out. And we anticipated that the European students would show even less dissatisfaction with their bodies, since they wouldn't be as vulnerable as Americans to the cultural trends we've described above.

We were dead wrong on both predictions.

Although the three groups of students didn't show major distortions on the measurements of fat, they showed even more profound dissatisfaction with their muscularity than the men in our local gym—and this dissatisfaction was just as prominent in Europe as in America. Specifically, when asked to select the body that they ideally would like to have, the three groups of college students, on average, chose a body with about *28 pounds* more muscle than they had themselves. And when asked to choose the body that women preferred most, the men in all three countries chose a body *30 pounds* more muscular than their own! The illustration below shows the actual body size of an average man from the study, side by side with the body he thinks women would like.

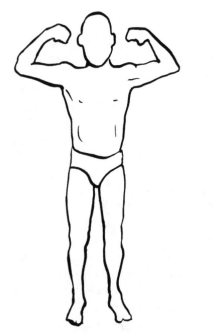
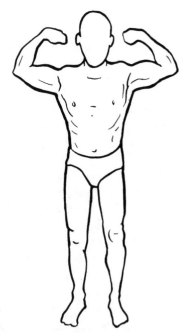

Body reality vs. body ideal in Western college-age men.

WHAT DO WOMEN REALLY WANT?

But do women actually *want* a very muscular male body? Not at all. We gave the computerized Body Image Test to groups of women college students in Austria and the United States, and asked them to choose the male body they liked the best. The Austrian college women chose an ideal male body with 14.9 percent body fat and a perfectly ordinary FFMI of only 20.3; the college women in Boston chose a somewhat more muscular ideal male, with 16.5 percent body fat and an FFMI of 22.9. But in both countries, these levels of muscularity were well below those that the men thought the women would prefer. In other words, there was a difference of 15 to 20 pounds of muscle between what men *thought* women wanted and what women *actually* wanted!

Other researchers have also found similar results. In earlier studies using figure drawings, men tended to err in estimating that women preferred a male body with a heavier stature than what women actually prefer. Women, on the other hand, erred in thinking that men wanted them to look thinner than what men actually liked. In fact, men overestimate the male body size that women prefer as much as women underestimate the female body size that men prefer. In the same vein, anthropologist Alan Klein found in a street-corner survey that 94 percent of women ranked photographs of bodybuilders as "extremely repulsive" on a 5-point scale, where 1 was "extremely attractive" and 5 was "extremely repulsive." Or consider the fact that modern teenage heartthrobs, such as Leonardo DiCaprio or Ricky Martin, aren't particularly muscular. But the men in our studies seemed to think that women wanted them to look like Sylvester Stallone or Jean-Claude Van Damme.

In a recent study from Pennsylvania, researchers Shawn Lynch and Debra Zellner have come out with similar findings. These investigators used a set of male figure drawings with the same level of fat but with increasing muscularity. College men in this study, just like our college men, chose an ideal body much more muscular than themselves, and also estimated that women preferred a highly muscular male body, much bigger than their own. By contrast, actual college women, when presented with the same figure drawings, didn't prefer big muscles.

Lynch and Zellner then tried their figure drawings on a group of older adults averaging around forty-five years of age. The older men, interestingly, did not show the same discrepancies as the college students; there was practically no difference between these men's estimates of their actual bodies, their ideal bodies, and the bodies they thought women preferred. Similarly, when the older women were asked to select the ideal male body, their choice corresponded closely to what the older men had guessed that women would like. This study supports what we've said in the first two chapters of this book: muscle preoccupations are much greater in younger men. Growing up in recent years, these younger men have been saturated with steroid-pumped media images and aggressive advertising from the new body image industries. They perhaps have also experienced "threatened masculinity" as a result of eroding traditional masculine roles. Older men, who grew up in the sixties and seventies, weren't exposed to these societal forces in their youth, and consequently don't have as many muscle hang-ups. Maybe this is why the younger men in the Olympic Gym seemed so much more uptight than the older men about removing their clothes for a shower.

HOW DO YOU SCORE ON THE COMPUTERIZED BODY IMAGE TEST?

What's the significance of our findings with the computerized Body Image Test? If you're a boy or man, and you took the abbreviated version of this test—or if you offered the test to a male friend or loved one—you'll want to know what the results mean. But to get the full benefit of the results, you're going to have to do a little math. First, if you were able to obtain your own height, weight, and body fat measurements, you can calculate your fat percentage and your FFMI, using the formula in Appendix I. We'll call this your "actual body." Next, the image that you chose in response to question 1 of the test represents what you perceive your body to look like. We'll call this your "perceived body." Finally, the image you chose in response to question 2 of the test represents the body that you ideally would like to have. We'll call this your "ideal body."

Now, write down the percentage of fat and the FFMI level for each of these three items: your "actual," "perceived," and "ideal" bodies. If you're a man comfortable with your body appearance, you should find that the three sets of measurements are fairly close together. Specifically, if your actual, perceived, and ideal bodies are all within a range of, say, plus or minus 5 percent on body fat and plus or minus 1 unit on the FFMI scale, then you're a pretty accurate observer, and you're unlikely to have any serious conflicts about your fat or muscularity. Even a difference of 10 percent in body fat or 2 units of FFMI on these three measures is probably not terribly significant in terms of your day-to-day feelings about your appearance. But more than a 15 percent fat discrepancy, or more than a 3-unit FFMI discrepancy on these items may suggest problems. For example, in a new study of 150 college men that we're completing right now, we looked specifically at the difference between perceived and ideal FFMI. Men with a discrepancy of more than 3 units on this measure scored lower on measures of self-esteem, higher on levels of depression, and higher on a test of eating disorder pathology than men with a smaller discrepancy.

On question 3 of the test—estimating the body of an average man of your age—the correct answer depends on your age and nationality. An average thirty-year-old American man, in our experience, has about 20 percent body fat and an FFMI of about 20—in other words, a body like that in row 2, column B in the chart on pages 68–69. Europeans average a few percent lower on body fat and about 1 unit of FFMI lower on muscularity than Americans. So a thirty-year-old European man would be about one-third of the way up from row 2 toward row 1 in the chart, and also about one-third of the way to the left from column B toward column A. Teenagers on both continents are about 4 to 5 percent thinner than thirty-year-olds, but their muscularity is about the same. Using these guidelines, you can judge whether your estimate of an average man of your age is accurate or distorted. If your estimate is off by one whole row or one whole column (in other words, if you made an error of at least 12 percent in body fat or 3 units in FFMI), then you probably have a distorted idea of the body size of other men around you. As we noted above, the men in our locker room study showed a lot of distortion on this item, estimating that average American men were much more muscular than they actually are.

On question 4—estimating the body that women prefer—we've already noted that most men greatly overestimate the amount of muscle that women like. Specifically, both American and European men chose an image in the chart that was between rows 1 and 2 and about halfway between columns C and D—close to the upper limit of muscularity of all the images shown in the chart. In contrast, women tended to choose a figure with body fat between rows 1 and 2 and with muscularity between columns B and C. We've also found that the more a man overestimates the figure preferred by women, the more likely he is to exhibit pathology in other areas, especially eating disorder pathology. These findings become even more dramatic when we calculate the difference between the muscularity a man thinks women want and the muscularity he perceives himself to have. This number is the difference between the FFMI chosen in response to question 4 and that chosen on question 1. If you came out with a difference of more than 4.5 units of FFMI between questions 1 and 4, you're likely to have much higher levels of depression, lower levels of self-esteem, and higher levels of eating pathology than average.

There are limits to these interpretations, however. In particular, it should be remembered that even large discrepancies on the computerized Body Image Test don't necessarily prove that a given man, or even a whole population of men, has a serious form of the Adonis Complex. The test results become important only if the differences between a man's body reality and body ideal result in distress, or keep him from attaining what he'd like in life.

Another limitation of the computerized test is that it looks at only two measures of body appearance: fat and muscularity. Some men may be reasonably content with their levels of fat and muscularity, but still feel miserable about some other aspect of their appearance. For example, they may worry (correctly or incorrectly) that they have thinning hair, ugly facial features, or a small penis. These types of preoccupations, which are forms of what's called "body dysmorphic disorder," wouldn't be picked up on the computerized Body Image Test at all.

THE ADONIS COMPLEX QUESTIONNAIRE: ANOTHER NEW BODY IMAGE TEST

To actually measure the distress the Adonis Complex causes men, we've devised a second type of test, consisting of thirteen simple questions and answers. We call this paper-and-pencil test, shown on the next three pages, the Adonis Complex Questionnaire, or ACQ. The ACQ asks specifically about the ways in which body image concerns may affect a boy's or man's day-to-day life. You'll notice that the test questions cover a broader range of body image concerns than the computerized Body Image Test, which looks only at muscularity and fat. On the ACQ, we have phrased the questions for a reader who is testing himself. If you aren't testing yourself but are instead applying the questions to a man you know, just substitute "he" in place of "you." As in the case of the computerized test above, if you want to try the test, you should take it now, before reading our study results from various groups of men, in order to avoid biasing your answers.

Also, in answering these questions, it's important to be totally honest. For some men, body-appearance concerns and associated behaviors have become so familiar that they hardly even notice them anymore. So

The Adonis Complex Questionnaire

1) How much time do you spend each day worrying about some aspect of your appearance (not just thinking about it, but actually worrying about it)?

   a) less than 30 minutes

   b) 30–60 minutes

   c) more than 60 minutes

2) How often are you distressed by your appearance concerns (that is, feeling upset, anxious, or depressed)?

   a) rarely or not at all

   b) sometimes

   c) frequently

3) How often do you avoid having all or part of your body seen by others? For example, how often do you avoid locker rooms, swimming pools, or situations where you have to take off your clothes? Alternatively, how often do you wear certain clothes to alter or disguise your body appearance—such as a hat to hide your hair or baggy clothes to hide your body?

   a) rarely or not at all

   b) sometimes

   c) frequently

4) How much total time do you spend each day involved in grooming activities to improve your appearance?

   a) less than 30 minutes

   b) 30–60 minutes

   c) more than 60 minutes

5) How much total time do you spend each day on physical activities to improve your body appearance, such as lifting weights, doing sit-ups, or running on a treadmill? (Include only those sports activities in which one of your major goals is to improve appearance.)

   a) less than 60 minutes

   b) 60–120 minutes

   c) more than 120 minutes

6) How often do you engage in dieting, eating special foods (for example, high-protein or low-fat foods), or taking nutritional supplements specifically to improve your appearance?

a) rarely or not at all

b) sometimes

c) frequently

7) How much of your income do you spend on items designed to improve your appearance (for example, diet foods, nutritional supplements, hair products, cosmetics and cosmetic procedures, workout equipment, or gym memberships)?

a) negligible

b) a more substantial amount, but never to the point of creating financial problems

c) enough to cause financial problems at some point

8) How much have your appearance-related activities undermined your social relationships? For example, have your workout activities, dietary practices, or other appearance-related behaviors compromised your relationships with other people?

a) rarely or not at all

b) sometimes

c) frequently

9) How often has your sex life been compromised by your appearance concerns?

a) rarely or not at all

b) sometimes

c) frequently

10) How often have appearance-related concerns or activities compromised your job or career (or academic performance if you are a student)? For example, have you been late, missed work or school, worked below your potential, or lost opportunities for advancement because of your appearance-related needs or self-consciousness?

a) rarely or not at all

b) sometimes

c) frequently

11) How often have you avoided being seen by other people because of your appearance concerns (for example, not going to school, work, social events, or out in public)?

a) rarely or not at all

b) sometimes

c) frequently

12) Have you ever taken any type of drug—legal or illegal—to gain muscle, lose weight, or otherwise improve your appearance?

a) never

b) only legal drugs purchased over-the-counter or by prescription

c) illegal use of steroids, diet pills, or other substances

13) How often have you used more extreme measures (other than drug use) to change your appearance, such as excessive exercising; working out even when injured; fasting or other unhealthy dietary activities; vomiting, use of laxatives or other "purging" methods; or unconventional techniques for muscle development, hair growth, penile enlargement, etc.?

a) rarely or not at all

b) sometimes

c) frequently

before you give a reflex answer of "rarely" or "never" to some of these questions, stop and think carefully. Are you sure that you're being truthful with yourself?

To get your ACQ score, give yourself 0 points for each question answered "a," 1 point for each question answered "b," and 3 points for each question answered "c." Adding the points together yields a total score that will range from 0 to 39.

Now for how other men score. We've given the ACQ to seven different groups of boys and men, each in a different setting. We were careful to administer the questionnaire under completely anonymous conditions, to make sure that participants would tell the truth, without fear of embarrassment. They were instructed not to put their names on the questionnaire but simply to deposit it in a large sealed box stating PLACE ANONYMOUS QUESTIONNAIRES HERE.

To begin, we stood at the front doors of two different gyms—one a "serious" gym for dedicated weightlifters and the other a big health club, similar to the Olympic Gym described in Chapter 1. In the two gyms, we collected responses from fifty-three men and fifty-four men, respectively. Next, we gave the questionnaire to two groups of students—one a group of forty-three boys ages thirteen to eighteen at a private secondary school and the other a group of fifty-four college men, ages eighteen to twenty-six, at the same university in Boston where we administered the computerized Body Image Test described above. We also gave the questionnaire to fifty-four male baby boomers ranging in age from thirty to forty-four, and thirty-six men ranging from forty-five to seventy-five—surveyed on a typical street corner in Cambridge, Massachusetts.

Finally, we gave the ACQ to a seventh group: fifteen patients who were seeing us for treatment of various body image disorders. In these cases, the questionnaire was not anonymous, but it was still of course confidential. We thought that it would be important to include a patient group to get an idea of the range of scores for men who had sought treatment for these problems.

INTERPRETING YOUR SCORE ON THE ACQ

The results from the first six groups of men are shown in the "scattergrams" on the next page. In this figure, each dot corresponds to the score of one man. If you've just taken the ACQ yourself, you'll be interested to see how your score compares with the scores of other boys or men in your age group. For example, if you look at the fifty-four college students, you'll see that three got a score of 10, two got a score of 11, and one got a score of 15. So if you're a college-age man, and you got a score of 10 or above, you're probably around the top 10 percent of college men in terms of appearance-related concerns, whereas if you got a score of 5, you're around the middle of the pack. For comparison, the men in treatment with us had an average score of 27.

Scores on the ACQ, like discrepancies on the computerized Body Image Test, give only a rough index of the severity of a boy's or man's body image concerns. Here's an approximate numerical guide to interpreting the scores:

- Scores of 0–9: You may have some minor concerns about body image, but they probably do not seriously affect your day-to-day life.

- Scores of 10–19: You probably have a mild to moderate form of the Adonis Complex. Body image concerns may or may not seriously compromise

Scores on the Adonis Complex Questionnaire in six groups of men.
*This "scatterplot" shows the range of scores on the Adonis Complex Questionnaire
that we obtained in six groups of men. Each dot represents the score of one man.
See the text of Chapter 3 for further details.*

your day-to-day life, but you may well be a victim of some of the social and psychological forces described in this book. If you're toward the upper end of this range, you need to take a serious look at the effect that the Adonis Complex is having on your life.

- Scores of 20–29: The Adonis Complex is likely a serious problem for you. You should strongly consider some of the treatment options described in the last chapter of this book.

- Scores of 30–39: You undoubtedly have a serious problem with body image. We would urge you to have a consultation with a knowledgeable mental health professional and to try some of the treatments described in this book.

The two tests in this chapter should give you an idea of whether you, or a man you know, may be experiencing features of the Adonis Complex. But still, the test score represents only a crude general measure, because the Adonis Complex can manifest itself in so many different ways in different men. Some men may be driven by dissatisfaction with their muscularity; others may focus primarily on their level of body fat; still others may become focused on specific parts of their bodies, such as thinning hair or facial features. And each of these various forms of body preoccupation may range from mild annoyances to devastating illnesses.

In the next four chapters, we'll go into greater detail about the diverse ways in which the Adonis Complex can manifest itself. By introducing you to men who have participated in our studies and clinical treatment, as well as men with more ordinary body image concerns, we'll offer some insight into the ways in which the Adonis Complex has touched their lives. We'll focus in on more severe cases in the next four chapters, since these are often the most striking and most illustrative. But remember that severe cases are simply more extreme examples of problems that far larger numbers of men have experienced to a lesser degree. We'll also talk about the body image concerns of more ordinary men. In the chapters that follow, you may recognize features that you've experienced yourself, or that you've witnessed in a man you know.

CHAPTER FOUR

Muscle Dysmorphia
Muscularity Run Amok

Bart, a big blond man in his early thirties, worked as a personal trainer in a well-known gymnasium south of Boston. He'd gotten a degree in exercise physiology from a junior college in Massachusetts about ten years earlier, and since then had been working in different jobs in various gyms around the area. Affable and gregarious, Bart knew the Boston gym scene intimately from his long experience; he had great stories to tell about the fitness scene, and especially about some of the local celebrities who had hired him as a personal trainer. An experienced anabolic steroid user, he had competed successfully in a couple of local bodybuilding competitions. He even showed us a picture of himself standing onstage holding a trophy almost as tall as he was.

At one point during his interview with us, when he was talking about his relationships with women, Bart began to reminisce about a former girlfriend who had suffered from anorexia nervosa. With obvious compassion, he spoke about his endless attempts to convince her that she was dangerously thin and that she shouldn't be so obsessed with losing more weight.

"You know, I think I was really able to understand how her mind worked, because I've got exactly the opposite problem from what she had," he said. "When she looked in the mirror, she thought she looked fat even though she was incredibly skinny. But when I look in the mirror, I sometimes think that I look really small, even though I know I'm actually muscular. You'd be amazed at how hard it is, sometimes, for me to actually convince myself that I'm big."

It was astonishing to hear Bart admit to such a problem. At 6 feet 3 inches in height, and weighing 270 pounds, he had a 52-inch chest and 20-inch biceps—putting him close to the size of the biggest competition bodybuilders illustrated in Chapter 2.

"When you look in the mirror, isn't it obvious that you're bigger than practically any of the other guys in the gym?" we asked.

"Yeah, you'd think it would be. But even though I know, on an intellectual level, that I'm actually big, I can get really preoccupied that I look small. I've had times when I wasn't even willing to go outside where people might see me, especially if it was a place where I had to have my shirt off, like at the beach or a swimming pool. And I'm not the only guy who has this problem. There are lots of other guys I've talked to in the gym who have the same thing. I call it 'bigorexia nervosa.'"

KEVIN'S CASE OF "BIGOREXIA"

As Bart recognized, he isn't alone. We've heard countless stories like his in our research studies over the last ten years. For example, we remember Kevin, another guy we met early on in Los Angeles. A tanned California native in his early twenties, Kevin lifted weights at a major gym in Venice Beach, the world epicenter of bodybuilding. When he arrived for his interview, he was dressed in heavy, baggy sweats, even though the temperature on the streets of Los Angeles must have been close to 80 degrees.

Kevin was an accomplished bodybuilder who had used anabolic steroids multiple times during his career. A little under 6 feet tall, he weighed about 230 pounds, with only a 34-inch waist—similar in proportions to the competitive bodybuilders illustrated in Chapter 2. And yet, when it came time for the physical exam at the end of the interview, he seemed a little apprehensive about taking off his shirt.

He started to apologize. "I'm not really in my best shape right now. I competed in a contest a month ago, but since then I've been pigging out on a lot of junk food and not getting enough protein. I guess I always have a slack-off period like this after a contest."

But when he actually took off his shirt, Kevin was spectacularly lean and muscular. We couldn't help saying something to reassure him: "Looks like you've managed to stay in pretty good shape under the circumstances."

He brightened up instantly. "You really think so?" he asked, seeming relieved that we hadn't found something wrong with him.

Having witnessed several previous cases of "bigorexia," we recognized the signs in his behavior. After we had asked a few more questions, he relaxed and began to talk more openly about his worries.

"When I get a bad shot of myself in the mirror, sometimes I actually stay home for the rest of the day and don't go outside, because I'm afraid people will think I look too small," he admitted. "Even when I'm feeling okay about the way that I look, I still wear sweats at all times when I'm working out at the gym."

"Do you take them off in the locker room when you change?"

"Funny that you would ask. I can't even remember the last time that I've taken off my sweats in a public locker room."

Gradually, Kevin began to spill out some of his other secrets. He never wore sleeveless or short-sleeved shirts in public situations, fearing that people would think that his arms looked like "sticks." On one of his shirts, he had deliberately sewn a button on the cuff so that the shirt would wrap tight around his wrist. He thought this would give the illusion that his arms were bigger. He had even tried to purposely shrink a couple of his other shirts in the laundry, hoping that this would make him look bigger as well. He had certain shirts in his drawer that he would never wear, for fear that they would make him look too small. Seeing the huge bodybuilder sitting in front of us, it was hard to believe that he was so tortured by such preoccupations.

So striking were these stories that in 1993 we wrote a small scientific paper describing the cases of nine men with bigorexia. We thought it was a curious new syndrome that might interest other researchers. For the paper, we decided to rename it "reverse anorexia nervosa"— since we felt that this phrase described the syndrome pretty accurately, as Bart himself had pointed out. We thought it must be a rare condition.

But to our surprise, our little published report of nine cases stimulated a flurry of response from the media. Journalists from around the United States and Canada called, wanting to interview us about the findings. We began to think that perhaps reverse anorexia nervosa was not as rare as we had thought. The word "bigorexia" was even selected by Oxford Dictionaries, the section of the Oxford University Press that publishes the prestigious *Oxford English Dictionary*, as one of the "most interesting" new words to enter the English language in the last ten years!

Now, we've come to realize that the rise of the "bigorexia" syndrome is a warning signal—it's a bellwether of what our society is doing to contemporary men's views about their bodies. Of course, Bart and Kevin represent extreme cases—but their stories testify to what is happening, on a lesser scale, in the minds of millions of today's boys and men.

"IS HE BIGGER THAN ME?"

One of these men is Eddie, an accountant who works out at a downtown Boston health club. We met him in the course of one of our studies. "It's amazing—nobody's ever asked me about this before," he said in response to our questions. "But it sounds like you must have heard the same stuff from other guys before me. Yes, I've definitely got a little of that 'bigorexia' thing. I guess it sounds sort of weird, but just a week ago I was at Crane's Beach with my wife, and I was looking around at the other guys on the beach. I saw a guy who was pretty muscular, and I couldn't help but think that he was bigger than me. Finally, I couldn't control it, so I turned to my wife and sort of casually asked, 'You see that guy over there? Is he bigger than me?' My wife immediately started to laugh and said, 'Are you kidding? You're twice his size!' But even that didn't quite convince me. I still found myself thinking that maybe my wife had just said that to humor me, even though she secretly thought that the other guy was bigger than I was."

"How often do you find yourself comparing your size to other guys?" we asked.

"Probably more than I'd admit. I think I do it almost automatically. Any time I see a guy who's muscular, I guess I almost unconsciously start to wonder if he's bigger than I am. It's funny—my friend Bill, whom I've known for years, always notices when I look at other guys. Bill told me that when he first met me, he thought I must be gay because I checked out other guys so often! Actually, I've never had a gay tendency in my life, but the amount of time that I spend looking at other guys is probably greater than the time that I spend checking out girls."

"Do you think you're unusual?"

Eddie smiled and shook his head. "You know, actually I don't think so. When I look around in the gym—especially when I'm looking at the reflection of some guy in the mirror, and he doesn't know he's being watched—I often notice guys comparing themselves with each other. Nobody talks about it, but I think it's common. I'd guess that probably lots of guys think about their muscularity much more than they'd admit to you."

We're convinced that Eddie is right. Admittedly, men with extreme cases of "reverse anorexia nervosa," like Bart and Kevin, probably account for only a few percent of men who go to the gym. But a much larger percentage of men have experienced at least some irrational thoughts about their muscularity, like Eddie's when he was with his wife at Crane's Beach.

To quote some specific numbers, we found 16 men with prominent symptoms of reverse anorexia nervosa in one survey of 160 men from gyms in the Boston and Los Angeles areas—a 10 percent rate. But if we were to add in all those with less serious muscle obsessions, the percentage would probably be double or triple that figure. When we consider that at least 5 million men currently have commercial gym memberships in the United States alone, it's clear that hundreds of thousands of men experience some aspect of this problem.

DO YOU HAVE MUSCLE DYSMORPHIA?

A couple of years ago, after having met dozens of men with this syndrome, we decided to change its name once again, from "reverse anorexia nervosa" to "muscle dysmorphia." We now feel that the latter term is better, because the men with this condition don't really have an eating disorder, as might be implied by the term "anorexia nervosa." Rather, they have misperceptions and/or obsessions about their muscularity. We use the word "dysmorphia" because these men appear to have a special case of a more general condition, already recognized in psychiatry, called "body dysmorphic disorder." In Chapter 7, we'll talk more about body dysmorphic disorder in general; suffice it to say for the present that it represents a condition in which people of either sex develop unrealistic preoccupations that some part of their body looks unattractive, ugly, or disproportionate. In typical cases of body dysmorphic disorder, for example, people become overly concerned that their nose is ugly, that their ears are too small, that their stomach protrudes too much, or that some other aspect of their appearance "isn't right" in some way. Muscle dysmorphia, therefore, is technically the "muscle" subtype of the larger category of body dysmorphic disorder.

We've now published formal diagnostic criteria for muscle dysmorphia, following the format used by the American Psychiatric Association in its diagnostic manual, *Diagnostic and Statistical Manual of Mental Disorders, 4th Edition*, known in the trade as DSM-IV. These formal diagnostic criteria are written almost like a "menu," so that different professionals can agree reliably on whether or not an individual has a particular psychiatric condition. For readers who are interested, we've supplied these criteria in Appendix II. For practical purposes, however, here's a list of some of the questions we ask to determine whether a man is experiencing features of muscle dysmorphia:

Clues to Muscle Dysmorphia

---

1) Do you often worry that your body isn't sufficiently lean and muscular?

2) Have you given up social opportunities that you might have otherwise enjoyed, specifically because you needed the time to work out at the gym?

3) Has your need to work out interfered with your job—for example, causing you to miss work, take too much time off from work, or give up career opportunities?

4) Have you frequently eaten special diets, such as very high-protein or low-fat diets, or used large amounts of protein or other food supplements to improve your muscularity?

5) Have you spent a lot of your money on special foods or dietary supplements, such as protein powders, amino acids, creatine, or other substances that are advertised to boost muscularity?

6) Have you turned down invitations to go to restaurants, parties, or dinners because of your special dietary requirements?

7) Do you avoid situations where people might see your body, such as beaches, swimming pools, locker rooms, or public showers, because you worry that you don't look muscular enough?

8) Do you sometimes wear heavy clothes, such as baggy sweatpants and sweatshirts, to cover up your body because you worry that you don't look muscular enough?

9) Do you sometimes wear several layers of clothes, such as three layers of shirts, because you hope that this will make you look bigger?

10) Do you deliberately choose clothes that you think will make you look more muscular?

11) Do you frequently measure your body, for example using a tape measure to check your waist, chest, or biceps?

12) Have you continued to work out even when you had an injury, because you were afraid that if you stopped you would lose muscle mass?

13) Have you taken drugs (either legal drugs like androstenedione or black-market drugs like anabolic steroids) to make yourself more muscular?

14) Do you frequently compare your muscularity with that of other men around you, because you worry that they may be bigger than you are?

15) If you see a man who is clearly more muscular than you are, do you think about it or feel envious about it for some time afterward?

Men with some degree of muscle dysmorphia will typically answer yes to at least four or five of these questions. If a man answers yes to more than half of the questions, we'd strongly suspect that muscle dysmorphia is significantly affecting his day-to-day life. Men meeting the full-scale formal diagnostic criteria for muscle dysmorphia, shown in Appendix II, will often answer yes to almost every question. In other words, like all forms of the Adonis Complex, muscle dysmorphia ranges in severity from a minor annoyance to a devastating psychiatric condition.

MUSCLE DYSMORPHIA AT ITS WORST

To better understand the psychological features of muscle dysmorphia, we've conducted a new "controlled" study in which we compared men who had this condition with ordinary weightlifters who did not. We wanted to understand why some men in the gym developed severe muscle dysmorphia, whereas others showed practically no symptoms at all. Our experiences with this study have given us new insights into the lives of men who suffer from this syndrome.

For example, the first man to arrive for the study was a bright and sophisticated guy in his late twenties named James. He told us that he had previously held a lucrative job, with the promise of rapid career advancement, in a large accounting firm. But because of his compulsion to train, he would often leave work an hour earlier than he was supposed to, or take two-and-a-half-hour lunch breaks to get enough time at the gym. Because he was spending so much time in the gym, he eventually got fired from his job. Soon thereafter he gave up his accounting career entirely to work as a personal trainer.

"I'd estimate that I'm making about a third as much money as I previously did in my accounting job," he confessed, "but it makes me feel much better to be able to be continuously at the gym. First, it means that I can work out myself during all of the periods when I have spare time. Also, if one of my clients cancels, I can sneak in an extra workout then. And even when I'm demonstrating an exercise to one of my clients, I'm managing to get a little workout just doing that."

Another man had also been fired from his job. He had a good position working as a paralegal in a big downtown law firm. But he had one special requirement: he needed to keep a blender at his desk, in order to make a protein shake for himself every 90 minutes. The noise disrupted his fellow workers, but he refused to alter his ritual for fear that it would compromise his muscularity. Finally, his boss told him that either his blender had to go or his job would go. He chose the second option, and left to become a fitness trainer.

Other men didn't even wait to get fired. We've met men with Ph.D.'s, law degrees, and an M.D. who had voluntarily left their professions because of a compulsive need to work out.

Equally striking were muscle dysmorphia's effects on the social lives of many of the men. Bryan, a man in his late twenties, told us that before he traveled anywhere he had to ascertain whether there were any gyms at his destination. Once, before going to the Virgin Islands, he discovered that there was no gym in the area where he could work out. Desperately, he shipped some of his dumbbells and weight equipment to the hotel in advance, so it would be waiting for him when he arrived. The shipping cost him hundreds of dollars. His girlfriend thought he was "insane." Another man reported that he simply couldn't travel at all; he refused to schedule any social activities too far from home, because he needed to be close to his own equipment and to a supply of food of precisely known caloric and protein content.

The men's sex lives were often disrupted as badly as their social and occupational activities. One man reported that he scrupulously tried to avoid any "unnecessary" physical labor in order to conserve energy for working out. As a result, he limited himself to sex twice a month. Another, when he was training for a bodybuilding competition, wouldn't even kiss his girlfriend for two weeks, fearing that she might transmit calories to him through her saliva. Even the men with less extreme concerns often reported that their muscle preoccupations had cost them their girlfriends.

Equally impressive was the shame and self-depreciation that some of these men revealed. Hunter, a twenty-eight-year-old engineer, had eagerly wanted to attend his fifth college reunion but didn't go at the last minute because he was so afraid that his classmates would think he looked too small. And this was a man who could bench-press 315 pounds—an amount greater than 90 percent of the men in his gym could lift! Jackson, an equally muscular car mechanic, confessed that he hadn't worn shorts for seven years because he felt that he had "chicken legs." Another man told us that he wouldn't take his shirt off in his doctor's office when getting a physical, and instead insisted that the doctor place the stethoscope under his shirt. Another revealed that he wouldn't even take his shirt off in the privacy of his own back yard to tan, despite the fact that no one could see him there. "What were you afraid could happen?" we asked.

"What if a plane went by and looked down?" he replied, perfectly seriously.

It may seem almost comical to think of big, muscular bodybuilders expressing such strange insecurities. But for many, these wildly irrational thoughts were terribly painful. In a particularly graphic case, one study volunteer was so embarrassed about his body size that he called us from the lobby of our building to say that, after thinking about it, he really wasn't big enough to deserve to participate in the study at all. It was only with difficulty that we persuaded him to overcome his fears and come upstairs. When he walked in, it was almost impossible to believe that he could have such a distorted body image. His FFMI was more than 24, and his body fat was only 6 percent—similar to the figures for the impressively lean and muscular drug-free bodybuilder in the first set of pictures in Chapter 2.

The men with muscle dysmorphia described an almost limitless number of strategies to deal with their insecurities. One man held his body rigidly in a certain posture to try to look bigger. Another spent three hours a day on his diet—planning what he would eat, shopping for food and supplements, weighing his food, and painstakingly apportioning exact amounts into small plastic bags. Variations on the compulsive exercising theme were also common. For example, Mike, a handsome, muscular young man who worked as a cook, grabbed every possible opportunity to exercise while he was at work. He always insisted on carrying heavy beer kegs, compulsively performed chin-ups on a rack in the kitchen, and repeatedly and rapidly lifted huge stacks of heavy dishes—all in an attempt to build up his muscles while on company time. He even sneaked into the bathroom at work to quickly do fifty or so push-ups before anyone came in. "When people came into the bathroom and saw me doing push-ups on the floor, or when they saw me lifting the dishes, I was totally embarrassed," Mike told us. "I felt like an idiot. But I *had* to do it—I couldn't stop! I was so desperate to build myself up."

Our numerical data bore out these anecdotal impressions. For example, the men with muscle dysmorphia reported that they checked themselves in mirrors an average of 9.2 times per day, and some reported checking themselves in the mirror more than 50 times a day. Perhaps most telling was another question that we asked: "How many minutes in a day would you say you are preoccupied with thoughts of being too small, not being big enough, or getting bigger?" The ordinary weightlifters in the comparison group reported that they spent about 40 minutes per day thinking about such things—which already seems like a lot. But the men with muscle dysmorphia averaged 325 minutes—

more than five hours per day—with such preoccupations. Several replied that they spent essentially every waking minute worrying about their size.

None of the thirty ordinary bodybuilders in the comparison group ever worried about his appearance to the point that he had been afraid to take his shirt off in public. But twenty-one of the twenty-four men with muscle dysmorphia reported this problem, sometimes to an extreme degree. One twenty-year-old man, for example, recollected that he had always refused to be on the "skin" team playing football with friends, and had instead always insisted on being on the "shirts" team. If he got stuck on the "skin" team, he would invariably come up with an excuse for not being able to play.

"What did your friends make of it?" we asked.

"They never could figure out what was going on with me," he replied. "I'm sure it never occurred to any of them that I was trying to escape from being on the 'skin' team simply because I was worried that I was too small. I think that if you had asked my friends, they would have said that I was the most muscular guy of the bunch."

We also asked our weightlifters to rate themselves on several multiple-choice items. When asked whether they were satisfied with the way that their bodies were proportioned, 47 percent of the men with muscle dysmorphia responded that they were "totally dissatisfied" or "mostly dissatisfied." On the question "How fat do you feel?" 74 percent felt "somewhat," "mostly," or "extremely" fat. And 74 percent stated that they would feel "extremely uncomfortable" if they could not exercise for a week.

Many of the men with muscle dysmorphia had also taken serious risks with their health, or even damaged their health, because they couldn't shut off their preoccupation with being too small. About half of the men in our study had used anabolic steroids, even though many admitted that they worried about the dangers of these drugs. Many said that they had continued training even when they had an injury and should have stopped for a period of time. Some could recall instances when they had steadily worsened an injury because they insisted on continuing to work out. One man, for example, developed a hernia from doing excessive and intense squats—an exercise in which he rested a 405-pound barbell across his shoulders, then squatted down to a position where his thighs were parallel to the floor, and then stood back up again, for eight or ten repetitions.

"I realized that it could be a hernia," he admitted. "But I didn't want to do anything to let up on my workouts, so I kept right on training. If the pain got really bad, I lightened up on the weights, but when the pain got a little better, I immediately went back to heavy squats again."

He kept training until the pain got so severe that he was forced to remain home for five weeks. After the five weeks, he felt ashamed that he might have gotten smaller, and he didn't dare to go back to the public gym for months. Instead, he worked out privately in his basement.

MUSCLE CONFESSIONS OF ORDINARY MEN

The astonishing stories of the men in our study gave us a detailed picture of muscle dysmorphia in its most severe forms. But from this experience, we also became aware of the milder, but still problematic, muscle concerns that commonly afflict other boys and men—both those who go to the gym regularly and those who do not. In talking to these men, we continued to be struck by how the "feeling and talking taboo" had prevented them from ever revealing their obsessions. Typically, both in formal interviews and informal conversations, we found we had to break the ice by telling a few anecdotes about other men with muscle dysmorphic symptoms. Then they would often quickly light up and say, "You know, I've had a little bit of that, too."

Keith, a sophomore at a prestigious local college, showed this instant recognition. "I can understand how those guys feel immediately," he told us. "I've gone through times when I get quite hung up about it myself. I remember in my dorm room last year, there was one place where the light came down from above, and when I stood under the light, I could see my reflection in the bathroom mirror through the open door. I really liked how muscular I looked with the light shining on me at exactly that angle. I got to the point where I used to routinely check myself out at least once a day, sometimes more, with my shirt off, standing in exactly the same spot and looking in the mirror. Once my roommate walked in unexpectedly and caught me standing there and posing. It was wicked embarrassing!"

"Did you have any other problems along those lines?"

"Well, actually, I did. There was one time that I looked at myself in the same mirror, and for some reason I just looked really out of shape. I was supposed go out on a date in about an hour with a new girl that I'd just met. After looking at myself in the mirror for a while, I got so hung up that I didn't look good enough that I called her and told her that I had come down with pneumonia, and that the doctors at the health service had advised me that I shouldn't go out. As soon as I hung up the phone, I felt incredibly dumb, but then it was too late. I couldn't very well call her back and tell her that my pneumonia was suddenly cured."

"Did you go on another date later?"

"Yes. As a matter of fact, we've been seeing each other for about six months now. But I've still never told her the story. She believes to this day that I actually did have pneumonia."

Dante, a student at the same college as Keith, had similar confessions. "I have a great relationship with my girlfriend Maura, but I still wonder all the time if she's more attracted to my friend Matt, who works out at the gym every day and has a better physique than me. It's stupid. She gives me no indication of that. But I can't help but wonder if a part of her is attracted to his muscles. Maybe I'm just thinking that more muscles is automatically more appealing to women, just like bigger breasts are more attractive to a guy, or at least to me."

Dante seemed reassured when we told him that his preoccupations were mild in comparison to those of the men in our study. He went on, "You know, now that I remind myself about it, I spend quite a lot of time worrying in one way or another about my muscularity. For example, I've always been careful never to select a roommate who was more muscular than me, for fear that my girlfriends might find my roommate more attractive. And I've frequently tried to get into a regular pattern of going to the gym. But my schedule's just too busy to be able to put in enough time. It *really* bothers me when I see guys who can afford to spend a couple of hours at the gym every day and who get really buff."

In reality, it emerged, Dante's problem wasn't a lack of time. It was that he was embarrassed to have his body seen in the gym. "There are times that I've looked in the door of the gym at school and seen that it was crowded," he admitted, "and I've just turned around and gone back to my dorm again. It just made me too self-conscious to lift weights when there were a lot of other guys around who might be looking at me."

He described the same problem in other situations. "There are a lot of times in the summer when other guys had their shirts off at the beach or someplace like that, but I've deliberately kept my shirt on because I was afraid I didn't look big enough. Sometimes I was sweating like a pig, but I still wouldn't take my shirt off. I remember telling somebody that I had to keep my shirt on because I had a problem with sun sensitivity.

I don't think it sounded very plausible, considering how dark and Mediterranean I look."

"Have you revealed these concerns to your close friends?"

"No way."

Darren, a thirty-year-old financial analyst, had been more successful at overcoming the feeling and talking taboo. He came up to us one day in the gym, introduced himself, and asked, "I know you're experts on bodybuilding. Tell me, does creatine really work?"

"Are you thinking of trying it?"

"Well, as a matter fact, I've been on it for the last six weeks. But I can't tell for sure whether it's making a difference or not."

As the conversation continued, it emerged that creatine was only one of a long series of muscle-growth supplements that Darren had tried over the years. "How much money have you spent on supplements?" we asked at one point.

"I'd be afraid to add it all up," he said, "but it would be several thousand dollars over the last couple of years alone. It's worth it, though, if it improves my odds with the girls when I go out to a club."

"Actually, it may not improve your odds. We've done studies which show that women don't particularly like a very muscular male body."

"You know, that's probably true. But I'll still work out and take creatine anyway, because no matter what you say, or no matter what women say, if you're big and muscular, it still has an effect. I don't know exactly how to put it. I guess you could say it's the law of the jungle."

We doubt that thirty years ago many financial analysts took muscle-building supplements and regularly worked out at the gym in a calculated attempt to look more muscular to women. But today, we hear many men describe the same intentions as Darren. Perhaps, in his reference to the law of the jungle, Darren was trying to express the problem of "threatened masculinity" that we described earlier—the sense that in today's world of empowered women, a man needs muscles to distinguish himself as a man.

Even teenagers have told us stories that sounded like early signs of "threatened masculinity." One high school student reproduced for us a scene he witnessed at a table in the cafeteria with his friends from the soccer team.

"You know," said one, "I was reading in some magazine that the size of your wrists is a good measure of your genetic potential for how muscular you can get."

Another boy started looking despondently at his wrists. "Mine are really small."

Soon, the boys had cleared an area of the table, laid their forearms side by side, and started carefully comparing the relative size of their wrists.

"I can't see what the size of your wrist has to do with how big your chest or your shoulders could get," said the boy with the small wrists.

"Maybe. But I'll bet that the size of your wrists is connected to how big your forearms can get," said another. "And in the winter, the only part of you that the chicks can see is your forearms."

"Does anybody know a good forearm workout?" asked another immediately.

The discussion continued with a comparison of various forearm exercises. One of the boys pushed his chair back from the table and began to demonstrate the proper technique for performing wrist curls and reverse wrist curls.

"I've tried those for a while," said another boy. "But I could never see a difference in my forearms."

"Yeah. Maybe I'll just wear long-sleeved shirts this winter," said the boy with the small wrists, still looking despondent.

WHAT CAUSES MUSCLE DYSMORPHIA?

Of all the psychological problems that we've written about over the years, few have sparked such interest in the media as muscle dysmorphia. Why has the public become so fascinated with this problem? When we posed this question to various journalists, some told us that they were eager to do a story about body image in men, because they had been saturated with stories about body image in women over the years. Others were intrigued with the idea that even muscular weightlifters could have secret anxieties about their body size. Two or three male journalists privately told us that they'd experienced a bit of the problem themselves.

Certain questions come up regularly in our interviews. First, just how common is muscle dysmorphia? As we've said earlier, hundreds of thousands of men have undoubtedly experienced some of these symptoms. In the United States alone, the number of men with severe, full-blown muscle dysmorphia, meeting the formal diagnostic criteria in Appendix II, might be 100,000. But, as we've explained, this number is tough to estimate; it might be considerably greater than 100,000. By definition, muscle dysmorphia is associated with shame and embarrassment about physical appearance. Most men with muscle dysmorphia would dread coming to an office for an interview where they might be asked about their body image hang-ups—witness the guy who froze in our lobby and made it upstairs only with massive encouragement. Therefore, for every man who responded to our advertisements in the gym, many others might have chosen not to respond, specifically because they were too embarrassed about their bodies.

And this isn't the only factor that could affect our estimates. We must consider that many men exercise at home, or simply don't exercise at all, because they're too embarrassed about their muscularity to be seen in a crowded commercial gym. Even Dante in our story above, despite having only mild symptoms of muscle dysmorphia, was often scared away from the gym because he was self-conscious about his muscularity. Since we recruited most of our study participants in gyms, we may have missed a large fraction of the cases.

The 1997 *Psychology Today* survey, mentioned in Chapter 2, hints at just how many such cases there may be. You may recall that an astounding 63 percent of men were dissatisfied with their abdomen, and 45 percent with their muscle tone. We've also mentioned that many studies, including our own findings with the computerized Body Image Test, indicate that boys and men want to be much bigger than they actually are. So combining all of these lines of evidence, there may be far more men with symptoms of muscle dysmorphia than anybody has imagined.

In our interviews, journalists also invariably asked us: where does muscle dysmorphia come from? As we've already indicated above, we believe that muscle dysmorphia is one of the casualties of our society's increasing pressure on men to look lean and muscular. But why do some men develop profound symptoms in response to this pressure, whereas others do not?

In response to this question, we would hypothesize that muscle dysmorphia is not really a new disease, but rather a new manifestation of an old disease. In technical terms, we think that it may be related to a condition called "obsessive-compulsive disorder." This is a disorder in which people develop "obsessions"—recurrent thoughts that they can't get out of their heads—and "compulsions"—repetitive behavior patterns that they do excessively. For example, a patient with obsessive-compulsive disorder might develop an obsession with dirt, where he is tortured with recurrent thoughts that there might be dirt or germs on his hands. In response, he might develop a compulsion to wash his hands two hundred times per day.

But people can develop many other kinds of obsessions and compulsions. Suppose, for example, that you're a young woman in modern Western society who has grown up playing with impossibly thin Barbie dolls and looking at pictures of Twiggy. Now, if you're born with a predisposition to obsessive-compulsive symptoms, you might become obsessed with thoughts of being too fat. Then, in response to these obsessional thoughts, you might begin to compulsively diet and exercise to lose weight. In that case, you would probably be diagnosed as having anorexia nervosa. But if one substitutes "fat" and "dieting" for "dirt" and "hand washing," it becomes clear that anorexia nervosa is similar to obsessive-compulsive disorder, except that it focuses on body weight and food.

Now suppose that you're a boy who has grown up playing with muscular G.I. Joes and reading comics with muscular action heroes. As a young teenager, you start to watch professional wrestling on television and begin to look at muscle magazines. You see images of steroid-fueled bodybuilders in advertisements, on television, and in the movies. In this case, perhaps, if you have a predisposition to obsessive-compulsive symptoms, you might become obsessed that your body isn't muscular enough, and develop a corresponding compulsion to work out excessively at the gym. In short, the symptoms of muscle dysmorphia may represent a new "outlet" for obsessive-compulsive tendencies in modern men, assailed by unrealistic body images in the media, and perhaps also unconsciously threatened by the growing equality of women.

Psychological experiences may combine with these various biological and social factors to breed symptoms of muscle dysmorphia. For example, a boy teased by peers as a child, or repeatedly deprived of self-esteem about his body, might be particularly motivated to channel his obsessions into compulsive weightlifting—although this hypothesis has not yet been scientifically studied. We remember one boy who lost his father at an early age. By the beginning of his teenage years, he had already become identified as the "man of the house." Perhaps because of his anxiety about this unwanted role, together with an inherent tendency toward compulsive behavior patterns, he began to lift weights constantly, starting at the age of fourteen. Soon he started using anabolic steroids.

This brings us to another question we're often asked. Is all bodybuilding inherently pathological? Is there something a little wrong with people who lift weights at the gym six days a week? The answer is no. Weightlifting, in itself, is obviously healthy and beneficial. Muscle dysmorphia occurs only when this normally healthy activity becomes an unhealthy preoccupation, or becomes associated with distress or impaired social and occupational functioning.

Let's return to our example of hand-washing compulsions. If a man washes his hands five times a day, or even fifteen times a day, that's normal. But if he washes his hands two hundred times per day, then he's got a psychiatric disorder. By analogy, working out, even working out very hard and frequently, doesn't represent an illness. Indeed, it's much healthier than not working out at all—just as washing your hands five or even fifteen times per day is a lot healthier than washing your hands zero times per day. But when working out runs amok, as in muscle dysmorphia, then it becomes just as pathological as compulsive hand washing.

HOPE FOR MEN WITH MUSCLE DYSMORPHIA

What can be done to help men with muscle dysmorphia? In response to this question, one must first recognize that the vast majority of men with these symptoms never seek treatment in the first place. They're spending their time going to the gym, planning their diets, and worrying about how they look; the last thing they'd want is psychotherapy. Once again, this situation is analogous to the case of anorexia nervosa. Young women with anorexia nervosa don't often come voluntarily to a doctor's office complaining that they're too thin and need to gain weight. Instead, they're usually dragged to the office by anxious parents, or sent for treatment because their condition is diagnosed by a school counselor, a pediatrician, or some other professional. So with muscle dysmorphia, as with anorexia nervosa, the biggest hurdle is persuading the individual to consider treatment.

Indeed, the hurdle may be even higher in men with muscle dysmorphia than in women with anorexia nervosa. In anorexia nervosa, the compulsive dieting can be life-threatening. Every year, about 1 percent of patients with anorexia nervosa die as a result of malnutrition, increased vulnerability to infection, or suicide. Thus, Mother Nature will usually "force the hand" in cases like this. But muscle dysmorphia is different. Such individuals are usually in good *physical* health; after all, they're paying compulsive attention to their bodies, because that is part of their condition. A few may come to a doctor's attention because they get into trouble from side effects of drugs like anabolic steroids, or because they develop a serious orthopedic injury, but they still keep on training. But even men with severe cases, whose social lives and careers may be devastated by their disorder, are much too busy at the gym to even think of going to a doctor or therapist.

So for someone with serious symptoms of muscle dysmorphia, the most critical step is to get him to accept some kind of treatment in the first place. We hope that this book will be helpful in this respect. If you're a man seriously preoccupied with your muscularity, you may be surprised to discover that you have a recognized psychological condition that others share. If you're a woman reading this chapter, you may have witnessed this problem in a boy or man you love.

What treatment options are best? We can't say for sure, because muscle dysmorphia is such a recent condition that scientific treatment studies have not yet been published. But for men with full-scale cases of muscle dysmorphia, we often recommend cognitive behavioral therapy. This is a practical, here-and-now kind of treatment that helps people change their distorted view of their appearance, resist problematic behaviors such as reassurance seeking, and stop avoiding important obligations like social events. For some patients, we also sometimes recommend certain antidepressant medications known to be effective in treating obsessive-compulsive disorder. In our hands, these same medications have provided tremendous relief for some men who had uncontrolled obsessions about their muscularity. We'll talk more about both of these types of treatment in the final chapter of this book.

But what if you're one of the much larger number of men with milder, but still bothersome, preoccupations with your muscularity? You probably don't need formal psychotherapy, much less medication, but you may very well need to stand back and take a look at what society is doing to you. Are you surrounded by media images trying to persuade you that an ideal man should have a larger-than-nature, steroid-pumped body? Have you been assailed with advertising from the growing male body image industries, trying to convince you that somehow you *should* be unhappy with your present level of muscularity? Are you, perhaps unwittingly, equating muscularity with masculinity?

Of all of the forms of the Adonis Complex, muscle dysmorphia represents perhaps the most graphic casualty of our society's increasingly unattainable ideals for the male body. For men with mild symptoms of muscle dysmorphia, then, the best "therapy" may be simply to recognize these messages for what they are and not get taken in by them. With this book, we can't pretend to change society, but we do hope that for men with concerns about muscularity, whether mild or severe, we can offer some relief from incessant and unrealistic media messages that bigger is better.

CHAPTER FIVE

Anabolic Steroids
Dangerous Fuel for the Adonis Complex

Duke Nukem, a muscle-bound warrior with blazing automatic weapons in both hands, is the hero of a popular series of CD action games. On their Nintendos, Sony PlayStations, and home computers, at least 5 million boys have guided Duke through successive game levels—Hollywood Holocaust, Red Light District, Death Row, and Toxic Waste Facility—blowing away enemies at every turn and finding key cards to open doors into secret rooms. But from time to time, Duke needs extra power to boost his strength and speed. What does he do? Under the guidance of the game-player, Duke finds and ingests hidden bottles of *steroids!*

Some growing boys aren't content to take steroids only in virtual reality; they want the real thing. Remember that as younger children, these same boys played with supermuscular action toys like G.I. Joe, Batman, and the Wolverine. They fantasized about the Herculean heroes they saw in comic books and television cartoons. As adolescents, they looked to muscular actors and sports stars for role models. And eventually, they learned that they could make their puny bodies look more like the bodies of their heroes—just by taking a drug.

The Adonis Complex couldn't have reached its present proportions without anabolic steroids. As we've seen earlier, steroids have created athletes, actors, and models bigger and stronger than any ordinary man, and the media have promulgated their images everywhere. These images have glorified the steroid-pumped body, portraying it as a model of health, athletic prowess, hard work, and dedication—while almost never admitting that it was a product of dangerous chemicals.

The public health problem of steroid use would be minor if the victims were only a few professional athletes and actors. But millions of boys and men have looked to these men as role models, and have longed to have bodies like theirs. And though nonprescription steroids are illegal in the United States and many other countries, these drugs are widely available through a vast underground black market, in which even a young teenage boy can buy them if he has the right connections.

Men's dissatisfaction with body image, according to research studies, is the most powerful driving force behind this huge black market. For example, researchers Arthur Blouin and Gary Goldfield have found that improving looks was the biggest reason that athletes gave for using steroids. Kirk Brower, another steroid expert, has shown in a series of studies that dissatisfaction with body size is a strong predictor of both steroid use and of long-term steroid dependence.

As a result, in today's body-conscious boys and men, anabolic steroid abuse has grown into one of the most dangerous manifestations of the Adonis Complex. The medical hazards of steroids—the increased risks for heart disease, stroke, and possibly prostate cancer with advancing age—represent only part of this danger. The greater danger of steroids arises from their psychiatric effects: boys and men suffering from the Adonis Complex may develop dangerous irritability and aggression while taking steroids, and sometimes severe episodes of depression during steroid withdrawal. Men can become dependent upon steroids, and some go on to become dependent on other injectable and addictive drugs that are also sold in the gym. Users may continue to take steroids, even when these drugs have caused them to become uncontrollably aggressive, to abuse women, or even to commit violent crimes.

HOW COMMON IS STEROID USE?

In the sixties and seventies, anabolic steroid use was largely restricted to elite athletes. But with the rise of the Adonis Complex over the last ten to twenty years, illegal use of these substances has exploded among college-age men, high school boys, and even some aspiring boys in elementary school! Now hundreds of thousands of men and boys use steroids not for any athletic purposes but just to get bigger.

Let's look at a few statistics. The scientific world was shocked in 1988 when researchers published a study in the prestigious *Journal of the American Medical Association* reporting the results of a survey of 3,403 twelfth-grade boys in forty-six public and private high schools around the United States. In this study, 6.6 percent of the boys reported that they were using or had used anabolic steroids. That's one boy out of fifteen across the United States! And more than two-thirds of these kids indicated that they had started using steroids at age sixteen or younger. In 1993, in the equally prestigious *New England Journal of Medicine*, another research group reported survey results from 1,881 high school students in one county in Georgia. The findings were almost identical: 6.5 percent of boys reported having used anabolic steroids illegally, without a doctor's prescription. These students were even younger: on average, they were under fifteen years old. And when examining these data, we must consider that some boys who used steroids might have deliberately not responded to the questionnaire, or denied their steroid use, because they were afraid that they might somehow be exposed. If so, the true rate of steroid use among these boys might be even higher.

Think of what this means. Let's assume that the 6.5 percent rate of steroid use in high school boys has remained roughly stable over the last twelve years, and that boys who drop out of school have the same rate of steroid use as boys who graduate. About 25 million American men have turned eighteen during the last twelve years. That would yield more than 1,500,000 American men, presently between the ages of eighteen and thirty, who have used anabolic steroids before age eighteen. Then we would have to add all of the men in this eighteen to thirty group who also have tried steroids but didn't start until after age eighteen. Then add the hundreds of thousands of boys presently under age eighteen who have already started taking steroids; and finally add all of the men presently over the age of thirty who have used these drugs at some time in their lives. Putting all of these numbers together, the total number of American men who've used anabolic steroids could reach 2 million to 3 million.

Of course, such estimates are subject to error. Some survey respondents might have erroneously reported anabolic steroid use when they had actually used only corticosteroids (such as cortisone, which has no muscle-building properties) or "muscle-building" food supplements that were not steroids at all. In fact, some people confuse steroids with food supplements, such as protein powders and creatine. (We'll talk about supplements in more detail in Chapter 8.) But even allowing for such errors, we're still almost certainly left with well over a million American men who have used genuine anabolic steroids. And often they started taking these drugs as teenagers.

MYTHS AND REALITIES ABOUT STEROIDS

Why has steroid use become epidemic? The answer becomes more obvious as we clear up some myths about these drugs.

Myth No. 1:   *Steroids don't work, or they work only a little.*

Reality: Steroids are very effective in building up muscle.

If you've looked at the pictures in Chapter 2, you already know how ridiculous this first myth is. Taken in large doses, steroids are phenomenally effective. A mediocre athlete, with modest motivation, who sleeps badly, eats junk food, and even misses an occasional workout—but who takes anabolic steroids—can easily grow more muscular than a gifted, dedicated, and hardworking athlete who does not.

Practically any kid who has hung around a gym knows this. All he has to do is look around and see what has happened to guys who have used these drugs. We vividly remember one of the first steroid users we interviewed for our studies in the mid-1980s, a twenty-three-year-old man named Jay. An accountant for a mortgage company in South Boston, Jay was a dedicated weightlifter who had taken five or six "cycles" of anabolic steroids—courses of drugs lasting eight to sixteen weeks at a time—during the last five years. He had tried testosterone injections, another injectable drug called Deca-Durabolin, and various steroids in pill form, such as Winstrol, Anavar, and Hemogenin. But his favorite drug of all was Equipoise—an injectable veterinary steroid designed for use in horses. Equipoise also builds muscle in human bodybuilders, and it's very popular because veterinary steroids are often easier to get on the black market than their human equivalents.

At 5 feet 10 inches, Jay was 225 pounds of solid muscle. He wore a double-extra-large loose athletic sweatshirt because it was one of the few pieces of clothing that would actually fit him. But he hadn't always looked this way.

"When I was seventeen, in my junior year in high school," he began, "I'd guess I weighed about a hundred fifty-five pounds. I was just your basic, slightly skinny kid. Then I started lifting weights, and I began to really get into it. I'd guess that maybe I gained about ten pounds from weightlifting before I went on my first cycle. In fact, I can remember exactly—I weighed a hundred sixty-seven at the time I began my first cycle of Anavar and Deca-Durabolin. It was really amazing how quickly I started to get stronger. I gained maybe about five or ten pounds in six weeks on the first cycle. But then, when I was eighteen, the summer after I graduated from high school, I started doing Equipoise, taking three cc's twice a week, and then I got ahold of some Hemogenin from Brazil. I took one of those each day, and towards the end, I went up to two a day for a while. I would estimate that I went from about a hundred and eighty pounds to at least two hundred and ten, maybe even close to two twenty, between June and the fall of that year. I put at least two inches on my bicep and four to five inches on my chest, and I actually lost an inch of fat from my waist!"

"Didn't you worry about injecting a veterinary drug like Equipoise?" we asked.

"Are you kidding? They give that stuff to two-million-dollar racehorses. I ain't worth anything close to two million!"

Since then, we've interviewed numerous boys and men who described muscle gains like Jay's. Some were even more dramatic. There was Paul, who told us that he started out able to do only one or two squats with 135 pounds. As described in the previous chapter, this is an exercise in which you place a bar on your shoulders, and squat down to a position where your thighs are parallel to the floor. Even a guy who isn't in shape, and who has never trained with weights at all, could probably do at least one squat with 135 pounds. But from this starting point, and with the help of one long cycle of steroids lasting almost a year, Paul increased his squat from 135 pounds to 655 pounds—a weight so heavy that the steel bar, with six big iron plates plus a couple of smaller ones on each side, would bend into an arch over his shoulders. During that year, Paul's body weight went from 135 pounds to 235 pounds.

Such is the power of steroids. Another young man we interviewed put it very simply: "Why be Clark Kent when I can be Superman?"

In light of stories like these, how could anyone have fallen for the myth that steroids don't work? Part of the blame for this myth, we must confess, lies with the medical and scientific community. For years, many reputable books of pharmacology, endocrinology, and medicine have stated flatly that anabolic steroids have no proven ability to help people gain muscle mass. In fact, if you look up various anabolic steroids in the 2000 edition of the *Physicians' Desk Reference*, you'll still find statements such as "Anabolic steroids have not been shown to enhance athletic ability."

Indeed, to appreciate just how long it has taken for the scientific community to acknowledge the effects of steroids, consider this: in the summer of 1996, the *New England Journal of Medicine* published an elegant and carefully controlled study, in which a group of top-level scientists demonstrated that an anabolic steroid, testosterone enanthate, was effective in causing gains in muscle mass. To the medical community, this was *news!* A fact known to kids in the gym for the last twenty years was still considered sufficiently unproven by doctors that in 1996 it was featured as the lead article in the most prestigious medical journal in the world!

Why did it take decades to confirm the obvious? The mistake becomes clear when we read the earlier scientific studies conducted with steroids. Most of these studies used doses of steroids that were ridiculously low in comparison with those actually used by athletes. For example, there are more than a dozen studies, from the 1970s and 1980s, in which one group of men received between 35 and 140 milligrams of some type of steroid per week, and a comparison group of men received an inert placebo—a "sugar pill." Not surprisingly, with puny doses like this, most studies didn't show an effect. By comparison, a typical high school boy in the United States would think nothing of taking anywhere between 300 and 1,000 milligrams of steroids per week, and a hard-core competition weightlifter might take up to several thousand milligrams per week—up to fifty or a hundred times the dose used in many of these laboratory investigations!

Various other technical and methodological flaws invalidated the findings of many early steroid studies. Suffice it to say that the medical community, by being slow to recognize the power of these drugs, underestimated their effectiveness and appeal for men and boys. As a result, medical authorities often lacked credibility when they tried to persuade men and boys not to take steroids.

"My doctor doesn't know shit about steroids," said Vince, the eighteen-year-old steroid user from the Olympic Gym whom we described in the first chapter. Countless other men have told us the same. This lack of knowledge is unfortunate; nowadays, most health professionals are well trained about many areas of substance abuse—alcohol, marijuana, cocaine, and so forth. But steroids, drugs used by more than a million American men, aren't even mentioned in many substance abuse courses.

There's another reason the effects of steroids have been shrouded in secrecy: it was in the interest of athletes to keep it that way. Athletes were anxious to preserve the secret of just how effective these drugs really were, so they could continue to give the impression that their bodies and athletic prowess were simply the result of hard work and dedication. After all, it would be scandalous if the public figured out that some favorite 280-pound football lineman on television, a supposedly homegrown all-American hero, was a product of drugs.

Similarly, manufacturers of food supplements and other products for athletes had every reason to deny the effectiveness of steroids. By perpetuating the myth that steroids didn't work, they could argue that young men shouldn't waste money on these drugs, but should buy their products instead.

This shroud of secrecy extends all the way down to ordinary kids in the gym. Even scientists specializing in substance abuse have often had difficulty penetrating the steroid culture to hear what's going on. We remember one steroid user named Jack who told us, "My friends would tell you about using cocaine or heroin before they'd tell you they'd used steroids. I know some guys who'd tell you they'd robbed a convenience store, or raped somebody, before they'd tell you that they'd been on juice."

On the basis of our research experience, we agree with Jack. It's a testimony to the power of the Adonis Complex that a man is more willing to reveal that he's taken cocaine than to reveal that his body appearance is dependent upon steroid use.

Myth No. 2:   *The muscle gains from steroids quickly wilt away when you stop using them.*

Reality: Some of the muscle gains from steroids last for a long time.

Nowadays, most authorities have conceded that steroids really do work. But many people, especially those who lack firsthand experience with steroids, still seem to think that although you can bulk up by taking steroids, you'll quickly shrink back to your original size if you stop taking them. Again, a lot of athletes and a lot of supplement purveyors would like you to believe this myth—but if you work out regularly, you can retain a lot of the extra muscle you've gained. We can remember, for example, measuring the body dimensions of a thirty-year-old man named Anibal in one of our steroid studies. Anibal had won a major state bodybuilding contest three years earlier, and reportedly hadn't used any steroids since that time. Yet, when he took his shirt off for his physical exam, he was still huge. His FFMI, calculated by the method described in Chapter 2, was still over 28—a figure far above what could reasonably be expected for a non-drug-using individual.

Of course, we had no proof that Anibal had abstained from all steroids during the entire three-year period since his contest victory. But he had no reason to lie to us, because he got paid for his participation in our study regardless. Also, a close friend of his independently confirmed to us privately that Anibal had used no steroids over the last three years. Anibal's secret? He had simply continued to work out faithfully, maintained a high protein consumption, and as a result had held on to most of the muscle he originally acquired with drugs.

We've heard many similar stories. For example, Jay, the 225-pound accountant we've already mentioned, described a couple of year-long intervals during which he didn't take steroids but retained nearly all of the muscle mass he had previously gained.

These long-lived effects make steroids almost unique among drugs of abuse. With alcohol, marijuana, or other substances, the reward is delivered to the brain only during the period of intoxication. After the drug wears off, you're back to where you started—or worse, if you happen to be abusing a drug that induces craving and other withdrawal symptoms. But steroids offer the promise of muscle gains, athletic prowess, and the admiration of others long after they have left the bloodstream. Little wonder, then, that steroids would appeal to any boy or man willing to go onto the black market to buy a bigger body.

Myth No. 3: *Steroid abuse can be prevented by drug testing.*

Reality: Steroid use usually goes undetected by drug testing.

As we've discussed, men can take huge doses of anabolic steroids and gain thirty or forty pounds of extra muscle over six months or a year of training. But then, provided they're not taking certain long-acting injectable steroids, they can discontinue the drugs and clear them out of their system in a matter of weeks. After that, they can submit to a urine test anytime they want and come out completely negative—even though they'll still retain most of their muscle gains.

Admittedly, drug-testing laboratories can successfully detect steroids in a urine sample from a person who is currently taking them, or who stopped within the past few weeks. And some of the long-acting injectable steroids can be picked up on testing even months after they're discontinued. But testing for steroids is expensive, ranging from $100 to $200 a shot, and it must be performed several times a year, unannounced, at random, to be useful. Thus, a standard urine screen for drugs of abuse, like that performed for an employment application, would almost never include steroids. It follows that most men can take steroids as much as they want without worrying about ever getting busted on a urine test.

Myth No. 4:   *Steroids frequently cause immediate medical dangers.*

Reality: The nonpsychiatric medical dangers of steroids are primarily long-term, not short-term.

With this statement we aren't implying that steroids are safe. In fact, as we'll discuss below, steroids can be very dangerous. We're simply pointing out here that most young men who use steroids don't experience any obvious medical problems while they're taking them. Time and again, in our interviews with steroid users, we've had conversations like the following, with a thirty-two-year-old man from Venice Beach, California:

"How many cycles of steroids have you taken during your life?"

"Oh, I'd guess about eight or nine."

"So how many months in total in your lifetime would you estimate that you've been on steroids?"

"I'd guess thirty-six months, maybe more."

"And during that time, what medical or physical problems have you experienced from taking steroids?"

"Nothing to speak of. Maybe a few zits here and there."

"How many guys do you know who've taken steroids?"

"Dozens."

"Have any of them experienced any serious medical or physical complications from taking steroids?"

"Not that I know of personally. A couple of cases of bitch tits, but not much else."

This is typical. Of the hundreds of steroid users we've interviewed, most have never been conscious of a serious medical problem, nor do they know of any friends who have. Some men report that they have developed acne when taking steroids, and we've seen occasional cases of severe steroid-induced acne that didn't go away for a long time even after steroid use was stopped. Also, some steroid users have noted the growth of female breast tissue under their nipples, a phenomenon known medically as "gynecomastia" and in the gym as "bitch tits." But for most men the increase in breast tissue isn't visible to the naked eye, and if it is, it can usually be removed by a plastic surgeon. Many men also note that their testicles grow smaller while they're taking steroids. This is to be expected: putting artificial steroids into the body suppresses the testicles' impetus to make testosterone, and accordingly the testicles grow smaller. But when one stops taking steroids, the body's own system comes back "on line," and the testicles grow back to their original size after a while. We've never heard of a case in which permanent impairment of testicular functioning occurred as a result of steroid use.

Educational materials, attempting to deter men from taking steroids, often dramatize these short-term medical effects, even though actual steroid users rarely worry about them. The same educational materials usually go on to say that steroids can cause liver disease, even liver cancer. Technically speaking, this is true; there are a few documented cases of liver cancer clearly associated with steroid use. However, they are rare; we have never seen a steroid user in any of our studies who had serious liver disease. The same goes for hair loss. We've seen lots of warnings that men on steroids risk losing their hair. In theory, this sounds reasonable, since men are more prone to getting bald than women, and this may be related to testosterone. But the fact remains that we've never actually seen a steroid user with hair loss unequivocally due to the drugs.

We're not saying this to imply that steroids are safe. They *are* dangerous, as we'll explain in a minute. But the problem is that most boys and young men who take steroids have never witnessed any serious dangers firsthand.

Now that you understand the four myths described above, the appeal of steroids to high school boys and young men should be obvious. If you're still not convinced, imagine that a drug existed for women that (1) would rapidly make them more attractive, (2) had effects that lasted long after the drug was stopped, (3) wouldn't be picked up on routine random drug testing, and (4) had no obvious immediate medical dangers. How many women would take such a drug?

THE REAL DANGERS: STEROIDS AND YOUR HEAD

Even though steroids rarely cause immediate medical problems, they really are dangerous, especially because of their psychiatric effects. While taking steroids, some men develop serious mood changes, ranging from mild irritability to severe aggressiveness, often accompanied by grossly impaired judgment and grandiose beliefs. In rare cases, steroids can even cause so-called psychotic delusions, such as the belief that people are plotting against you, or the belief that you have special powers or abilities. Some steroid users experience sudden bursts of aggressiveness, a phenomenon that has now entered the public vocabulary under the term "'roid rage." Other steroid users may quietly simmer with anger for long periods of time and plan their aggressive acts in advance. We have seen or heard of many men who committed violent crimes—even murders—while under the influence of steroids.

In 1987, we published the first reported case series of steroid-induced psychiatric symptoms, in which we described a man who developed religious delusions while on steroids and who promised to show God to a friend. Another bought an old junk car and deliberately drove it into a stone wall while a friend videotaped him. Another became so annoyed when he was cut off on a road by another driver that he pursued the offender, cornered him, and smashed his windshield with a crowbar. All of these men had been perfectly normal before they used steroids, and they all eventually returned to their original state of normality within a few weeks after the steroids were stopped.

After we published our initial reports of steroid-induced mood changes and violence, we began to receive phone calls from attorneys across the United States, reporting that they had clients who had committed violent crimes while they were on the drugs. In most instances, no previous observer had made the connection between the steroid use and the violence. We agreed to consult on a number of these cases, and went out to interview these men directly. In many of the cases, the link between the steroid use and the violence seemed inescapable.

One of our first cases was a man who had worked as a prison guard. Prior to using steroids, he was a model citizen. He had no history of violence, no psychiatric problems, no criminal record. People described him as having a shy, mild-mannered personality. But when he started taking steroids, he became dramatically more confident, more irritable, and more aggressive. During the fifth steroid cycle, when he was taking a larger dose than usual, the symptoms started to get out of hand. One day, he stepped into a store to use a telephone because his car broke down. The lady in the store made a harmless joke—something to the effect that with so many people borrowing her phone, she ought to start charging for it. He became enraged at this little remark and continued to stew about it long after he left the store. Eventually, his rage got the better of him; he drove back to the store, dragged the lady outside, forced her into his car, and began to drive away. After a while, he had to slow down for a construction site. The lady seized the opportunity, leaped out of the car, and ran for safety. Grabbing his service revolver, he shot her, hitting her in the spine, leaving her paralyzed from the waist down for the rest of her life. He was apprehended and ended up with a sentence of twenty years in the state penitentiary. By the time we met him, he had already been in prison for several years, where he had been a quiet, even-tempered model prisoner with no suggestion of aggressive behavior. He had gone from Dr. Jekyll to Mr. Hyde and back to Dr. Jekyll again, and the only explanation that fit the facts was his steroid use. The case was so compelling that it was described in a national television show about violence among law enforcement officers who took steroids.

In another case, a highly respected police officer who worked on a SWAT team started going to a local gym to train for strength and endurance. He reported no history of psychiatric disorder or violent behavior. The worst thing he could recall ever having done was a prank where he set fire to a soap dispenser in a public bathroom. But all of this changed after he began to take steroids, apparently at the suggestion of a local pharmacist and with the help of a local doctor who was willing to prescribe these drugs (a practice now largely banned). He quickly became obsessed with his body and began working out for hours each day at the gym. He became cocky and irritable. His wife immediately noticed the drastic personality change and begged him to stop taking steroids, but he refused. While at a rock concert, he felt that one of his friends had insulted him; he attacked the man and beat him unconscious. When cut off in traffic, he forced the other driver off the road, dragged him out of his car, and beat him up. These acts were totally different from his usual character—but he never recognized at the time that they represented "'roid rage." Eventually, he became involved with a criminal gang, stealing money from drug dealers. During one such robbery, he shot and killed the victim.

Now he has languished in jail for the last six years. Looking back at the time that he was taking steroids, he is astonished that his character could have changed so radically—and that he was unable to detect the changes, despite warnings from his wife, parents, and friends. Recently, working from prison, he has helped to start an educational program to alert other men and boys to these dangers.

We've now consulted on more than twenty legal cases involving apparent steroid-induced violence. One of the most sensational was the case of a sixteen-year-old boy. This boy, too, had no history of violence or criminality prior to using steroids. In fact, he was a timid kid; once, when he was young, the other kids at his housing project locked him into a portable toilet and rolled him down the street. In school, he was withdrawn and often depressed. But then, at age fourteen, he started taking steroids. Suddenly, he began to have run-ins with the police—and these occurred precisely at the times when he was on the drugs. Once he trashed his whole bedroom in a fit of rage, and his mother brought him to an emergency room to find out what was wrong. Nobody asked about steroid use, and the diagnosis was apparently not considered.

Then one day, at age sixteen, he found out that his fourteen-year-old girlfriend had gone off to a nearby town with another guy. Right about that time, he had been taking big doses of testosterone, plus a second anabolic steroid in pill form. He couldn't control his rage. Stealing into his mother's kitchen, he found a long sharp carving knife with a mean, curved blade. After downing a few beers, he went and found his girlfriend, lured her out with him into the nearby woods, and stabbed her many times.

He is now in a state prison, where he remains for life without the possibility of parole.

As researchers, if we had seen only one or two such cases, we might be able to dismiss them as coincidence. But we've seen far too many to explain them away, and we've also been impressed that there's a pattern to them. In the typical case, a man with no prior history of violence or criminality takes steroids. He develops a personality change characterized by exaggerated self-confidence, greater energy, and markedly increased irritability and aggressiveness. Sometimes the aggressiveness comes out in the form of abrupt, impulsive acts of rage, but sometimes it can simmer for hours or days after an instance of provocation. Very often, as in the cases above, the victim of the aggression is a woman, often a girlfriend. Perhaps this is because steroids trigger or amplify some primal sense of sexual territoriality deep in the core of the male brain. Perhaps this biological message resonates with messages from our culture, where men sometimes obtain power over women through physical threats or violence.

If you think we're getting too speculative here, then let's turn back to the scientific data. In more than a dozen studies now, researchers have compared the psychiatric status of men while they were taking steroids to when they were not. In four of the studies, the largest of which was from our own laboratory, participants received either genuine steroids or an inert placebo under double-blind conditions—meaning that neither the study participants nor the scientists who assessed the participants knew which treatment was being administered until the end of the study, when all of the ratings were finished and the "blind" was broken. This method guards against the possibility that the participants, knowing when they were receiving real steroids, might bias their reports as a result of the power of suggestion.

A clear scientific consensus has emerged from these data. If men are taking only 200 to 300 milligrams per week of testosterone or an equivalent steroid, they rarely show psychiatric effects. But if they go up to 500 milligrams per week or 1,000 milligrams per week—doses commonly used illicitly—steroid users are increasingly likely to experience episodes of irritability, aggressiveness, and impaired judgment. And these psychological reactions can't be explained away as a mere personality quirk of bodybuilders, or an effect of the "gym culture," or simply a consequence of excessive weightlifting, because they have been observed, under double-blind laboratory conditions, even in men who haven't been near a gym.

Some examples will convey the nature of these reactions better than any statistical data. One man, while receiving testosterone in a laboratory study, became so short-tempered about the service in a restaurant that he got up from the table, elbowed his way past the waitress, and barged into the kitchen to complain to the manager. Previously, he reported, he had always been too polite to complain in a restaurant at all.

Another man, also receiving testosterone in a laboratory study, was standing in line at McDonald's. An elderly woman, a foot shorter than he, cut in front of him in line and ordered a hamburger. As she was walking away with her tray, he turned to her, clenched his teeth, and said very quietly, "If you do that again, I'll kill you!" A moment later, he caught himself and thought, "Did I really say that? I just threatened a five-foot-tall seventy-five-year-old lady!"

In one double-blind laboratory study, conducted at a research unit of the National Institute of Mental Health, men were administered 240 milligrams of methyltestosterone per day—a dose comparable to that used by many hard-core "gym rats." Two out of twenty men had bad reactions; one got so out of control that he actually requested to be placed in the ward seclusion room.

Remember: these anecdotes describe men receiving steroids under rigorously controlled laboratory conditions. Also remember that these men had been carefully selected to have no prior history of serious psychopathology, violence, or criminal behavior. In the real world, illegal steroid users don't select themselves with such exquisite care. And there are no limits on the doses or combinations of steroids they can take. They might take testosterone and "stack" a couple of other steroids in pill form on top of it—taking three steroids simultaneously is actually a common practice. And, like the sixteen-year-old boy who killed his girlfriend, they might toss down a few beers as well. So the rate of serious psychological reactions to steroids in the real world may be a lot higher than that observed in the laboratory.

Anecdotal experiences from studies of steroid users in the gym support these impressions. Countless men have reported to us and to other scientists that they have become uncharacteristically short-tempered, threatening, and even violent while on "juice." The smallest annoyance, particularly in situations like driving, can trigger attacks of "'roid rage." For example, one man, while on steroids, became enraged because the driver in front of him forgot to turn off his directional signal for several miles. He ran up to the other car at the next stoplight, smashed the windshield using a metal signpost, and screamed curses at the cowering driver inside. Another lost his temper because the driver in front of him was going only 25 in a 40-mile-per-hour zone. He forced the man off the road, ran up to the car, pulled the helpless driver out onto the street, and screamed, "If you can't drive more than twenty-five, you shouldn't be allowed to drive at all!" He then confiscated the man's car keys and dropped them down a grating.

"How often do you get so angry in driving situations?" we asked, after hearing this remarkable story.

"When I'm not on steroids? Never," he replied.

We've heard so many stories like these that now, every time we see somebody acting aggressively on the road, we look through the windows of his car to see if he has the disproportionate chest and shoulder muscles of a steroid user.

Sadly, in our experience, steroid-induced violence toward women is probably equal in frequency to steroid-induced violence on the road. We've already touched on this phenomenon earlier in our description of various cases. So serious is the problem of violence against women that we'll devote a whole section to it in Chapter 9.

We still don't know what happens inside the brain to cause steroid-induced violence. Perhaps the most puzzling finding—both in double-blind laboratory studies and in real-world surveys—has been that only a minority of men develop prominent psychiatric reactions to steroids. In the course of our research, we've done numerous statistical analyses to see if there was some particular personality variable, some biological test, or some aspect of family history that would predict who would develop these bad reactions. But none of our hypotheses has worked out: violent reactions to steroids seem to be completely idiosyncratic and unpredictable. Our hunch is that they're due to some biological predisposition, some sort of chemical quirk in the brain that certain people are born with and others not.

Even though only a minority of men have this predisposition, and even fewer men reach the point of having dangerous reactions, we are still looking at a significant public health problem. Many men—probably more than we realize—end up in jail every year for violent behavior or crimes that might never have happened if it were not for the steroids in their systems. And their victims, often women, may be harmed or even killed in the process.

But this isn't all. Men may experience not only aggressive and sometimes violent reactions while on steroids, but also depressive reactions while coming off steroids. Although steroids are not addictive drugs in the strict sense that heroin or alcohol is addictive, there is no question that users experience a withdrawal syndrome after they finish a cycle, especially if they stop the steroids abruptly. During mild withdrawal, a man may feel lethargic, with an increased need for sleep, decreased appetite, markedly decreased sex drive, and sometimes noticeable feelings of depression and anxiety. Severe depressive reactions to steroid withdrawal occur in only a small percentage of men—but when they do, the symptoms may be devastating. We have consulted on several cases in which a steroid user killed himself apparently as a result of depressive symptoms during steroid withdrawal. Indeed, in one study in Ohio examining seventy-seven current or former steroid users recruited in local gyms, the authors found that 6.5 percent of the men had made a suicide attempt at some time during steroid withdrawal.

There's another more common and more insidious consequence of steroid withdrawal: it may provoke a syndrome of dependence on steroids. Some users, experiencing an increase in depression and anxiety when coming off steroids, together with the disappointment of losing some of their muscle gains, are drawn back into using steroids over and over again. Thus, biological and psychological factors combine to perpetuate use of larger doses of these drugs, more frequently and for longer periods, than the user had ever originally intended. The resulting syndrome of "anabolic steroid dependence" is now widely recognized among scientists, and many research studies have addressed this topic. We understand the syndrome of steroid dependence much better than we did ten years ago, but we still don't know very much about how to treat it.

Steroid-induced aggression or violence, steroid-withdrawal depression or suicide, and severe or prolonged steroid dependence have likely affected well over 100,000 men in the United States alone. And in the case of the steroid-induced violence, we must count not only the users but also the victims of their irritability and aggression.

MORE REAL DANGERS: STEROIDS
AND YOUR LIFE EXPECTANCY

Psychiatric problems aren't the only wild card associated with steroid use. Steroids can also drastically alter the ratio in the bloodstream between the "good" cholesterol—technically known as the HDL cholesterol—and the "bad" cholesterol—or LDL cholesterol. This means that steroids probably accelerate hardening of the arteries, or atherosclerosis, eventually leading to heart attacks, strokes, and other complications at an early age. No one really knows the magnitude of this risk, because nobody has done a controlled study of heavy steroid users twenty or thirty years later, when they've reached middle age, to see what happens to them. As a matter of fact, we've just started doing such a study ourselves, probably the first of its kind, to try to get some answers to these questions.

And there's another wild card, even less understood by scientists—the possibility that steroids may increase the risk of prostate cancer. We know for a fact that testosterone and related steroids can accelerate the growth of prostate cancer, sometimes causing a tiny island of cancerous cells in the prostate to progress to full-blown, aggressively spreading disease. Conversely, in men afflicted with prostate cancer, surgical removal of the testicles—with a consequent drop in blood levels of testosterone—can slow or halt the progression of the cancer. Now, what if a man takes steroids, and he has even a few precancerous cells in his prostate?

We already know of two reports in the medical literature that describe bodybuilders who used steroids over a long period and came down with prostate cancer at an unusually young age. Again, there's no proof that steroids were the cause in these cases, but it's quite possible, given that the men were so young. Are there many more latent cases that will come to light over the next decade? What about the hundreds of thousands of kids taking steroids now, and who may continue taking them into adulthood? What's their risk of prostate cancer, in comparison to an average man, when they reach fifty or sixty years of age? The situation might prove analogous to that of cigarettes and lung cancer: people smoked cigarettes widely in the forties and fifties, but it wasn't until the 1970s that the link to lung cancer became increasingly clear. And by then, for an entire generation of smokers, it was too late.

MORE DANGERS: GETTING NEEDLE HAPPY

There's another, indirect risk of steroid use hardly mentioned in the scientific literature or the popular press: many steroids have to be administered by injection, usually into the gluteus muscle in the buttock. Virtually all users, in our experience, learn to administer the injections to themselves. Think for a moment about the implications of this fact: some hundreds of thousands of young American men, many of them teenagers just out of puberty, have learned to use needles on themselves, simply because they want so badly to make themselves look bigger and more muscular.

This fact immediately brings up the usual dangers of needles, such as the transmission of AIDS, hepatitis B and C, and other life-threatening diseases as a result of needle sharing, not to mention the risk of abscesses and other local infections from using dirty needles. Another serious consideration is that many of the "steroids" on the black market are actually counterfeits. Clever dealers may sell bottles with caps and labels virtually indistinguishable from the real thing, but actually concocted in the basement. The bottles may be filled with some other drugs, or maybe just cooking oil, perhaps contaminated with bacteria. In our studies, we've interviewed dealers who've claimed to have made up and sold tens of thousands of bottles of fake "injectables." Presumably, the contents of those bottles found their way into the bodies of countless boys and men. Whether any got infected or otherwise ill from these counterfeits is not known.

But perhaps the most malignant effect of needles is that they open the door to use of other injectable drugs. In the gym, the most popular new injectable drug seems to be Nubain, or nalbuphine, a prescription painkiller chemically related to morphine. Although nalbuphine is not supposed to be nearly as addictive as morphine, we have seen several men, all steroid users, who injected Nubain and became addicted to it. Some of these men reported that they started using Nubain in the gym, just as a way to treat aches and pains from weightlifting. Others admitted that they had tried it purely to get high. Ominously, we have now seen numerous men who progressed from nalbuphine to injecting more highly addictive opiates, including morphine and heroin. Several have required detoxification in the hospital. Some were teenagers.

OTHER DANGEROUS BODY-SHAPING DRUGS

Steroids and Nubain aren't the only drugs of abuse in the gym. In fact, with the rise of the Adonis Complex, dozens of other drugs, legal and illegal, have become popular among men seeking to reshape their bodies. The list on the next page documents the vast number of these drugs. One very popular drug is ephedrine, a substance that comes from a Chinese plant called *Ephedra* or *ma huang*. Ephedrine is legally available in various drinks and powders, and therefore is available in practically every nutrition store and gym as a "natural" fat burner. Natural though it may be, ephedrine is a close chemical relative of amphetamine, or speed, and it has the same side effects. In large enough doses, ephedrine can cause high blood pressure, racing heartbeat, insomnia, and sometimes severe cardiovascular complications. Like speed, it can be habit-forming. Medical complications of ephedrine, including fatalities, have recently been reported from around the United States, and the Food and Drug Administration has recently considered clamping down on ephedrine use.

Ephedrine is only one of many potentially dangerous drugs men can take to burn fat. There are other legal, over-the-counter drugs, like pseudoephedrine and phenylpropanolamine, that you can buy in any number of decongestant preparations in your local pharmacy. Then there are prescription-only stimulants like amphetamine and methamphetamine—the latter typically known as Methedrine, or crystal meth— that burn fat and can also be seriously habit-forming. Then there are thyroid hormones, which are Schedule V substances, meaning that they're not as rigorously controlled by law enforcement authorities as drugs like steroids and amphetamines. Thus, thyroid hormones are easy to get on the black market, even though they can be dangerous and even fatal if taken in excessive doses. Clenbuterol, a drug used largely for veterinary purposes, has both fat-burning and muscle-building properties. Although invented for use in pigs and cattle, clenbuterol is used illegally by thousands of boys and men in gyms everywhere. In large doses, it can produce dangerous and even potentially fatal cardiovascular complications. However, scientists know practically nothing about the extent or the risks of underground clenbuterol abuse.

Another potentially nasty category of abused drugs is the diuretics—drugs that increase urine output. Diuretics are particularly favored by competition bodybuilders, because they dehydrate the body, thus making the muscles look sharper and more defined. Taken in excessive doses, diuretics can occasionally cause sudden death as a result of cardiovascular complications. Indeed, over the last few years, there have

Drugs Abused by Athletes as Compiled from Underground Guides

Anabolic-androgenic steroids

Androstanolone
Boldenone (Equipoise)
Clostebol (Megagrisevit)
Dromostanolone (Masteron, Permastril)
Ethylestranol (Orabolin, Maxibolin)
Fluoxymesterone (Halotestin, others)
Formebolone (Esiclene)
Mesterolone (Proviron)
Methandienone (formerly called methandrostenolone) (Dianabol, others)
Methandriol (Andris, Methyldiol)
Methenolone (Primobolan)
Methylandrostenediol (Methandriol)
Methyltestosterone (Android, others)
Mibolerone (Checque Drops)
Nandrolone (Deca-Durabolin, Durabolin, Laurabolin, others)
Norethandrolone (Nilevar)
Oxandrolone (Anavar, Lipidex)
Oxymetholone (Anadrol, Anapolon)
Quinbolone (Anabolicum Vister)
Stanozolol (Stromba, Winstrol)
Stenbolone (Anatrofin)
Testosterone esters (Depo-Testosterone, Sten, Sustanon, others)
Trenbolone (Finajet, Parabolan)

Beta agonists (drugs that stimulate "beta-adrenergic" neurons)

Clenbuterol

Central nervous system stimulants

Amphetamine (Pervitin, others)
Diethylpropion (Tenuate)
Ephedrine (Dymetadrine, Theodrine)
Phentermine (Fasten, Ionamin)
Theophylline

Diuretics ("water pills")

Acetazolamide (Diamox)
Furosemide (Lasix, others)
Hydrochlorothiazide (Aldactazide)
Metolazone (Mydox)
Spironolactone (Aldactazide, Aldactone)
Triamterene (Dyazide)

Anticatabolics (drugs supposed to decrease muscle breakdown)

Aminoglutethimide (Cytandren)

Narcotic agonist-antagonists (painkillers)

Buprenorphine (Buprenex)
Butorphanol (Stadol, Torbugesic)
Nalbuphine (Nubain)

Other hormones

Dihydroepiandrosterone (DHEA)
Erythropoietin (Epogen, Procrit)
Human growth hormone (Protropin, Humatrope, others)
Insulin
Thyroxine (Synthroid)
Triiodothyronine (Cytomel, Triacana)

Growth hormone stimulants (drugs supposed to stimulate growth hormone secretion)

Clonidine (Catapres)
Gamma-hydroxybutyrate (GHB)
Levodopa (L-DOPA)

Testosterone stimulants (drugs supposed to stimulate testosterone secretion)

Clomiphene (Clomid)
Cyclofenil (Fertodur)
Human chorionic gonadotropin (HCG)

Miscellaneous

Danazol (Danocrine)
Fenfluramine (Pondimin)
Isotretinoine (Accutane)
Pentoxifylline (Trental)
Phenformin (Debeone)
Probenecid (Benemid)
Tamoxifen (Nolvadex)
Testolactone (Teslac)
Ticlopidine (Ticlid)
Yohimbine (Yocon, others)

been cases of highly ranked bodybuilders who have dropped dead on the day of a competition because they overdid their diuretics.

Collectively, these many body-shaping drugs are abused by millions of boys and men. But we know little about the full extent of their dangers—because few men will reveal that they are dependent on these substances for the appearance of their bodies, and consequently little research on abuse of these drugs has been published. Thus, the fallout from the Adonis Complex may be even greater than we realize.

THE DILEMMA OF STEROIDS: WHAT CAN BE DONE?

To today's body-obsessed man, body-changing drugs have enormous appeal. Steroids, in particular, work well and superficially seem to have few nonpsychiatric short-term side effects. But as we've discussed, steroids carry severe but less visible dangers—psychiatric effects, long-term medical complications that we're only beginning to understand, dangers associated with injections, and the risk of being introduced to other dangerous drugs through experience with the steroid culture. And worse, steroids aren't just hazardous to the men who use them, but also to the victims of steroid-induced violence—especially women.

What can be done to control steroid use or to treat men who have developed long-term dependence on steroids? We discuss below the three methods most often proposed: educating students about the dangers of steroid use, interdiction of steroids by law enforcement authorities, and psychiatric treatment of steroid users. We'll then point out why we're not very optimistic about the success of these three techniques, based on our experience with interviewing hundreds of users. Finally, we'll propose one strategy that we think really *might* work, over the long term, to reduce steroid abuse in our society.

Education

On the surface, education seems like an obvious technique. There's no question that we should tell kids about the dangers of steroid use. And we could go further: for example, we could insist that young male athletes attend a compulsory class on how steroids can be harmful to them. Education has been widely used to dissuade kids from experimenting with other types of drugs; kids all over the country are systematically taught about the dangers of cocaine, opiates, and other drugs. Why wouldn't the same approach work for steroids?

If you've read this far, you can guess what we're about to say. Unless you're prepared to lie to kids, you can't hide the fact that steroids really *will* make them bigger, leaner, and stronger—closer to the ideal male body images that they see daily in the media. And unless you're prepared to lie again, you can't tell them that steroids will frequently cause serious nonpsychiatric medical side effects in the short term, because that's also simply not true. The threat of developing bad acne or female breast tissue may deter some kids, but many are prepared to trade these risks for the promise of bigger muscles.

The remarks of many steroid users, as we've quoted above, illustrate how "authorities" lose their credibility with kids when they understate the efficacy of steroids or exaggerate their short-term dangers. So we're not surprised to hear that antisteroid educational programs have produced mixed results. One specialized program in Oregon has come up with fairly promising statistics. But another steroid prevention program, using scare tactics to dissuade adolescents from using these drugs, may actually have led to an increase in steroid use.

Perhaps we can do better by avoiding scare tactics and trying to educate young men about the real dangers of steroids—the psychiatric effects, or the potentially life-threatening long-term medical effects. Certainly, we think it's important for parents to take an active role in this. But boys aren't likely to be deterred from steroid use by the thought that they might become uncontrollably aggressive, or the possibility that they might get heart disease or possibly prostate cancer when they're fifty or sixty years old. Adolescent boys who want to look bigger in the next few weeks don't spend a lot of time worrying about what their health will be like in forty years.

Certainly, we're not opposed to education. Of course we should tell kids what science knows about steroids. But as a method for preventing steroid use, education is a tough battle.

Interdiction

If we can't persuade boys and young men to abstain from steroids voluntarily, why not beef up law enforcement efforts and cut off the supply? The United States Congress reasoned along these lines when it passed the Steroid Trafficking Act in January of 1991. The act didn't get a lot of publicity—most people were tuned in to the Gulf War at the time—but it raised steroids to the level of Schedule III controlled substances, which means that they were brought under the jurisdiction of the Drug Enforcement Administration, or DEA, along with certain diet pills, sleeping pills, and other drugs of abuse.

The DEA has worked faithfully to carry out its new mandate to control the underground steroid trade. We've talked to several DEA agents, and they're a hardworking and dedicated group. But it's an uphill battle for them, because steroids can make for an attractive form of drug dealing—as several steroid dealers have told us in the confidentiality of our research interviews. The fact is that federal authorities, for all of their dedication, can't stop the flow of steroids into high schools and gyms all over the country.

Treatment

If we can't prevent boys and men from obtaining steroids or from trying them, can we at least offer people treatment for their steroid problems? Why not a treatment group for steroid users, similar to treatment groups for cocaine or heroin users, or perhaps a twelve-step program like Alcoholics Anonymous?

If you've read this far, you'll already realize how naive this suggestion would be. Steroid users, overwhelmingly, don't *want* treatment. They rarely see their drug use as a problem; in fact, they may even see it as a positive aspect of a program of trying to stay maximally healthy and fit. Most would scoff at the idea of seeing a mental health professional. Admittedly, we've seen a handful of steroid users who have sought treatment. These were men who developed severe episodes of depression when they tried to stop taking steroids, or whose muscle dysmorphia symptoms caused them severe distress, and we've treated a few of them successfully with antidepressants. But they're a tiny minority of the total population. So once again, although we're certainly in favor of treatment, we wouldn't pretend that it will change the rate of steroid use among boys or men as a whole.

EXPOSING THE TRUTH

So is there anything that actually would reduce the number of steroid users? We suggest one strategy that, over time, might actually help: to educate the public about what really is going on. This strategy would deprive steroid users of their most valuable asset—secrecy.

Secrecy allows many steroid users to enjoy the admiration of people around them, because most people don't realize that their levels of leanness and muscularity were achieved by taking drugs. If every man and woman recognized that these muscular guys were just taking drugs, their mystique would be gone.

By way of illustration, consider a scene that we once witnessed at a gym. A highly muscular personal trainer was coaching a man in his thirties on weightlifting exercises. The trainer had obviously taken a good deal of "juice."

"What does it take to get to look like you?" asked the wide-eyed client.

"Long, hard work," said the trainer, dead seriously.

The client actually appeared to believe him.

But what if the general public could be educated to realize the truth? What if the client in the gym realized that his trainer was actually a felon—someone who had taken drugs illegally, in violation of federal law, to look the way he did? Would the client have still hired that trainer for $60 per hour?

And what about the man with a sculpted body who advertises exercise machines on infomercials, or the hunk who hawks fitness programs or protein supplements? Would the public still flock to buy their products if they knew that they'd used chemicals to look that way?

Perhaps even more important, what about the men whose 'roided bodies appear in magazines, on television, and even in person—sometimes before audiences of impressionable teenage boys—as models of health? *Health?* What if every boy in the audience knew that these guys had taken drugs that might cause them to drop dead from a heart attack or stroke thirty years from now?

Such widespread public awareness would not eliminate steroid use. Many professional athletes, and some nonathletes, would probably still use them, even if they realized that everybody would know. But at least, if people stopped glorifying the steroid-pumped body, erroneously thinking that it was a monument to hard work and dedication, much of the impetus for steroid use would be removed.

It is for these reasons that we've offered clues in previous chapters to help you to recognize a steroid user when you see one. As we've illustrated with the photographs of steroid users in Chapter 2, and explained with our FFMI formula in Chapter 2 and Appendix I, our research tells us that there's an upper limit to the muscularity that a man can attain without drugs. With a little practice, you can look at a man and often guess fairly accurately whether he has exceeded these limits.

This thought brings us back to a larger issue that we stress throughout this book. The Adonis Complex fundamentally boils down to an exaggerated and unrealistic view of what the male body should look like. If the media continue to convince American men that the ideal body is supermuscular, steroid use will continue to flourish, no matter how much money we spend on education, and no matter how many new DEA agents we assign to interdiction. But if men in this country could come to realize that they don't need to emulate these unrealistic, supermuscular images, then the steroid problem would cease to be an issue.

What is the evidence for this? Consider that in many Latin American countries, as we have mentioned, steroids are legally available without a prescription in any pharmacy. And yet, paradoxically, most of these Latin American countries (with the partial exception of Brazil) have few problems of steroid abuse, whereas the United States has a serious problem of steroid abuse despite rigid legal enforcement. The reason, we suspect, is that men in most Latin American countries aren't so insecure about their muscularity as North American men who have become victims of the Adonis Complex. If North American men could achieve a similar realization—could get back to the more realistic body-image attitudes of our fathers and grandfathers—then abuse of steroids and other body-shaping drugs would largely evaporate.

CHAPTER SIX

Fear of Fat

Men and Eating Disorders

"I hate my body," said Grant, a young salesman from the Cleveland suburbs. "I've always hated my body. I guess it goes back to when I was a kid. I was a little chubby. I can still remember my aunt, when I was about ten years old, pinching my fat little cheeks and saying that I was 'husky.'" He winced. "Husky is just a nice way of saying you're a fat pig. I decided I didn't want anybody—*anybody*—to ever call me husky again."

"So what happened?" we asked.

"When I started high school, I decided I was too fat, and I resolved to go on a diet. I called it the 'Gummy Bear diet.' You know Gummy Bears—those little candies for kids that are made of some stuff like hard Jell-O? Well, I bought about five hundred packages of Gummy Bears. Each day, I would eat a normal breakfast, whatever I wanted, but from that point on, I would allow myself to eat only Gummy Bears for the rest of the day. My theory was that I'd get so sick of Gummy Bears, and my stomach would get so full of them, that I couldn't possibly eat as many calories as my body was using."

"Did it work?"

"Yes, it did. I lost over thirty pounds, until I weighed only a hundred fifty-eight at a height of six feet. And whoever manufactures Gummy Bears made a *lot* of money."

"Were you satisfied with the way you looked at that point?"

"For a little while, I guess. But most of the time, I still thought I was too fat. I went on the track team in high school and specialized in middle-distance running. I got pretty good. People thought the main thing I loved was the competition. But secretly, my biggest motivation was that I was trying to stay thin."

"What happened when you got to college?"

"I stopped running. I got fat. Or at least I thought I looked fat. Along with some of the other guys in my fraternity, I'd have eating binges when I felt bad. We'd order seventy-two Buffalo wings and pig out. It was gross, but we loved it."

"Did you try to lose the weight?"

"Yeah, I did a lot of weird things. Believe it or not, I started smoking cigarettes. I guess that must sound pretty strange, considering that I was a runner on my high school track team. But the smoking definitely helped keep my weight down. And sometimes, when I drank alcohol, I would deliberately drink until I was so sick that I'd throw up, just so I wouldn't gain weight. There were even a few times when I was sober that I tried to make myself throw up, just because I felt guilty about having eaten too much. But mostly, I just got depressed."

"How do you feel about your weight now?"

"I'm still depressed. Especially in the morning, when I look at myself in the mirror to put on my tie. I keep swearing that I'll get back into a regular gym schedule, or go running. And I've tried all the usual diets and weight-loss supplements, of course. But nothing works, at least for long."

"How much do you weigh now?"

"This morning, a hundred ninety-nine pounds."

"That's not particularly fat, for someone six feet tall."

"That's the same thing that my girlfriend keeps trying to tell me. But when I'm alone, looking at myself in the mirror, I pinch my stomach and there's a big thick roll of fat between my fingers."

"So what are you going to do?"

"I don't know. Maybe I'll go back to Gummy Bears."

FAT FIXATIONS

The Adonis Complex breeds different kinds of problems in different men, depending upon their particular vulnerabilities. Muscle dysmorphia and anabolic steroid abuse arise in men concerned that they aren't muscular enough. But millions of other men become concerned that they aren't thin enough. These men, constantly battling to lower their body fat, may develop another common and often secret manifestation of the Adonis Complex: abnormal eating behaviors. These behaviors range from mild dietary preoccupations to outright psychiatric illnesses, such as anorexia nervosa and bulimia nervosa. Although these various conditions—especially the more severe ones—are generally called "eating disorders," the term can be somewhat misleading, because they usually stem from an underlying body image problem. In other words, an individual's eating often becomes abnormal only because he has developed an excessive preoccupation with his body shape and weight.

Most people have heard of the two most serious eating disorders. *Anorexia nervosa* is a syndrome of compulsive dieting to the point of emaciation or even death; *bulimia nervosa* is a syndrome of compulsive eating binges, followed by self-induced vomiting, laxative abuse, or other extreme measures to prevent weight gain. More recently, researchers have added a third major diagnostic category, *binge-eating disorder,* to describe people who suffer from compulsive eating binges but don't make themselves vomit or otherwise "purge" the calories they've just eaten. For the reader who's interested, we've provided the standard diagnostic criteria for these three disorders in Appendix II. But remember—for every individual with a full-scale eating disorder meeting one of these sets of diagnostic criteria, many, many more suffer from other problematic eating behaviors and weight concerns. Many more experience uncontrolled cycles of weight gain and weight loss; idiosyncratic dietary patterns that cause them problems; or patterns of compulsive running, aerobic workouts, or other exercise to control weight. The common root of most of these conditions is a preoccupation with fatness and overall body shape.

We've been studying eating disorders of many types for the last twenty years, and we've written more than eighty scientific papers and a couple of books in this field. But until recently, most of our work, like that of other scientists, involved eating disorders in women. For years, the conventional wisdom held that eating disorders in men were rare—limited to a few ballet dancers, gay men, or wrestlers who vomited to try to make weight for a meet.

But now that wisdom is changing. We're seeing more and more eating disorders of all types in men. Part of this increase, we think, is because these conditions are more common among men today—probably in response to changing societal standards of male body image. As we noted previously, the ideal male body in our society has not only gained muscle but has also lost fat over the last few decades. Look back to Chapter 2 and compare the sharply chiseled body features on the modern G.I. Joes with those of their earlier counterparts. Or consider that the centerfold men in our study of *Playgirl* magazine lost an average of 12 pounds of fat between the mid-1970s and the present. Or think about the six-pack of sculpted abdominal muscles that has now become standard for male models in fitness magazines and advertisements. As a matter of fact, consider that the very expression "a six-pack of abdominal muscles" entered our cultural vocabulary only in the last ten years or so. Our society increasingly extolls the low-fat look in men, and it's likely that some men develop eating disorders in response to this pressure.

But the apparent increase in male eating disorders may also have another explanation: we and other scientists are becoming more sensitive to eating and weight preoccupations in men, and we're learning how to ask the right questions. As we have begun to inquire more carefully about men's eating and weight-control behaviors, and as men have overcome the "talking taboo" to reveal their concerns, we've been stunned by the number of male eating problems we've uncovered.

EATING DISORDERS IN MEN:
NOT SO RARE AFTER ALL

One of our first such experiences occurred ten years ago in a study of weightlifters. Earlier statistics have suggested that only about 0.02 percent—2 out of 10,000—American men have had anorexia nervosa at any time in their lives. So if you were to interview, say, 100 men, your chances of finding even a single case would theoretically be only about 2 percent. Imagine our surprise, then, when in a study of 160 weightlifters, we found *four* who reported a history of full-scale anorexia nervosa! If we were to accept the 0.02 percent rate at face value, the chances of finding four cases in a sample of 160 men would be less than one in a million. Even more remarkably, we found that a couple of these men started out with anorexia nervosa as teenagers and then "flipped over" into the reverse problem—muscle dysmorphia—later on.

One man from New Hampshire named Steve told us that when he was seventeen years old and 5 feet 6 inches tall, he dieted down to 89 pounds. Even then, he said, he still looked in the mirror and thought he was too fat—a classic feature of anorexia nervosa. Then, around his eighteenth birthday, Steve discovered weightlifting. Within six months or so, he was up to 145 pounds, but by this point he had decided that he looked too small. He began to take anabolic steroids, and continued to grow bigger. By the time that we saw him for his interview, when he was almost twenty years old, he was up to 189 pounds—precisely 100 pounds bigger than he had been only a couple of years earlier—and yet his body fat was still an ultralean 7.3 percent. But now, Steve revealed, he worried both that he had too much fat and not enough muscle. He worried so much that he had recently refused even to be seen outside of his house with his girlfriend for a period of several days.

Another man named Geoff, also recruited from the same sample of weightlifters, was twenty-seven years old at the time of his interview. "I guess it was when I was about fifteen," he told us, "that I decided I looked too fat. I had been growing a lot taller over the last year, but I thought I still looked pudgy. It bothered me more and more, so one day, I just decided to stop eating completely, and I went down from around a hundred and forty pounds to a hundred and fifteen."

"How did you feel at that point?" we asked.

"I still thought that I was too fat. My mother started to get really scared because she could tell I wasn't eating anything. Sometimes I ate a little bit in front of her just to please her, and then I tried to make myself throw up afterwards when I was alone. But I couldn't get myself to do it."

"Then what happened?"

"It went on for at least a year, and sometimes it got really out of control. There were times when I remember that I didn't think about anything all day long except that I wanted to be thinner. And then one day in eleventh grade—I can still remember the exact moment—I was looking at myself in the mirror alone in my bathroom, and I decided that I had a worse problem, that I looked too flabby and weak. I figured that girls would like me better if I put some more muscle on my chest and shoulders. So I asked my mom if she would buy me some weightlifting stuff."

"How did she react?"

"She was delighted. She thought it would be good therapy for my eating problem. That same day, she ran down to the department store and bought one of those beginner's weightlifting sets—the ones where the weights are made of concrete and covered with plastic. But I loved them. I took them all down to my basement, to a place where no one would see me, and set up my own private little weightlifting room. And then after only about six weeks or so, I was examining my shoulder in the mirror, and I could see that it was actually bigger. I got an incredible rush from seeing that, and from that point on I got more and more into the weightlifting."

Geoff quickly outgrew his little concrete weight set, and soon

joined a commercial gym near his house. His preoccupation with thinness had become eclipsed by an equally intense preoccupation with muscularity. He soon became one of the biggest men in his gym. But now,
instead of obsessing that he was too fat, he obsessed that he was too
small and wimpy.

Stories like these have helped to convince us of the hypothesis we
presented earlier: when a young man with obsessive-compulsive tendencies is exposed to today's messages of the ideal male body, any of several
different forms of the Adonis Complex may develop. If his obsessions
first get focused on being too fat, he may diet compulsively, and perhaps
even develop full-scale anorexia nervosa, or binge eating and vomiting.
Tweak the obsessions a little differently, change the focus to being too
frail, and he may shift into a trajectory of compulsive bodybuilding, and
sometimes develop full-scale muscle dysmorphia accompanied by anabolic steroid abuse. Had this same man been born a generation earlier,
we suspect that he probably still would have developed some type of
obsessive-compulsive behavior—but it is unlikely, we think, that he would
have embarked on a frantic campaign to overhaul the shape of his body.

SECRET EATING PROBLEMS

Steve and Geoff represent extreme examples of these body obsessions.
But many of the other men in our study were also preoccupied with their
body fat, leading to all manner of secret eating and weight-loss rituals.

"I'm fine when I make my own food," said one man, named Bob,
"but it sometimes bothers me when I go to a restaurant, because I can't
be sure how much fat there is in a particular dish."

"Has this ever created problems for you?"

"Well, one night I spent over an hour driving around with my girlfriend, trying to pick out a restaurant, just because I couldn't find one
where I thought the food was healthy enough."

Most of the time, Bob told us, he prepared all of his food for the
day and packaged it in small plastic containers—8 ounces of tunafish in
one, 6 ounces of raw carrots in another, a 6-ounce chicken breast with 8
ounces of brown rice in a third. "I keep them in the back seat of my car,"
he explained. "Then I can eat them at just the right intervals throughout
the day."

"Why do you try to eat them at particular intervals?"

"Because it's much better for muscle growth to absorb protein in
many small doses throughout the day," he said authoritatively. "The

body just can't handle more than about twenty or thirty grams of protein at once."

He went on to describe several other theories of how and when different types of food should be eaten for optimum fitness. At one point, he produced for us a frayed notebook, filled with notes on the protein and calorie content of foods that he had eaten each day for the last several weeks. It was clear that he spent several hours of every day simply attending to his diet. In Bob's life, eating preoccupations had obviously crowded out many other potential activities and social contacts—experiences that might have given him pleasure and fulfillment. But remarkably, Bob didn't even seem to believe that he had an eating disorder.

Two slightly overweight weightlifters in our study also initially denied that they had any serious eating concerns. But on further questioning, both admitted to problematic dieting patterns. Saul worked the evening shift as an emergency ward technician. "I'm very careful to diet all day, but when I get to work, I lose it," he explained. "When you're under all that stress, you can't control what you eat. Most every night, I'll end up pigging out on hamburgers, fries, a shake, and more fries."

Saul wasn't seriously overweight. But as he told his story, it was obvious that he was very depressed and self-critical about not being able to control his eating.

Dave seemed more resigned to the 10 pounds of fat that he'd accumulated since college. "I went through a phase where I actually carried a calculator around with me, everywhere I went, to add up the exact number of calories I was eating," he confessed. "Now I'm not quite so hung up about it. But I still go through phases where I get pretty weird about food."

Dave went on. "If I see another guy my age at the gym with perfectly defined abs, it really ruins my day. I've never admitted this to anybody, but I've had times where an experience like that would make me so depressed that I could hardly think about anything else for the next hour. I couldn't get any work done."

Dave had tried all kinds of dietary supplements, but most had failed. Recently, he had used a combination of high doses of ephedrine plus caffeine, purchased in a nutrition supplement store. These drugs are perfectly legal, but taking them in high doses can cause insomnia, tremors, and sometimes more serious side effects such as heart arrhythmias. Dave had had some problems with insomnia himself, but he had managed to lose 10 pounds.

"I did really well for a while, but then I had a heavy period at work where I had to go out of town almost every week. I couldn't get to the gym every day, and I stopped taking the pills. So I put most of the ten pounds back on. But now work has lightened up again, and I'm going to go back to the ephedrine and caffeine and increase my aerobic workouts. I'm sure that if I can just get down by fifteen pounds, then probably I can just keep the weight off. That's my plan anyways. Do you think it will work?"

Although we cautioned Dave about the risks of depending upon these drugs, he made it clear that he was determined to resume taking them. He was also eager to know whether he could come back to our lab to have us recheck his body fat in a couple of months. He was delighted when we promised to do so—and since the time of the initial interview, he's been back several times, even though our lab is a long distance from his home.

Weightlifters, like Saul and Dave, aren't the only group of men who may harbor secret eating problems. Bodybuilders and runners are other groups of men who may be at particularly high risk of developing abnormal eating patterns and excessive preoccupation with their weight. The National Runner's Survey on Dieting and Eating found that 21 percent of the 2,640 men who responded said they were "terrified" of gaining weight either "often," "usually," or "always." In addition, nearly one-quarter of the men said that they were preoccupied with a desire to be thinner, and two-thirds admitted to dieting, even during peak periods of running. Another study found that male runners had a higher level of eating disturbance than male nonrunners. These studies indicate that a surprising number of runners—a group we suspect many people would consider free of such concerns—may suffer from the Adonis Complex.

FOOD AND SELF-LOATHING ON CAMPUS

Although we were struck by the number of eating problems in our weightlifters, we wondered if our findings might simply be a result of "selection bias": men who go to gyms probably aren't representative of men as a whole. Therefore, to get a different sample, we decided to advertise in college newspapers around the Boston area. We recruited twenty-five men with serious eating disorders, meeting the formal diagnostic criteria listed in Appendix II of this book, and compared them to a "control group" of twenty-five college men without eating disorders, also recruited by newspaper advertisement. This was our chance to hear about body-image and eating problems in a general population of men out in the community.

The college men with eating disorders turned out to have a lot in common. Most impressively, the great majority of them had never previously revealed to any other human being that they suffered from an eating disorder, and only four of the twenty-five had ever sought any kind of treatment.

These four men had all attended Overeaters Anonymous meetings, but none had experienced any improvement. Only two of the twenty-five men had actually engaged in psychotherapy for their eating disorder; most of the others had never even come close to seeking treatment for their condition. Some didn't even realize that effective treatment was available, and of those who did, many were too embarrassed to see a doctor or therapist for what they considered a "women's disease."

It was sobering to hear of the misery that these men had silently endured. Barry, a twenty-one-year-old man with a history of anorexia nervosa, exemplified this secret pain. As a kid, he had always been a little plump. "I don't think I was ever really fat," he recalled, "but I got sick of being plump in comparison to the other kids in school."

As Barry passed puberty, his concern with being too fat escalated into an all-consuming obsession. He reached the point where he routinely ate only a piece of lettuce for breakfast, another piece of lettuce for lunch, and as a special treat for dinner, a piece of lettuce with ketchup on it. At one point, at a height of 5 feet 10 inches, his weight fell to a dangerously low 85 pounds. His brain screamed for the food that he was denying himself. He would walk into McDonald's, just to smell the food, then leave. He became obsessed with cooking and recipes. He subscribed to *Gourmet* and *Bon Appetit* magazines, clipped recipes from newspapers, and faithfully watched Julia Child's cooking show every day on television—but never indulged his own appetite. Even when at his thinnest, he would still constantly squeeze the "love handles" that he was convinced hung on his sides. "They were always there, no matter how much I lost everywhere else," he said. " I couldn't see that I was thin. All I focused on were my love handles."

By the time we met him, Barry was up to 117 pounds, and the symptoms were mild in comparison with what they had once been. But still, he confessed, he spent most of his day thinking about food and wondering whether he was too fat. As he spoke, he half-consciously brushed the side of his abdomen with his hand, no doubt duplicating a motion he had repeated tens of thousands of times over the years, checking his "love handles."

Other men with anorexia described similar experiences. Rob reduced his diet to a single ham-and-cheese sandwich per day. Rolando

drank Slim-Fast for breakfast and lunch, and ate a single piece of skin-
less chicken for dinner. Tony allowed himself no more than one piece of
fruit, a cup of cereal, and two pieces of licorice per day. Paul started out
as a vegetarian, then went on to become a vegan. A vegan (pronounced
vee-gan) avoids not only meat but all animal products. No dairy products, no eggs, not even honey, since honey is made by a bee.

But eventually, even a diet of rice, tofu, and salads seemed too in-
dulgent. "I began to eliminate even more things," Paul went on, "to the
point where eventually I wasn't eating anything at all." He paused to reflect on that period of his life. "I wanted to be invisible. I hated myself. I
didn't want to be noticed. It was a form of slow suicide."

Paul was one of the two men in our study who had actually seen a
therapist, and he credited much of his recovery to the improved self-
esteem he developed through treatment. But, like Barry, he still harbored
shame and self-criticism about his body, and at 5 feet 6 inches in height,
he still weighed only 110 pounds.

Ben also started out with symptoms of anorexia nervosa, but then
went on to develop bulimia nervosa as he grew older. He experienced
eating binges at least twice a week, always vomiting afterward, and
often taking huge doses of laxatives as well. Like most of the other men,
he had never revealed this secret to anyone, managing to disguise it even
from his college roommate, who shared the same bathroom. "I plan the
binges for hours in advance," he explained. "It's easy to get the food. I
live near a street where there are three fast-food joints right together—
Kentucky Fried Chicken, McDonald's, and Burger King. I stop at each
one in succession and buy a load of food. Sometimes I get suspicious
looks."

Once at home in the security of his room, Ben would polish off
four Big Macs, three Whoppers, six pieces of chicken, four large containers of french fries, and two milk shakes. "Sometimes it takes only
twenty minutes to scarf down so much food," he said. "I feel so out of
control when I binge. I can't stop. I feel primitive, like an animal, like I
never ate before. Then, as soon as it's over, I feel guilty, repulsive, glut-
tonous, stupid, lazy, and fugly—that's my word for 'fucking ugly.' I immediately make myself throw up so that I won't gain weight."

For many of the men, binge eating had all of the features of drug
addiction. "It feels like a rush, like snorting a line of cocaine," said a
man named Luis. "I can't wait to binge. I look forward to it more than
I do sex." He revealed that he spent anywhere from $20 to $150 per
week on food for binges. "Sometimes I've even stolen money to support
my food addiction," he admitted.

Other men described the binge-eating experience as an altered state of consciousness. "When I'm bingeing, I'm almost in a trance, like I'm hypnotized," said one. "I feel numb. When the binge is over, I look down at all of the wrappers around me, and I can't quite believe that it really happened. I can't believe that I actually ate all that food."

The primitive, animal-like feelings described by Ben were echoed by many other men. "When I binge, I physically shove the food down my throat, almost as madly as when I throw it back up," said one. Another said, "I eat like a baby, smearing food on my face, letting the onion dip drip from my chin."

The men's accounts of "purging" behaviors were equally graphic. "I would vomit at least fifteen times a day," said one. "It had to be at least fifteen. The enamel on my teeth rotted, and I got inflammation of my esophagus from the vomiting."

Luis, the man mentioned above, first developed bulimia nervosa in high school, but eventually reached the point at which he achieved some control over the eating binges and no longer induced vomiting afterward. But he was able to recall the vomiting experience in graphic terms. "I would have to make myself vomit at first. Then I would vomit at the sight and smell of my own vomit. That would happen until I was spitting up bile. It was gross."

"Did you have any medical problems as a result of throwing up so often?" we asked.

"Nothing serious, I guess. But my eyes would water and get inflamed when I was throwing up," he continued. "And I popped so many blood vessels in my face. It looked like I had some kind of rash."

"Didn't other kids notice the burst blood vessels when they saw you at school?"

"They may have noticed, but they never figured out what the reason was."

Virtually all of the other bulimic men in the study told us the same thing: no one had ever guessed, and we were the first people they had ever told. Bingeing, as one of them put it, was "like a secret relationship."

Curiously, the men with eating binges often described a sense of relief when they binged and purged. "I had no control over whether my mother beat me when I was a child," said one, "but I have control now. Eating like a slob and puking is according to my rules."

"I was so lonely," said another. "I had no girlfriends. I wasn't getting laid. Food became my girlfriend." Similarly, another described that if he went on a date and it didn't go well, he would immediately come home and go on a binge. Another used binge eating as a way to relieve stress from his job. "Everybody at work treats me like a doormat," he said. "Eating binges make me feel better."

Nevertheless, even for those men who described a temporary sense of relief, one unrelenting mantra ran through their stories: they loathed their bodies. Many of the men weighed themselves many times a day, and often chastised themselves if they gained even a pound. Virtually every man regularly examined himself in the mirror; most condemned the image they saw. As one put it, "I've always felt uncomfortable in my skin."

MALE EATING DISORDERS IN THE ALPS

After hearing these confessions from men in the Boston area, we wondered whether men with eating disorders were underrecognized in other Western societies as well. So we contacted our colleague, Dr. Barbara Mangweth, at the University of Innsbruck in Austria, and she set about doing an almost identical controlled study of men with eating disorders—the second to be performed anywhere.

The setting of Innsbruck, Austria, is as different from downtown Boston as could be imagined. A compact little city of only about 150,000 inhabitants, Innsbruck sits on the river Inn in one of the most beautiful settings in the world, with a wall of mountains, the Nordkette, rising 6,000 feet right out of the city and up into the snow. In the core of the town is the *Altstadt,* or Old City, which still retains the ancient buildings and narrow streets of six centuries ago. Outside of the Altstadt, a ring of newer buildings has sprung up, but the town gives way quickly to farmland, dotted with quaint alpine villages extending up the valley. Could life in this idyllic countryside possibly breed serious eating disorders in men, comparable to those we saw in Boston? We wondered whether our colleagues, drawing from such a small population, could find enough cases of male eating disorders to create a statistically meaningful study.

Our doubts were quickly resolved. Dr. Mangweth quickly rounded up thirty college men with eating disorders and a comparison group of thirty ordinary college students who didn't have eating disorders. And when she analyzed the data, the results were strikingly similar to what we had seen in the United States. The Austrian men with eating disorders described the same severe food and eating rituals, the same chronic preoccupations with thinness, the same disgust and shame with their bodies.

One of the Austrian men described bulimic symptoms so severe that he often had to take time off from work to be able to cook, eat, and vomit. He estimated that he vomited fifty to seventy times per week. Remarkably, he didn't believe that he had a problem and saw no reason to change his behavior. Another man described a secret place, in the cellar of his family's home, where he kept a wooden cooking spoon that he could put into his throat to induce vomiting. The vomiting became a lonely, daily ritual, filled with shame and self-loathing, in the darkened cellar.

Another Austrian man described long-standing symptoms of anorexia nervosa. All week long, he kept himself on a very strict diet, with the exception of Friday nights, when he engaged in a rigid eating ritual. At exactly 5 P.M. on Fridays, he would buy a large container of strawberry ice cream and a package of cookies, always at the same store, on his way home. Then, having secured himself in his room, shielded from all possible disturbances or interruptions, he would eat in a very slow, systematic manner, standing as he ate, on the theory that the food would flow through him more quickly, and be less likely to accumulate as fat, than it would if he were sitting down.

All of these men confessed that they had never told a soul about their problem. Dr. Mangweth emerged from her study with the same impression that we had formed earlier in Boston: the most striking feature of these men was their secrecy.

As a result of this secrecy, we're convinced that severe eating disorders are probably much more common in both America and Europe than usually supposed—because men with these conditions rarely come to professionals. Consequently, we believe that estimates of the prevalence of serious eating disorders, derived from observations in clinics, grossly understate the number of men who are suffering in the general population. In clinics, among patients coming for treatment of eating disorders, only about one in fifteen is a man. But in the community at large, according to a recent scientific paper by leading researcher Arnold Andersen, the proportion of men with anorexia nervosa and bulimia nervosa may be as high as one in six.

BINGE EATING: THE BIGGEST MALE EATING PROBLEM

Our studies in Boston and Austria focused only on more severe eating disorders. But beyond these extreme cases is a far larger number of men with other distressing eating problems. Perhaps the most common of these is simple uncontrolled binge eating, but without the purging behaviors seen in bulimia nervosa. Such binge eating problems may be just as common in men as in women. Men who binge eat often feel distress over their body image, as well as the same shame, secrecy, and self-depreciation that occurs with the more severe eating disorders.

Researchers are only beginning to learn about binge-eating problems. In one recent study, for example, Paul Garfinkel and his colleagues interviewed 4,285 women and 3,831 men in Canada. They found that 3.2 percent of the women reported a history of binge eating at least twice a week at some time in their lives, whereas among men the rate was just as high—3.3 percent. These numbers would lead to an estimate of several million North American men who have experienced problems with binge eating.

Some men with uncontrolled eating binges simply gain weight, but many make some attempt to compensate for the calories that they have consumed. Some, like Saul, the emergency room technician we described earlier, develop a daily cycle in which they scrupulously diet for most of the day, only to binge in the evening or at night. The next morning, they'll begin the cycle all over again. Others tell us that they have binges and then immediately start exercising to burn off the weight they just gained. For example, we can remember one man who would go directly to the gym after a binge and run on the treadmill for as long as two or three hours. "By the end, I would almost pass out from exhaustion and dehydration," he said.

Jeremy described huge late-night binges that typically consisted of a tub of vanilla frosting, several handfuls of raw cookie dough, four bags of Doritos, and a dozen Mars bars. "I couldn't go back to sleep with so much food in my stomach," he told us. "So I would go out for a run at midnight. It wasn't very smart. I didn't live in a safe neighborhood."

We talked to several other men with serious binge-eating problems when we studied an antidepressant and antiobsessional medication called fluvoxamine, or Luvox, as a potential treatment for this condition. All of the men described distress over their binge eating, and most confessed that they had totally lost control over food consumption. One told us that he found a restaurant near his house where he could buy day-old pizzas by the bag—a strategy that at least managed to keep down the cost of his binges. Another described such powerful urges to binge that he once broke into his neighbor's house, stole all of the ice cream out of the freezer, and ate it on the spot.

Luvox helped both of these men. Indeed, when the overall data from the study were analyzed, the patients who received the Luvox experienced a much greater reduction in their eating binges than those who received the identical-looking inert placebo pills. However, the patients in this study were chosen according to strict diagnostic criteria, similar to those for binge-eating disorder shown in Appendix II. Therefore, we can't assume that Luvox or drugs like it are necessarily effective for all types of binge eating.

OTHER WORRIES ABOUT WEIGHT

Many men who binge eat are not overweight, or are only a little overweight. But still, they usually tell us that they're constantly worrying about their body shape and their level of fat. One man named Dale, who had this form of the Adonis Complex, summed it up very simply: "If I didn't worry about what I looked like, I'd just eat whenever I wanted. But instead, I'm constantly dieting to keep my weight under control. The eating binges are just the times when I blow my diet and everything breaks down."

Dale was actually quite thin. In fact, we suspect that if he didn't diet so constantly and aggressively, and maybe allowed himself to gain just a few pounds, he wouldn't have been so chronically hungry—and then perhaps he would have been less prone to eating binges in the first place. But he didn't dare stop his diet to try such an experiment, because he was scared that he'd get too fat. And so he remained trapped in a vicious cycle of dieting, binge eating, and dieting again.

We should add an important clarification at this point: in contrast to the men described above, who suffer from various forms of the Adonis Complex, there are other men who are seriously overweight and are concerned with their problem for perfectly legitimate reasons. We would say that these latter men don't have the Adonis Complex, because their concern with their weight, unlike Dale's, has a rational basis. But even though we don't classify ordinary obesity as part of the Adonis Complex, we do not question the suffering it may cause. Indeed, it's estimated that up to a third of patients with obesity who seek treatment in weight-loss clinics suffer from depression or other psychological problems.

In our experience, many men who are overweight or obese may suffer not only from depression but from severe self-criticism, because they feel that they have only themselves to blame for their weight. In our society, it's still commonplace to assume that obesity is the fault of the individual—due to bad dietary habits, laziness, lack of willpower, or other character flaws. This is similar to old-time beliefs about alcoholism—that it was due to some lack of "moral fiber" rather than being a legitimate illness. In the same vein, scientific evidence now shows that obesity isn't simply due to "bad behavior"; there's a strong underlying genetic component. But still, it's common to blame the overweight person for his weight problem.

The medical, social, and psychological consequences of actual obesity go far beyond the scope of this book. We are restricting our discussion here to men with the Adonis Complex: those whose weight is in the healthy range but who nevertheless worry that they're too fat. It is these men, we believe, who have fallen victim to media images, advertisements, and other societal messages extolling the lean, fit male body.

CLUES TO EATING DISORDERS IN MEN

As the above studies and anecdotes have shown, men with eating problems experience a wide variety of different dietary patterns, weight-loss behaviors, and forms of distress. Below, we've assembled a list of clues covering all of the various forms of eating disorders discussed above. As elsewhere in this book, we phrase these clues in terms of "you." But if you're someone applying these clues to a man you know, you can simply substitute "he" in place of "you."

1) Do you regularly binge eat—that is, do you eat, in a discrete period of time (for example, during a two-hour period), an amount of food that is definitely larger than most men would eat during a similar time period and under similar circumstances? Do you feel that you can't control your eating during the binge—for example, do you feel that you can't stop eating or that you can't control what kinds of food you eat or how much you eat?

2) Do you often eat much more rapidly than is normal?

3) Do you often eat until you feel much too full?

4) Do you often eat alone because you'd be embarrassed if others saw how much you were eating?

5) Do you feel disgusted with yourself, depressed, or very guilty after overeating?

6) Do you make yourself vomit to prevent weight gain, especially after binge eating?

7) Do you use laxatives, diuretics (pills to induce fluid loss), enemas, or other medications that were not prescribed by a doctor to cause weight loss?

8) Do you often fast to lose weight, especially after you feel you've eaten too much?

9) Do you often exercise excessively to lose weight, especially after you feel you've overeaten?

10) Is your opinion of yourself, or your self-esteem, heavily influenced by your body shape or weight?

11) Have you ever refused to maintain your weight at (or above) a minimally normal weight for your age and height?

12) Have you ever been intensely fearful of gaining weight or becoming fat, even though other people thought you were underweight, or you weighed less than normal for your age and height?

13) Do you eat much less than other people think is normal? For example, do you restrict yourself to only one meal a day, or restrict your calorie consumption to a specific amount, even though you're still hungry?

14) Do you have weight concerns that interfere with your functioning, even though others think your weight isn't a major problem? For example, does your concern with your weight interfere with relationships, social activities, your job, or schoolwork?

15) Do you eat a special diet that interferes with your normal activities or your relationships with other people? For example, because of your special diet, is it difficult to eat out with other people, or do you avoid eating out with other people?

16) Do you sometimes turn down invitations because of the food that will be present at the event?

17) Do you ever go on a weight-loss diet that makes your doctor or your friends concerned about your health?

18) Do you smoke, use street drugs, or use large amounts of diet pills to control your weight?

19) Do you wear certain clothes (for example, big bulky clothes that cover you up) even if the situation doesn't call for it, or do you avoid wearing certain clothes (for example, shorts) because you're afraid you'll look too fat?

20) Do you often weigh yourself or check out your body in mirrors because you're afraid that you're fat or have gained weight?

If you answered yes to more than one or two of these questions, you may well have a form of the Adonis Complex. If you answered yes to a larger number of these questions, or have experienced one of the more serious eating problems in the above list, then you might want to consult the formal diagnostic criteria listed in Appendix II to see if you qualify for a diagnosis of an eating disorder.

WHAT CAUSES EATING DISORDERS IN MEN?

Why are so many contemporary men, in both America and Europe, developing pathological eating patterns and attitudes? For many years, the dominant theories about the origins of eating disorders focused on psychological conflicts within the individual, or on so-called "family dynamics." These theories argued that eating disorders were a response to adverse childhood experiences, such as bad parenting, dysfunctional family patterns, sexual conflicts, childhood abuse, and pathological attitudes toward food and dieting acquired while growing up. But in our studies, we've found few differences between men with eating disorders and comparison men in our assessments of family and childhood background. Some men with eating disorders, of course, have reported adverse experiences in childhood, such as physical or sexual abuse, conflicted relationships with their families, or idiosyncratic familial attitudes toward eating and food. But these same experiences were reported by comparable numbers of men without eating disorders. Therefore, childhood and family experiences don't seem adequate to explain all of what we're seeing.

Do male eating disorders develop in response to sociocultural pressures? At first, this theory might seem unlikely: our Austrian men with eating disorders, growing up in remote farming villages in the Alps, would seemingly be exposed to cultural influences very different from those affecting college students growing up in suburban America. But as we have already demonstrated with our computerized Body Image Test in Chapter 3, men's dissatisfaction with body image is similar in Innsbruck and Boston.

Upon reflection, this similarity isn't surprising. Action toys with washboard abdominal muscles populate the toy chests of Austrian boys just as they do in America. Boys from both cultures grow up seeing similar male models in pictures and magazines, watching the World Wrestling Federation matches and other muscular males on television, and watching the same Hollywood movies. Indeed, the Austrian men could hardly have missed seeing action thrillers starring their own countryman, born only 600 kilometers from Innsbruck—Arnold Schwarzenegger.

Advertising is another likely culprit. Vast body image industries, hawking everything from exercise machines to diet aids to nutritional supplements, stand to profit from convincing boys and men that they should be uncompromisingly fit and lean. Having saturated the women's market long ago, many of these industries are trying to tap the other 50 percent of the population. Images of perfectly trim male models are now broadcast to boys everywhere, from the American inner city to Alpine farming communities. The ideal male, as portrayed by these images, has not only been putting on muscle, but has also been dieting.

In short, our theories on the origins of male eating disorders closely parallel our theories about the roots of other forms of the Adonis Complex, such as muscle dysmorphia. Throughout Western cultures, the societal ideal of the male body, transmitted by increasingly international and uniform media messages, has grown more and more difficult for the average boy or man to attain. Men with a biologically or genetically based predisposition to obsessional preoccupations or compulsive behaviors may be particularly vulnerable to these messages. These men respond with mounting anxieties about their degree of body fat, and may develop a wide variety of eating disorders in response. Some, through rituals of dieting, purging, and exercise, manage to stay thin. Others fail—or at least perceive themselves to fail—and descend into low self-esteem and depression.

RELIEF FOR MEN WITH EATING PROBLEMS

What can be done for these millions of men, from those secretly binge eating or vomiting to those overly distressed about their love handles? First, they must be willing to reveal their problem. Secrecy and embarrassment are the single greatest impediment to getting help. The current predicament of men in this respect is similar to that of women with eating disorders twenty years ago: in the 1980s, women with these conditions also usually kept their problem secret, thinking that no one else could have a similar problem. Fortunately, the widespread publicity about eating disorders in the 1980s helped to liberate many of these women, allowing them to overcome their embarrassment and reveal their problems to professionals. Self-help organizations for women with eating disorders mushroomed around the country; many of these organizations opened multiple chapters in different localities, so that a woman with an eating disorder did not need to go far to find others who shared her experiences.

But comparable self-help groups for men are lacking. And few men are comfortable joining a self-help group in which every other member is a woman. Most men with eating disorders today, like women in the 1980s, still live under the illusion that they are unique, that no other men could have such a problem. We hope that this book, along with increasing public recognition of the problems of male body image, will help to make it easier for men with eating disorders to come forward and reveal their body concerns and eating behaviors to professionals who can help them.

Help may include certain antidepressant medications and/or certain types of psychotherapy, depending upon the severity of a man's symptoms. To start with an example of a serious eating disorder, Christopher, a graduate student in one of our men's therapy groups, comes to mind. Although he came from a loving family, Christopher always harbored a feeling that he wasn't quite good enough.

As he grew up, Christopher found that his perfectionist tendencies led him to start obsessively thinking about his body. "I remember thinking that no matter what I did for a living or how well I could do my job, it wouldn't mean anything unless I looked perfect. My body became my biggest preoccupation, at the expense of everything else. I became obsessed that I looked fat; then I got obsessed with counting calories, then fat grams, then with counting how many times I would chew food. I couldn't help it."

Christopher began to diet at the age of twelve, to the point where he was starving himself. He started to cut out many foods from his diet but eventually found starvation too negative an experience. His bout with anorexia nervosa lasted five months. Then, instead of resuming normal eating habits, he began alternately binge eating and fasting.

Christopher seemed a likely candidate for Prozac. Prozac is a drug chemically similar to Luvox, the medication that we used in the binge-eating study described above. Prozac and Luvox are usually called "antidepressants," but they are also often effective for obsessive-compulsive symptoms and bulimic symptoms. Indeed, after six weeks on Prozac, Christopher's eating binges decreased substantially. Even more exciting was the fact that his obsession with food also declined. For the first time in years, Chris told us, he was no longer devoting every waking thought to his love handles, food, or having to be the best.

Still, Christopher experienced some remaining eating binges, so we added cognitive-behavioral therapy. One technique we used was mood monitoring: we taught Christopher to be aware of his thoughts and emotions throughout the day, and to identify situations that triggered bingeing and purging. Oftentimes, men and women with eating disorders have difficulty recognizing their emotions. Mood monitoring helps people to recognize what they are feeling and to connect their feelings to their behaviors. We also used a technique called "behavioral tips." These were specific behaviors that Christopher could adopt to reduce the likelihood of a binge. Anger management techniques, relaxation exercises, avoiding the supermarket when hungry, calling a friend when he felt like bingeing, and listening to music were some of the many alternative strategies Christopher learned. With these techniques added to the effects of the Prozac, Christopher managed to get rid of the binge eating entirely.

CHOOSING TWO THIN PARENTS

Serious eating disorders like Christopher's require extensive treatment. Such treatment is especially important for men with anorexia nervosa, an illness that may kill more than 10 percent of its victims. But what about the much larger group of men who are reasonably well adjusted but still excessively worried that they look too fat? This form of the Adonis Complex doesn't represent a full-scale psychiatric problem, but it can still cause a lot of distress. We have seen many men attempting to diet excessively, or spending vast sums on dietary or nutritional supplements, or compulsively exercising in an endless attempt to work the fat off of their abdominals. They seem convinced that they'll be happy only if they can become permanently thin.

If you're a man in this category, we can suggest one good way to stay permanently thin: *choose two thin parents*. Ideally, *choose four thin grandparents* as well. We apologize for being facetious, but the fact remains that genetics plays a powerful role in determining body fat, even though many men don't like to admit it. We see lots of men who eat a healthy diet and get plenty of exercise, but still carry a moderate amount of fat because nature made them that way. These men sometimes feel that they ought to be able to become model-thin, in spite of the messages of their own DNA.

Some men ask if there's a medical technique, some drug perhaps, that will help keep weight off permanently. The answer, technically speaking, is yes—but only at the price of new dangers, if not death.

Smoking several packs of high-nicotine cigarettes every day or taking large doses of amphetamines or other diet pills every day will reduce weight—but we certainly wouldn't recommend these approaches. Furthermore, even if these drugs were safe, you would have to take them every day, and never stop, to remain thin. This is because these drugs lower the body's "setpoint"—the level of body fat that your brain wants you to maintain—only while you are taking them. As soon as you stop, your setpoint goes right back up, and you'll put the fat back on again.

Anabolic steroids also promote loss of body fat. After all, it's nature's own anabolic steroid, testosterone, that is largely responsible for men having less body fat than women. If you give testosterone to a woman, she will grow leaner and more muscular, and begin to look more like a man. If you give testosterone to a man, to the point where his levels are far higher than those secreted naturally, he will grow even more lean and muscular than an ordinary man. But steroids, like all other fat-burning drugs, stop working when you stop taking them. Although the muscle gains from steroids may persist for months or even years after use, the fat tends to go back on in a matter of weeks.

For men who already have a healthy eating pattern, there remains only one further method for sustained weight loss that we can recommend: regular, moderately intense exercise. Running and other aerobic activities, and even supposedly "anaerobic" activities such as weightlifting, will cause most men to lose some body fat. But many men who faithfully follow an exercise regimen may be disappointed to find that they lose only 10 pounds or so, and then hit a plateau. Often these men will refuse to acknowledge that this plateau probably represents the minimum that Mother Nature intended for them. They feel that if they can't get any thinner, they must be failures.

And that brings us to caution about an almost useless method of permanently losing weight, namely *going on a diet*. We especially advise against some of the more extreme weight-loss diets that are perennially popular. In fact, an extreme decrease in caloric intake will result in a reduced metabolic rate, which actually impedes weight loss. Of course, we admit that most men can lose a significant amount of body fat by dieting. But unless a man remains on an aggressive diet for all of his life, and lives in a constant state of mild hunger, he is eventually going to put the fat back on. There's nothing particularly controversial about this fact in scientific circles—yet, once again, many men are simply unwilling to accept it.

Upon reflection, it's not surprising that men with the Adonis Complex try to resist scientific realities about weight. Remember that these men have been subjected since childhood to images of lean, ideal male bodies. In fact, some of these bodies are lean because the men in the images took anabolic steroids to get that way. In addition, a growing industry of diet foods, diet books, and diet plans reaps billions of dollars from nurturing men's insecurities about fat—just as a similar industry has preyed for decades on the body image insecurities of women.

Many men aren't conscious of these forces. They've become so fixated on losing fat that they haven't stopped to think carefully about why they feel they *need* to lose more fat in the first place. So if you're a man who doesn't really have a problem with obesity, but who still constantly worries about fat, we would encourage you to stop, take advantage of the body you were born with, and enjoy it! If you're someone who is modestly overweight, try regular exercise and a healthy diet, but don't be tempted to try extreme weight-loss measures. You may never have washboard abdominals. On the other hand, your body may be gifted in other respects. For example, you may well be capable of becoming extremely strong—far stronger than your thinner male friends. But if you remain fixated on becoming something that you aren't, and remain a captive of media images and the messages of the body image industry, you'll torture yourself needlessly.

This same advice applies to all men with eating problems, from mild preoccupations with fat to extreme cases of anorexia or bulimia nervosa. It's similar to the advice we've offered in previous chapters for men who worry about their muscularity or men tempted to try anabolic steroids. In all of these forms of the Adonis Complex, men could be relieved of much suffering if they could only be liberated from society's unrealistic ideals of what they *should* look like. Of course, it's good to try to eat well, exercise well, and maintain a healthy body, but it's unhealthy to use extreme measures to maintain a body completely different from the one that Mother Nature gave you. If men could accept this truth, much of the burden of the Adonis Complex might be lifted from their shoulders.

CHAPTER SEVEN

Beyond Muscle and Fat
Hair, Breasts, Genitals, and Other Body Obsessions

Steve was rugged-looking, tall, and muscular, with a bright smile and thick brown hair. A construction worker in his mid-thirties, he lifted weights every day and mountain-climbed on weekends. He was in great shape, and many men envied his good looks. He often got compliments about his fitness. In fact, his friends—and even strangers—told him he looked like Arnold Schwarzenegger and should consider an acting career.

But there was a big difference between the way Steve looked on the outside and felt on the inside. "Everyone tells me how great I look, but I don't agree with them," he told us in the privacy of our office. "Some people even tell me I should be an actor, and once this famous photographer came up to me and started snapping my picture. I was totally humiliated! I covered my face with my hands and begged him not to develop the pictures. I even got a little threatening. Why would he take pictures of me? Something must be wrong with his eyes!"

In response to his relentless worries, Steve spent hours trying to improve his supposed appearance flaws. A typical day went like this. "I get up at six in the morning to try to make myself presentable for work, which is pretty near impossible. I take a shower, and then the hair routine starts. I comb it, spray tons of mousse on it, blow-dry it, then the hair gel goes on till it's as stiff as concrete. Then I comb it over and over, trying to cover the bald spot and make it look okay. Sometimes I put some hair thickener in to create an optical illusion. Then, after I've done this for maybe half an hour, I look in the mirror and I think, 'I can't go out like this! I look like a jerk! It's sticking up and looks bizarre, and I look naked on top of my head.' So I do the hair thing again . . . and again . . . and again. Then, believe it or not, it's about eight o'clock and

I'm gonna be late for work. So I force myself to leave the house, just hoping no one takes a close look at me. Things are a little better at work, because it's just guys, but I still feel uncomfortable.

"It's embarrassing to tell you this, but I bring a pocket mirror with me to work. I keep it on hand so I can sneak some peeks at my hair during the day. I have to make sure that I haven't lost any more and it looks okay. I'm petrified that one of the other guys is gonna catch me looking in the mirror—talk about humiliating!"

Hair was Steve's biggest appearance concern, but not his only one. He also constantly worried that he had "love handles." "I realize I'm pretty built and all," he explained, "but I still can't get rid of these fat pads around my waist. I've been embarrassed to take my shirt off since I was a kid. I had a potbelly when I was a kid, and I was teased a lot. I hated it. Now I have these handles. I don't lean sideways or against a wall because I don't want my shirt to lie on them and make them more visible. I'm one thousand percent self-conscious without my shirt on. I seriously considered liposuction; I've even priced it, but it's pretty expensive."

The next time we saw Steve, we asked that he bring his fiancée with him, so we could get her view of the problem.

"This is Steve's biggest issue," Alison told us. "He's a great guy, and you can see how handsome he is. But this is driving both of us crazy. No matter how many times I tell him how good he looks, he won't believe me."

"Well, I know what I see when I look in the mirror." Steve interjected. "It jumps out at me!"

"This is what we go through every day," Alison said. "It's eating away at our relationship. We argue over this. Sometimes he won't go out with me. Especially when it's windy and his hair might get messed up. He's afraid the bald spot will be exposed. And that stupid hat he wears all the time . . . We can't get into certain restaurants because he won't take it off."

She nervously glanced at Steve. "And it's affecting the intimate part of our relationship, because he doesn't want me to get too close to his hair—he's afraid I'll mess it up if I touch it. And even though he's got a great body, he thinks he has love handles, which he doesn't, but it makes him really self-conscious and uncomfortable."

"You know, I feel ridiculous hearing Alison say this stuff, but it's true," Steve added. "And she doesn't even know half of it. On the inside, it's actually worse than anybody knows. I've got to admit it. It's making me pretty miserable."

Steve went on, at first sheepishly, but gradually more openly, as we listened. He described his experiences with dozens of hair ointments and several hair clubs. "I tried hair thickeners and medicines that are supposed to make your hair grow. Some of them were supposed to increase your metabolism, and others were supposed to increase your blood supply or kill bacteria. I'd say I've spent at least three hundred dollars a month for the past three years, and none of them has done a thing for me. I've just wasted a lot of money."

"I'm so glad you can finally tell these things to someone," said Alison with a sigh of relief.

As Steve's story illustrates, men with the Adonis Complex worry about parts of their bodies other than muscle and fat. Hair, as in Steve's case, is a particularly common preoccupation, but men frequently develop worries about their skin, facial features, breast fat, and, commonly, penis size. For some men, like Steve, these appearance concerns are profoundly disturbing, causing them emotional distress and taking much of the pleasure out of life. For others, the concerns don't cause such major problems, but they can still be upsetting, and they can consume lots of energy and money.

These observations shouldn't seem surprising in light of the study results we've discussed earlier. Consider the *Psychology Today* survey results, which revealed that 43 percent of male respondents were dissatisfied with their overall appearance—almost triple the 15 percent rate reported by men in the same survey back in 1972. For example, as you may recall, 38 percent of men were dissatisfied with their chest/breasts, 63 percent with their abdomens. Also remember our own results with the Adonis Complex Questionnaire, described in Chapter 3. The first question on this test asked, "How much time do you spend each day worrying about some aspect of your appearance (not just thinking about it, but actually worrying about it)?" In response to this question, about 10 percent of the secondary school and college men responded "more than 60 minutes." That means that there are millions of young American men who spend more than an hour a day not just *thinking* about their appearance, but actually *worrying* about it.

What about the many individual features of the male body not specifically covered in these general questionnaires? On the basis of our clinical experience, we know that countless men worry about other, more private, aspects of their bodies as well. Probably the biggest secret fear is penis size; we've treated countless men with this concern. And the men who come to us and to our colleagues for consultation represent a tiny group in comparison to the vast numbers who harbor such preoccupations but who wouldn't dream of admitting them to a professional. The penis-enlargement industry—just like the bodybuilding and dietary supplement industries we've described in previous chapters—is yet another part of the huge and growing men's body image industry, catering to and amplifying men's fears and insecurities about their bodies. As we noted in Chapter 2, the American Academy of Cosmetic Surgery calculates that men received 690,361 cosmetic procedures in 1996 alone, and that figure doesn't include the even larger number of men who sought cosmetic treatments from nonprofessional sources, such as the hair treatments and penis-enlargement techniques advertised in the backs of magazines or on the Internet.

Now that the baby boomers are aging, moving into the decades when hair thins and buttocks sag, these kinds of products, the hopes they inspire, and profits they reap will proliferate even more. As aging men become more insecure about their appearance, they spend more and more money in pursuit of looking youthful. It's ironic that as women have become increasingly aware of—and a little more liberated from—society's unreachable standards of beauty, men are increasingly and unknowingly falling prey to the very same forces.

BODY DYSMORPHIC DISORDER: ANOTHER
TROUBLING BODY IMAGE PROBLEM FOR MEN

Many men experience body image concerns but manage to keep them under control. Bad hair, jowly cheeks, and hairy backs may be annoying, cause passing distress, or consume paychecks, but they don't usually seriously interfere with daily living. But for many other men, this distress can consume their time and emotional energy, depriving them of other pleasures in life. And for some men, identical body concerns can escalate into a serious, full-scale psychiatric condition called "body dysmorphic disorder," or BDD. Men with BDD develop health-threatening worries that something is terribly wrong with how they look, when in fact they look fine to others. In reality, their appearance defects are minimal, even nonexistent. Yet they worry, for example, that their hair is too thin, their skin is scarred, their nose is crooked, their breasts are too fat, or that they aren't tall enough. Any body part can be the focus of concern. Others try to reassure them that they look fine, but the reassurance fails.

When this form of the Adonis Complex gets severe, men don't just dislike their appearance—they become obsessed with it. Some men with this problem tell us that they think about their perceived body flaws virtually every minute of the day. As one of our patients said: "I spend ninety-nine percent of my time thinking about my hair and the fear that I'll soon be bald." In addition, the appearance preoccupations cause significant distress (such as anxiety or depression) or interfere with functioning—for example, making it hard to be around others or difficult to concentrate at work. We have provided the official diagnostic criteria for BDD, taken from the American Psychiatric Association's *Diagnostic and Statistical Manual of Mental Disorders,* in Appendix II. But remember that these criteria, like the official diagnostic criteria for other conditions listed in Appendix II, describe only the more severe cases. For every man whose symptoms meet these full diagnostic criteria, there are many others who aren't as impaired but are still hurting.

If our description of BDD sounds a lot like our earlier description of muscle dysmorphia, that's because muscle dysmorphia is a specific type of BDD. The general category of BDD refers to all types of serious unfounded body image concerns. Muscle dysmorphia is simply the form of BDD in which muscularity, as opposed to some other aspect of the body, becomes the focus. We've devoted a whole previous chapter to muscle dysmorphia because it has proliferated so much in recent years and provides such a graphic example of the effects of society's body ideals on today's man. But other forms of BDD cause the same shame and distress, and the same attempts to improve or hide the body, as muscle dysmorphia.

Some people confuse BDD with vanity, which can make it difficult for men with this problem to talk about it. BDD isn't vanity. People with BDD suffer. Most don't want to look great—they just want to look acceptable.

We have kept track of the specific body preoccupations of ninety-five men with BDD whom we evaluated. The illustration on the next page shows the percentage of these men who reported a preoccupation with each body area. As you can see, the percentages add up to far more than 100, because virtually all of the men were preoccupied with several different body areas. Typically, they considered three or four different parts of their bodies unattractive.

These statistics were compiled from men who had full-scale BDD, but men with less severe body image problems can also become preoccupied with any of the same body parts shown in the figure. These millions of other men with milder appearance concerns may superficially

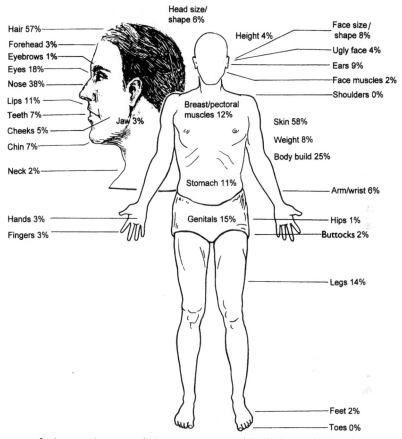

Hair 57%
Forehead 3%
Eyebrows 1%
Eyes 18%
Nose 38%
Lips 11%
Teeth 7%
Cheeks 5%
Chin 7%
Neck 2%
Hands 3%
Fingers 3%

Head size/shape 6%
Height 4%
Jaw 3%
Breast/pectoral muscles 12%
Stomach 11%
Genitals 15%

Face size/shape 8%
Ugly face 4%
Ears 9%
Face muscles 2%
Shoulders 0%
Skin 58%
Weight 8%
Body build 25%
Arm/wrist 6%
Hips 1%
Buttocks 2%
Legs 14%
Feet 2%
Toes 0%

Body areas that cause distress among men with body dysmorphic disorder.

function so well that their secret concerns and hours of distress aren't even detectable to those closest to them.

Tom was one of these men. He was fixated on his receding hairline, even though he tried to disguise his concerns. "I really can't stand what's happened to my hair," he told us in the privacy of the office. "I feel self-conscious, and I certainly wish I had more of it like when I was in college. Sometimes when I catch a glimpse of myself in the mirror, I think 'Where's it going?' and I wish I had more. I try to hide my worries from my wife, but she can't help but recognize that I think about it. She keeps telling me to forget about it. I spend extra time combing it each morning, trying to cover up the thinner areas. It doesn't stop me from doing things. Still, my friends and coworkers would never guess how much I dislike it."

Ted, an investment banker in New York City, was highly successful and had an air of self-confidence. In most respects, Ted really did feel good about himself—except for the potbelly that had materialized over the past several years. "My stomach used to look fine," he said. "I never even thought about it. But as I reached middle age, it started expanding. Now I must think about it twenty times a day. I don't like it, and I'm always dieting. Sometimes I feel self-conscious, especially at the beach. I'm checking out the other guys' stomachs, seeing how big they are compared to mine. As a matter of fact, I've had a couple of times that I deliberately didn't go to the beach for just that reason."

Bob, an equally successful attorney, had another type of secret preoccupation. "It's my beard shadow," he said. "I hate to admit it, but I spend close to an hour every morning trying to look the way I want. I spend more time in the bathroom than my wife does! And then I shave at least one more time during the day, trying to get rid of every hint of my beard. If I catch a glimpse of myself in the mirror and I see a shadow, it bothers me."

Tom, Ted, and Bob would not technically meet the official diagnostic criteria for BDD because their body image concerns aren't severe and problematic enough to qualify. But they, like countless other men with the Adonis Complex, have nagging worries about their appearance.

SILENT SUFFERING

Ten years ago, we didn't hear much about BDD, just as we didn't hear about muscle dysmorphia or eating disorders in men. One reason, we believe, is that practically no one realized how common this problem was. Therefore, most professionals—including ourselves—didn't routinely ask about it when they saw patients. But once we started systematically asking questions about body-appearance concerns, we were amazed at how many men began to open up about their anxieties over their looks.

Zach was one of them. He came into treatment because of serious drug and alcohol abuse. But the underlying problem, which he had never previously revealed to anyone, was his preoccupation with the appearance of his nose, jaw, and other facial features. "I could have had a much better job at work, but I couldn't get promoted because I was way too anxious around other people about how I looked, so I quit," he said. "I dropped out of college because of this problem. I have no sex life or love life. It's made my life really unbearable that I look so bad after all these years!" The only time that Zach felt any relief from the pain, he told us, was when he was drunk or stoned, or preferably both.

We remember meeting Tony, a student at a college in Rhode Island. Tony had been admitted to the hospital because he'd tried to kill himself. "My nose job was the beginning of all of my problems," he explained to us. "That's why I'm here. I wanted my nose shorter. I wanted it to look more masculine. I looked nerdy, like a little professor with a long nose. But the surgeon changed the whole shape. He took my whole nose off! Now I look infinitely worse! It's too short and thin, and it looks like a woman's nose. I'd rather be dead than have my nose look like this!"

Tony's nose actually looked fine to us and to all of the rest of the hospital staff. But no amount of reassurance made his obsessions go away.

Jon, a man in his early forties, worried that his skin was too pale. He wore a bronzer at all times. "I absolutely can't go out without it," he explained. "Once I was in severe pain from a gallbladder attack that I think was caused by the tanning pills I was taking. But before I went to the hospital, I had to put on my bronzer. It didn't bother me that I might die from the operation; the only thing I was really worrying about was that the surgeons would think I looked too pale when they saw me on the operating table."

Jeremy hated his calves, thinking they looked too big. To decrease their size, he tied them up with a rope at night while he slept, to the point that they turned blue due to lack of circulation. He also slept with a clothespin on his nose, trying to make it smaller. In desperation, after several plastic surgeons had refused surgery, he deliberately smashed his nose with a hammer. "That way, they'd have to fix it," he said.

With all the suffering it causes, why did BDD remain "underground" until recently? The answer isn't entirely clear, but our experience suggests that a major reason is the feeling and talking taboo we've described previously. In our society, "real men" aren't supposed to worry about what they look like, much less go around confessing such concerns to others.

The feeling and talking taboo adds insult to injury for these men. Even though they may be internally tortured by their preoccupations, many feel compelled to deny or minimize them to others. Often, despite their silent suffering, they won't reveal their concerns to anyone—their doctors, their wives or girlfriends, or their best male friends. As one man said to us, "I thought I was the only one in the whole world with this problem. I couldn't tell anyone about it, not even my wife. I was too embarrassed and ashamed."

If only these men could realize how many others around them were hiding similar feelings! BDD is as common in men as in women, affecting an estimated 1 to 2 percent of the population. That's well over a million men with full-scale BDD meeting the official diagnostic criteria in Appendix II—which means that there are millions more men with appearance concerns that don't meet the full diagnostic criteria but are still troubling. Furthermore, BDD may be even more common in men than in women who seek cosmetic surgery. In one study that looked at this question, only 7 percent of women seeking cosmetic surgery were found to have BDD, whereas one-third of men had the disorder.

DO YOU HAVE BODY DYSMORPHIC DISORDER?

On the basis of our experience with hundreds of men with BDD, we've developed a list, shown below, of some of the more common clues to BDD. Some of the behaviors in this list can be fairly normal—but in BDD they're carried to an extreme. Most men with BDD exhibit at least several of them. We've phrased the questions in this list in terms of "you," but if you're thinking of a man you know, you can easily rephrase these questions in terms of "he."

Clues to Body Dismorphic Disorder

1) Do you worry a lot about how you look? For example, do you spend at least an hour a day thinking that you don't look right?

2) Does some aspect of your appearance really upset you? For example, does it get you down or make you anxious, frustrated, or angry?

3) Do your appearance concerns cause problems for you—for example, problems at school or work, or in relationships?

4) Do you sometimes miss things (such as social events, work, or school) because you feel too unattractive to be seen?

5) Are you sometimes late for things (such as a social event) because you dislike your appearance or you're trying to improve it (for example, by grooming)?

6) Is it hard to concentrate on your schoolwork or job, or are you less productive than you should be, because of your appearance concerns?

7) Because of your self-consciousness over your appearance, do you feel more comfortable going out at night, or when fewer people will be around?

8) Do you feel self-conscious around others because of how you look? Do you feel especially uncomfortable in social situations?

9) Do you find yourself often checking mirrors or other reflecting surfaces (such as windows), trying to check out how you look?

10) Do you often check your body directly, without using a mirror?

11) Alternatively, is it hard for you to look in mirrors—and or do you even try to avoid looking in them—because you're so upset by what you see?

12) Do you try to hide the body areas you dislike—for example, wearing sunglasses or a hat, covering yourself with clothing, or combing your hair in a way that hides areas you don't like?

13) Do you try to hide certain parts of your body by keeping yourself in a certain position—for example, turning your "bad side" away from others, or sucking in your stomach?

14) Do you spend a lot of time grooming? For example, do you spend lots of time trying to get your hair just right, or shave several times a day to get rid of any hint of your beard?

15) Do you spend too much time in the bathroom trying to fix how you look?

16) Do you pick at your skin, trying to get rid of any blemishes or imperfections?

17) Do you ask other people whether you look okay, or how a certain part of your body looks? If they say you look fine, do you think they're just being nice?

18) Do you try to convince other people that you don't look right when they tell you that you look fine?

19) Do you often compare yourself to other people, checking out their looks? Do you often compare yourself to models in magazines or to actors in the movies or on TV? Do you usually think that others look better than you?

20) Do you emphasize certain good parts of your body, trying to distract people from the ugly parts (for example, getting a dark tan so they don't notice your nose)?

21) Do you sometimes worry that people are looking at you, staring at you, talking about you, or making fun of you because of how you look?

22) Do you measure parts of your body, hoping to find that they're the size you want?

23) Do you eat special diets to change your appearance?

24) Do you exercise excessively to improve how you look? (This behavior is especially common among men with the muscle dysmorphia form of BDD. If you answer yes on this item, you might want to take another look at our clues checklist in Chapter 4.)

25) Do you do other things to try to improve your appearance—for example, using a bronzer to darken your skin?

26) Do you go to dermatologists, surgeons, or other health professionals for an appearance-related problem, only to have them tell you the treatment you're requesting isn't necessary?

27) Have you had cosmetic surgery and been dissatisfied with the results? Or have you had multiple surgeries, hoping the next procedure would finally make you look good?

28) Do you pad your clothes in an effort to make certain body areas look bigger (such as your shoulders or genitals)?

As you go through this list of clues, you'll see that some of the items are more serious than others. Many men and boys would probably answer yes to at least one or two of the items, so a couple of yeses aren't a big deal. But if you answered yes to more than one or two items, you may be having at least some difficulties with the Adonis Complex. And if you answered yes to questions 1 and 2 *plus* any one of questions 3 through 7, your appearance concerns are more serious, and you may have BDD. Most men with full-scale BDD also answer yes to at least several of the other questions as well.

LIVING WITH SEVERE BDD

As the above list of clues implies, there's a broad spectrum of body image concerns in men, ranging from mildly annoying worries to a severe and even life-threatening psychiatric condition. Severe BDD can be devastating. Though outsiders may recognize that something is wrong, they may not guess that BDD is the reason. Men with severe BDD may have trouble getting their job done; they may even quit their job or get fired because their symptoms interfere with their concentration and productivity. They may refuse to attend social events and shy away from dating or relationships because they think they look unattractive. Some men's symptoms lead to divorce. Men with severe BDD may even attempt suicide. One man we know, who's now doing well with treatment, attempted suicide nearly twenty times. "The pain was unbearable," he said. "My life was a devastation. It was so painful I couldn't put it into words. Every day was hell."

For nearly ten years, we've carefully interviewed men with more severe BDD to assess the frequency of these complications. What we've found brings home how serious this form of the Adonis Complex can be. In studies comprising more than a hundred adolescent and adult men we've interviewed,

- 98 percent said that BDD had substantially interfered with their social life.
- 82 percent said that BDD had substantially interfered with their job or schoolwork.
- 15 percent were not currently working because of BDD.
- 44 percent wanted to be in school but were not because of their BDD symptoms.
- 33 percent had been completely housebound for at least one week because they felt too ugly to be seen.
- 88 percent were currently dissatisfied with their life.
- 17 percent had attempted suicide.

We've also used a scale to measure these men's quality of life and found that it was terribly compromised. In fact, mental-health-related quality of life was much poorer for people with BDD than has been reported for people with a variety of other psychiatric disorders, for people with a chronic medical condition (such as diabetes), and even for people who had had a recent heart attack. A couple of stories from our patients, better than any statistics, tell of this pain.

Dan was a successful journalist for a nationally known newspaper. He had been happily married for twenty years to his high school sweetheart, an accomplished dancer. He had three healthy children. Highly respected in his community, Dan had won national acclaim for his work. He was friendly, outgoing, and had lots of friends. Each year, he hosted his city's charity golf tournament, and he served on the board of one of the city's teaching hospitals.

No one, except Dan's wife, had any idea that Dan actually had BDD and that life was a struggle for him. Dan worried that his beard growth was too heavy and uneven, and he felt compelled to shave at least three times a day. He also worried that his skin was badly scarred— although no one but Dan could see his minor imperfections.

"Sometimes it's hard to do my job," he conceded in the privacy of the office. "Some days my beard and skin look worse than other days. I can feel very self-conscious when I'm around people, because I'm thinking they might be noticing what's wrong with how I look. Sometimes the thoughts are distracting, and it takes me longer than it should to get an assignment done. The other thing is that I've spent many thousands of dollars getting my skin worked on."

Mary Ann was painfully aware of the money Dan had spent. "I can think of lots of better things we could have done with it," she said with resignation. "And it didn't really help you feel any better."

She tried to explain the problem to us. "The biggest effect of this is on our marriage. Dan's a wonderful man, but sometimes he gets withdrawn and moody. He doesn't want to burden me with how he's feeling, but after twenty years, of course I can figure it out. It's always about how he looks. I try to reassure him that he looks fine, and I know he tries to force himself to cheer up, but it never really works. And sometimes when we go out with friends or to a social event, he just isn't himself. Sometimes he doesn't even want to go. Other people might not notice, but I can tell it's constantly weighing on him. The amazing thing is, even though Dan tells me everything that's going on with him, and this is his biggest problem, he kept it a secret from me for fifteen years! He was too embarrassed to tell me."

Through a huge investment of time and money, Dan had at least managed to keep his life and his marriage outwardly successful, even though he constantly suffered. Others were not so fortunate.

Joe was a good-looking young man who had everything going for him. He had just graduated from a well-known midwestern university and was an outstanding athlete, having won several state tennis competitions. But recently, he revealed to us, his life had dramatically changed. "I've lost everything to this hair problem," he told us. "It's my whole life. All my life consists of now is coming up with strategies to deal with it—and none of them work. It takes up all my time."

Joe used to like his hair. "I used to get lots of compliments on it," he said. "It was one of my better attributes. But when I was nineteen, I heard this girl say to this guy that he was going bald. I can remember the exact moment of hearing that remark. The thought suddenly came over me, 'If someone said that to me, that would be it.' Hair is the most important part of a guy's appearance.

"Well, no one ever did say it to me, but I started worrying anyway. I started thinking that maybe my hair didn't look so good. And the thought just grew and grew on me. It started crowding out all my other thoughts. Now the only thing I can think of is that I look gross. Looking at myself in the mirror is like looking at a horror movie.

"I constantly monitor myself for hair loss—I have to keep complete track of each and every hair I lose. Checking the mirror is part of it. I also check my pillow every morning to see if there's any hair there, and I'm always counting the hairs that fall into the sink when I'm doing my hair, or the ones in the shower drain. If I lose more than ten a day, I go ballistic.

"My grades really bottomed out after the problem started, and I can't look for a job because I can't compete, the way my hair is. I can't be in a relationship with a girl because I look so bad. I lost my last girlfriend over it. All I did all day long was ask her if my hair looked okay— we'd discuss it literally for hours at a time. We fought over my constantly discussing it. I kept having her put hair-growth medicines in my hair. Finally, she couldn't take it anymore, so she left."

Tears began to well up in his eyes. "This problem has completely ruined my life. I can't imagine any greater suffering than this. No one understands how painful it is. It's like having cancer—I'm paralyzed with fear. I've even threatened suicide over it. I purposely drive recklessly, without wearing my seat belt, hoping I'll get into a car accident and die. If I have to go through life looking like this, I don't want to live."

Charlie got even closer to suicide than Joe, and all because he was devastated by his hair. "I even had the whole thing planned out, how I would kill myself," he revealed to us. "I even started giving my stuff away. But the one thing that stopped me was thinking that when I was dead in my casket, people would look in and say, 'Oh, God, look at his hair!' Seriously, that's the one thing that's kept me alive!"

HAIR FEARS

It may seem hard to believe that a man could become suicidal about his hair, but we're even aware of some men who have actually killed themselves because of BDD. Admittedly, these cases are more extreme, but we see evidence of men's growing concern with thinning, balding, or graying hair everywhere around us. For example, a recent article in a major news magazine blared the headline ONLY HIS HAIRDRESSER KNOWS FOR SURE. The article went on to say that "older gentlemen, once considered classically handsome in a Phil Donahue way, are paying more attention to hair color these days too. In a tech-driven work force more youth-obsessed than ever, salt-and-peppered men are reaching for familiar products like Grecian Formula and Just for Men."

A recent fad is something called "tipping," in which guys bleach or dye just the tops of their short, spiky strands, leaving their roots long and exposed. This is catching on among men of all ages and socioeconomic classes—stockbrokers as well as construction workers. Over just the past five years, sales of men's home hair-color kits increased by 50 percent, reaching $113.5 million in 1998.

While tipping is a recent trend, messages about hair's vital importance have targeted men for years. If only you get rid of that ancient-looking gray, banish those snowy flakes from your shoulder, or fill in those shiny bald spots, you'll instantly be more youthful, sexy, and successful. Women will flock to your side. Now, as the baby boomers contemplate their growing bald spots, the hair industry is having a field day. Men have let their insecurities get the better of them, joining hair clubs in droves. More than 200,000 men receive hair transplants or restorations annually, and hundreds of thousands more receive hair weaves and other nonsurgical procedures. More recently, medications with the potential to slow hair loss, or even regrow hair, such as Rogaine and Propecia, have become drugstore blockbusters. We're unaware of any studies that have determined just how common hair concerns are among men, but these numbers alone suggest that millions of men dislike their hair and are trying to improve how it looks.

Hair is one of the most common preoccupations described by our patients with BDD. For example, Jason wore a $1,200 hairpiece that cost him $100 a month to maintain. "I hate the thing," he said in frustration. "It doesn't really make me feel any better. I see people with rat's nests on their head—and they don't care! Why can't I stop worrying? I don't want to go out on dates because some woman will run her fingers through my hair and know it's fake."

As a result of his hair concerns, Jason had given up on dating entirely. He told us, "I worry I'll always be alone because of how I look."

At age twenty-three, Paul didn't wear a hairpiece and had never given up on dating. But like Jason, he lived in dread that a woman would run her hands through his hair and disturb the precise way he had arranged it. "I recently was going out with this girl," he told us, "and she just loved to run her hand through my hair. I kept telling her that I didn't want her to do that. Finally, one time she really messed it up, and I lost my cool. I grabbed her arm and jerked it away from my head and yelled, 'How many times have I told you not to do that?' I was so upset that I frightened her. After that, our relationship began to fall apart, and now we've broken up. Looking back on it, I think that my reactions to her touching my hair ruined the whole thing."

We've heard many other men, who aren't patients at all, tell stories of their distress about their hair. For example, we remember one discussion at lunch with three men who were all attending the same business meeting. When they heard that we were doing research on male body image, they all started asking questions. Then, bit by bit, each began to reveal his own private obsessions. It turned out that all three of them experienced hair preoccupations to varying degrees—even though none of them had ever previously mentioned his troubles to either of his friends.

"I've never told this to anyone," began Chuck, "but I worry that someone in another car will look at me driving by and see the bald spot I have in the back. Sometimes I even run red lights because I don't want to be stopped next to somebody in an adjacent car. I'm afraid they might look in through my car window and see my bald spot—seriously!"

"This is pretty unbelievable, but I've got the same thing," said Clark. "I'm always noticing which way the wind is blowing across my head. I'm afraid it will blow my hair the wrong way and expose the bald area." He parted his hair to show a thinning area that was almost unnoticeable. "When I'm in a taxi and the window is open, I always sit on the side where the wind will blow my hair across the bald spot instead of exposing it. Just last week, I insisted on switching places with my fiancée in the back seat of the cab. I wouldn't reveal why, because I was afraid she'd think I was too weird."

"It's the same for me," added George. "My biggest problem is that I get really bent out of shape if someone's standing behind me in a line, because I'm afraid that they'll be staring straight at the bald area in the back. I tried some of those sprays that you put on that are supposed to look like hair, but they look really fake. Now I'm thinking of joining a hair club."

SECRET ANXIETY OVER PENIS SIZE

Many men keep their hair concerns a secret. But far more secret—and yet very common—are men's worries about penis size. Of course, this is hardly surprising. Genitals symbolize virility, procreative potency, and power. As one man explained, "Penis size is what makes you a man. Guys don't talk about it, but they all think about it."

We don't know of any statistics indicating how many men worry about this part of their anatomy, and we suspect that accurate statistics about this secret preoccupation would be very difficult to obtain. But certainly, the numerous ads in men's magazines, encouraging the reader to have his penis lengthened or enlarged, indicate that many men harbor such concerns. A quick look on the Internet further reveals the plethora of marketed penile-enlargement techniques. One company markets the Magnum Extension System; another, the Extender Penis Enlargement Pump. Artificial gadgets such as these, we suspect, contribute to the impossible standards bombarding men today. They give men the message that what's natural and normal isn't okay.

Surgery is yet another approach. Some penile augmentation techniques use Gore-Tex or collagen. Another—and controversial—technique augments penis size by removing fat from the buttocks or thighs and grafting it into the penis. Some critics maintain it's an unsafe procedure that can result in permanent penile dysfunction, and others maintain that the penis can end up looking like a tired balloon.

We've heard about penis concerns from many men with BDD and from some without full-blown BDD. Although the diagram on page 155 suggests that only 15 percent of men with BDD are preoccupied with their genitals, we're convinced the true number is much higher, because many men would be far too embarrassed to tell us about this one. As one man told us, "I'll tell you about some of the things I don't like about how I look, like my teeth and my stomach, but I won't tell you about all of them because it would be too scary."

We particularly remember Hank, a quiet, likable young man who was focused on his penis size. "It's been a problem for as long as I can remember, since I was seven or eight," he began, with much hesitation. "I remember noticing it when I was in the locker room in junior high. I thought my penis was smaller than the other guys'. I constantly compared myself with them in the shower. Then this girl told me I didn't have any bulge. That sent me over the edge. I started thinking about it all the time. Ever since then, for the past fifteen years, I've constantly been worried about whether people are noticing how small I am. I've asked girls about it, and they say I'm fine and I shouldn't worry. I've seen three different urologists over the years, and they've all told me the same thing. But I was convinced they were just trying to get me out of the office. They just tried to humor me, even though they were secretly laughing to themselves about how small it was."

He paused, almost as though he were trying to judge whether we were laughing at him, too. But he seemed reassured that we sympathized with his plight.

"I always wear loose, long shirts to cover my crotch," he went on. "I even sewed an extra pocket in my underwear and stuffed my shorts to look bigger. I constantly worry that women will reject me because of it, and I never ask them out. There's this woman I met at work, and I can tell that she likes me, but . . ." He winced. "I'm afraid to ask her for a date. And it all comes down to this problem."

Another patient, a middle-aged man who had lived with the problem for years, described his affliction with almost clinical detachment: "This problem prevents me from having a normal sex life. I'm afraid to take off my clothes. When I was a kid, I always skipped gym class because of it, and now I won't work out at the gym because of it. I'm terrified people will make fun of my genital size. I worry so much about my size that it's made me impotent several times."

Jack, a younger man whom we saw, was furious at his parents because he felt they didn't have him circumcised properly. "All I think about is that my penis is disfigured," he told us, almost in tears. "I'm damaged. I think about it over and over again. I examine it at least twenty or thirty times a day. I check it in all different kinds of light and with mirrors. It will always be damaged."

Justin's concerns were less severe, but he was a little self-conscious about his penis size, and he wouldn't take a shower at his gym. "Sometimes I can go for a while and hardly think about it at all," he said. "But sometimes it really gets to me. I'm uncomfortable stripping down to my underwear in the locker room because the bulge doesn't look big enough. And a couple of times I've turned down chances to go away to sports competitions because I was afraid I'd be put in a situation where I might have to take a shower in a public place."

Al blamed advertisements for his worries. "Those guys in the magazine ads who model underwear," said Al. "When I see those ads, I always feel a little insecure about the way I look. I always find myself thinking that they probably stuffed something in the underwear to make the bulge bigger for the advertisement. Maybe they don't, but it makes me feel more secure to think that they do."

MORE WORRIES: BREASTS, BODY HAIR, AND HEIGHT

It may be surprising to hear that some men with the Adonis Complex worry about their breasts. Breast concerns—feeling that one's breasts are enlarged, fatty, or feminine-looking—are probably almost as secret among men as concerns about penis size. We've even had patients come to us specifically complaining that they had gynecomastia—the medical term for enlargement of the male breasts. Traces of gynecomastia are common in younger men, but it's almost never visible to the naked eye and rarely signifies anything medically wrong.

Nevertheless, we've had patients and research participants who were consumed with such preoccupations—and we're not surprised to hear that thousands of men receive breast-reduction surgery annually. For some men, such concerns are linked to worries about their masculinity. Does their body look masculine enough? Do they look virile enough?

A twenty-two-year-old man named Collin worried about his breast size and nipples, which he thought were swollen. "I feel like a freak, like I'm half man and half woman. I got worried to the point where I went to a doctor. But he told me I look fine. I still don't believe him. How can I go out with a girl looking the way I look?"

Body hair is another demon that can capture men's minds. Some worry about having too much, others too little. Max was afflicted with the latter problem: "I think it's related to manliness," he told us. "My skin is really smooth, like a woman's skin. I hardly have any hair anywhere. See?" He laid his arm across the desk, trying to get us to agree.

"I hardly have a beard, I'm perfectly smooth," he went on. "Men aren't supposed to look like this. I've been to some doctors to have my testosterone level checked and to see if there was any medicine I could take to grow more hair. But they all said I was fine. I just don't think the doctors really cared. Or else there must be something wrong with their eyes—they all need glasses!"

Height is another body concern for some men. Indeed, one out of every six men is dissatisfied with his height, according to the 1997 *Psychology Today* survey. Our society expects men to be taller than women, especially the woman they're dating or married to. One man we knew, Bruce, summed it up well: "In all the movies and on TV, the guy is always taller than the girl. How many short guys do you see who get a great-looking woman, except for Woody Allen? All of the media gives us the same message: guys need to be taller than their dates."

Bruce got very creative in his efforts to look taller. He wore lifts in his shoes, consciously stretched to stand up taller, and combed his hair sticking straight up (with a little hair gel as an aid). He would furtively search a room, looking for the highest chair. And, like many short men, he dated only women shorter than himself, hinting at the self-consciousness he felt. "I'm much too short for most women," he said with finality. "In our society, it's hard for a guy like me. All the presidents are really tall. And how often do you see a guy in an advertisement who's really short? Or in the movies? When you see a short guy in the movies, it's almost always in a comic role. Believe me, it's tough to be short."

As Bruce's story exemplifies, many men's body image concerns are linked to worries that a partner won't find them attractive. They tell us: "No woman will like me," or "Who would ever want to be with me?" Often these statements reflect their shattered feelings about their masculinity. Having large enough genitals, enough head and body hair, nonfeminine-appearing breasts, and being tall all evoke images of manliness—toughness, virility, strength. The irony is that for all their doubts and insecurities, these men typically look perfectly masculine to others. And furthermore, as you may recall, women tend not to like "hypermasculine" bodies anyway. They find men with a "hypermasculine" face less attractive than men with a more ordinary or even slightly feminized face. But as media images of the ideal male body have mushroomed and become more and more uncompromising, ordinary men increasingly criticize themselves for even the smallest personal imperfections. Tragically, they may avoid dating or initiating intimate relationships as a result.

TREATING BDD AND RELATED
BODY IMAGE CONCERNS

Among men concerned with their hair growth, penis size, or other body features, probably the most common choice of "treatment" is some type of cosmetic procedure. These procedures may range from shady hair-growth or penis-enlargement remedies to expensive, high-profile surgical clinics. Many men with full-scale BDD think cosmetic surgery is the only true solution to their plight. As one of our patients told us, "I was sure all my problems would be solved when I found the right surgeon." Studies have found that as many as one-third of men seeking cosmetic surgery have BDD and 12 percent of people seeking treatment from a dermatologist have this disorder. Indeed, by the time that we first see them at the office, most men with BDD have already sought and received treatment from surgeons, dermatologists, dentists, or other medical professionals. They've had ophthalmologists try to correct "cross-eyed" eyes, surgeons do nose jobs, and urologists try to fix "small" genitals. Some have done extensive doctor shopping, until they found one willing to do the requested procedure. One man begged for treatment from three dermatologists, three dentists, and sixteen plastic surgeons. They all turned him down, because they thought the treatments weren't needed and weren't likely to be helpful. One surgeon even told him it was fortunate he didn't have much money, because if he did he'd be "mutilated."

We've even seen or heard of some men with BDD who, in great desperation, did their own surgery. One man attempted to do his own nose job, by replacing his nose cartilage with cartilage from a chicken. Another man rubbed his face with caustic acid to smooth his skin. Yet another man attempted his own face-lift with a staple gun.

Of course, most men don't reach these extremes, and many men are pleased with the outcome of cosmetic treatments. But countless men, especially those with full-blown BDD, have endured disappointments with valueless or even dangerous cosmetic procedures. We've talked to many men who had never actually seen a professional about their body image concerns, but who had nevertheless spent thousands and even tens of thousands of dollars on potions, mail-order kits, fly-by-night "clinics," and many other types of quackery in an endless quest to perfect their supposedly defective bodies.

We could go on about many other treatments that usually don't help. These include hypnosis, special diets, and herbs. Even general counseling or psychotherapy, while often helpful for other types of problems, usually isn't very effective when used alone to treat men with full-scale BDD.

The good news is that most people with BDD can get better with the right treatment. The first step is to take BDD seriously. Simply telling yourself or someone else to stop worrying, or to just get over it, is usually unsuccessful. Thinking it's "a phase that will simply pass" also usually ends in failure. It's important to identify the person's concerns as BDD, to take their concerns seriously, and to encourage them to get professional help.

Scientific research, as well as our clinical experience, has shown that two types of treatment are effective for BDD. These are the same two approaches we've described for eating disorders. The first is antidepressant medication—in particular, the class of medications known as selective serotonin-reuptake inhibitors, or SSRIs (sometimes alternatively called "serotonin-reuptake inhibitors," or SRIs). These are antidepressant medications that also have antiobsessional properties. That is, in addition to treating depression, they diminish obsessive thoughts, like the appearance obsessions of BDD. They also help people stop their compulsive, repetitive behaviors, such as mirror checking and skin picking. The other treatment that appears effective is cognitive-behavioral therapy (CBT), in which the therapist focuses specifically on the BDD symptoms rather than on other current or past issues, and uses specific techniques to treat them.

It may be best to combine these two treatment methods. For example, we remember Pete, a man in his early twenties who constantly worried about barely perceptible "acne scars" on his face, and also about his body build—his "fat" stomach and his "small" chest, arms, and wrists. We started Pete on Paxil, one of the SSRIs, and simultaneously instituted CBT. Because he spent so much time in the mirror, we helped him stay out of the mirror by having him take it down. This approach is called response prevention—learning to resist compulsive or avoidant behaviors.

Next, we had him do exposure, a CBT technique that consists of deliberately confronting feared or avoided situations. For Pete, this was any kind of social situation, or any situation in which he had to get close to someone who might see his "flaws." We first made a list of specific situations that he avoided and that provoked his appearance concerns, such as going to a club, going to a store, and buying clothes. He rank-ordered these and other situations according to the amount of anxiety he felt in these situations (0 = no discomfort, 100 = extreme anxiety). He started by deliberately confronting the situation on his list that he had rated 30, which was walking into a store to buy something and standing in line at the cash register (this situation made him anxious because he thought the cashier would be examining the "acne scars" on his face as he approached the front of the line). With our encouragement, Pete did this many times and often deliberately stayed in the store for a long time—long enough for his anxiety to decrease. He then started doing things with higher ratings on his list, and the more he did them, the easier it got. We also offered Pete cognitive therapy, which challenged his negative and unrealistic beliefs about his appearance, helping him to develop a more realistic view.

With this combination of treatments, Pete got a lot better. He now routinely goes out in public situations, and his anxieties about social relationships have diminished greatly. It's hard to say what helped—the medication or the CBT. We think it was probably both.

If you or someone you care about pursues this type of treatment, it's important to find a therapist who is familiar with BDD and who has expertise in CBT (most therapists are not trained in CBT). For people with more moderate BDD—and definitely for those with severe BDD—an SRI is almost essential, whether or not CBT is used. Some sicker individuals are in fact unable to benefit from, or even participate in, CBT until their symptoms have partially improved with medication. We've treated many patients who've done very well with medication alone, whereas others, like Pete, benefit from a combination of medication and CBT.

If you're a man who doesn't have a full-scale psychiatric syndrome, but you still secretly worry about your hair, your penis, your stomach, or some other part of your body, take heart. Millions of men worry just like you do, and some—as you've seen in this chapter—worry far more. If your concerns aren't too severe, you may be able to step back and do a little of your own CBT. Try listing some situations in which you feel anxious about your appearance, and deliberately expose yourself to them in increasing doses. Try revealing some of your thoughts to a person you trust. You may get some relief from this alone. Most important, ask yourself where your beliefs come from in the first place. Have you been indoctrinated with unrealistic ideals that you see in the media? Have you fallen prey to the body image industries that stand to profit by convincing you that you should be ashamed of your body and that anything short of perfection is unacceptable? Have you been conned into thinking that your masculinity and sex appeal are measured by your body hair or genital size?

We don't mean to say that full-scale BDD will respond to these insights. But men with milder cases of this form of the Adonis Complex may achieve great relief simply by recognizing and standing up to the societal forces that are fueling their discontent.

CHAPTER EIGHT

Boys at Risk

Hello. I am a 13-year-old male. I am no hard body. I think I might be pudgy. But I don't know because I can't really ask anybody. I took a body fat test and got 22%. I'm not sure what this means. Is it good, okay, or bad? I used to have a six pack when I was 11. Since then I lost it. I still have muscle, but it seems buried under about a centimeter of fat. I can pinch about 1.2 inches of it under my belly button. When I sit a big roll of it appears, leaving a crease on my belly button. Nobody has ever told me that I am fat, but I need somebody's help. Thank you a lot!

I'm 14 years old and I'm thinking about taking 50 ml of Deca Durabolin per week for 4 weeks. I know about the side effects of steroids on adults, but not on teens. Is there any side effects that I should know?

I am 14, 5'11" and 132 lbs. I've been lifting since October. I have two 15 lbs dumbbells that I use every night. I want to put on some size and strength before I go to high school. I have 11 inch arms, 35 inch chest, 13 inch calves, 18 inch thighs, and a 30 inch waist. I have 7 months to gain some size before high school. If you have a program or diet please print it on this page. Thank you.

I'm a 15 year old male! I play football for my high school and I weight lift. But I'm seriously looking to become a new teenage model. I was wondering if anyone would give me some tips. I'm about 170 pounds and I want to lose pounds and I'm about 6 feet and I would like the Good-looking teen model body, the Ideal Model Body is what I mean! So if anyone has any real good tips or anything that would help me get started in the modeling industry, could you help?

These are a few quotes from among hundreds on the Internet, written by boys concerned about their appearance. In the anonymity of cyberspace, these boys are free to pour out their anxieties. Often, shame or embarrassment prevents them from revealing these anxieties to their peers. Like the thirteen-year-old above, they "can't really ask anybody."

Many boys suffer from the Adonis Complex. Alarmingly, many mothers and fathers, teachers, and coaches are unaware of these boys' worries—or of the harm boys may do to their bodies in pursuit of their appearance ideals. Any adult who deals with boys needs to learn about these problems: boys' body dissatisfaction is commonplace, increasing, and closely tied to their fragile and still developing self-esteem.

CAN'T I MAKE IT ANY BIGGER THAN THAT?

In a recent study, we documented how unrealistic—and even dangerous—boys' appearance ideals can be. For this study, we gave our computerized Body Image Test to boys aged eleven to seventeen who were participating in a summer sports camp, where they practiced soccer and lacrosse. Unlike any previous assessment given to boys, this test has the significant advantage of evaluating boys' attitudes toward *both* body fat and muscularity. Previous studies, by comparison, generally asked boys to choose from a simple series of male images of increasing size, without making any distinction between size due to muscle and size due to fat. Thus, if a boy wanted to have more muscle but not more fat, there was no suitable image he could choose to express his ideal. The boys in our study could choose images with both varying amounts of fat and varying amounts of muscularity, thus allowing us to tease apart these two components.

As we have already discussed in Chapter 3, the computerized Body Image Test revealed striking discrepancies between body reality and body ideal among adult men in both America and Europe. But when we looked at our results with the American boys, the discrepancies were even bigger and more alarming. As shown in the bar graph and drawing on the next two pages, boys of all ages, from eleven to seventeen, chose a body ideal that possessed about thirty-five pounds more muscle than they actually had themselves. And they also believed that women would prefer them to grow to this level of muscularity. Specifically, more than half of the boys chose as their body ideal an image with an FFMI of 25.5 or greater. This means that *a majority of boys chose a body ideal that most men could attain only with steroids!*

Our anecdotal experience with the boys bore this out. As they scrolled up through the more muscular images of the somatomorphic matrix, grins broke out on their faces. One boy, choosing the "ideal"

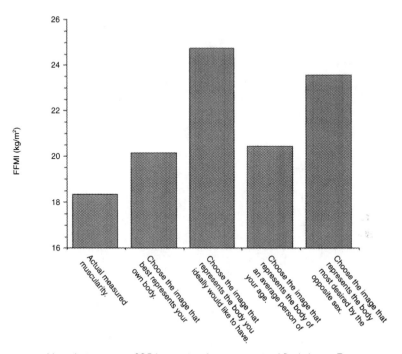

Muscularity scores of 35 boys using the computerized Body Image Test.

body for himself, immediately went right up to the maximum image that the computer could present him—a body already far beyond the limits attainable without steroids—and asked, "You mean I can't make it any bigger than that?"

The results of our sports camp study are disturbing. What will happen to a generation of boys, a majority of whom would like to have a body that could probably be attained only by using illegal drugs? Many boys in this new generation, unable to achieve their unrealistic ideal body through hard work and healthy eating habits, may turn to anabolic steroids or other dangerous substances to satisfy their aspirations. Others may not succumb to drug use, but may suffer devastating damage to their self-esteem and their physical and emotional well-being. Today's boys are at risk.

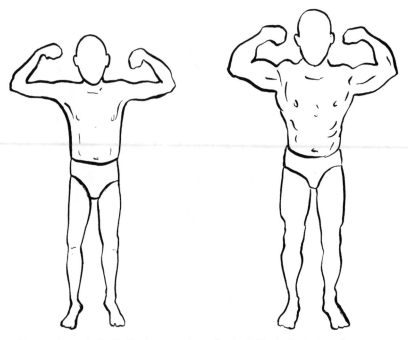

Body reality vs. body ideal in American boys. On the left is the body size of an average boy from our study at a suburban summer sports camp. On the right is the average body size that these boys would like to possess.

MORE SURPRISING RESEARCH FINDINGS
ON BOYS AND BODY IMAGE

Other clinicians and researchers have also begun to look inside the hidden realm of boyhood. Psychologists like William Pollack and Michael Gurian have opened an important new arena of inquiry into the emotional lives of boys—bringing to our attention boys' secret worries and conflicts. As part of this trend to better understand the feelings of contemporary boys, researchers have asked elementary and high school boys whether they like how they look, how they'd prefer to look, what their eating habits are like, and other questions about body image. Consistent with the findings from our sports camp study, these studies have found that many boys are indeed self-conscious about their bodies and unhappy with how they look. One study found that boys are even more dissatisfied with their weight than girls are. In addition, this body dissatisfaction may extend all the way down to boys who are only six years old.

In a recent study by researcher Dan Moore, 895 adolescent boys filled out a questionnaire that asked about attitudes toward body image. A surprising *42 percent* said they were dissatisfied with their weight, and *33 percent* were dissatisfied with their body shape. Nearly one-third of the normal-weight boys were dissatisfied with their weight, and more than two-thirds of those thought they were *underweight*. But they didn't want to get fatter. Instead, they were most likely to desire a bigger chest and arms, and a smaller stomach. In other words, just like many adult men, and just like the boys in our sports camp study, they aspired to the lean and muscular look of G.I. Joe, Duke Nukem, Batman, or the many similar images in the modern media.

Several other studies of boys have produced similar results. For example, in one study done more than thirty years ago, boys felt it was advantageous to gain weight, because they attributed extra weight to muscle and bone, not fat. Additional studies from the 1960s showed that male children and adolescents strongly preferred a muscular male body. In another large study done in 1991 by M. Elizabeth Collins, more than 1,000 elementary schoolchildren in Indiana were shown figure drawings of male and female children and adults of varying weight, ranging from very thin to obese. A majority of the boys picked an ideal boy figure different from what they thought they looked like, indicating dissatisfaction with their own appearance. Again, however, a large portion of the boys selected an ideal figure *heavier* than they thought they were, as compared to the number who selected a lighter figure. The boys often remarked that the ideal figure that they selected looked strong. One boy actually drew muscles on the arms of his ideal male figure!

This same study produced another interesting finding. The researchers had the boys in the study examine the adult male images and asked, "Which picture shows the way you want to look when you grow up?" When the girls examined the same images, they were asked, "Which picture shows the way you think it is best for grown-up men to look?" Strikingly, boys as young as six years old wanted to grow up to be bigger than six-year-old girls wanted them to be! This is the same result that we obtained in the sports camp with older boys.

Other studies comparing boys and girls have added to these findings. Like their adult counterparts, girls usually want to be thinner, whereas boys often want to be bigger and more muscular. For example, researchers Randy Page and Ola Allen, in an unusually large study of nearly 2,000 high school students, found that the most dissatisfying weight perception for boys was being too thin. Girls, on the contrary, were more upset by thinking they were too fat.

Another study of 6,500 adolescents, by Richard Levinson and his colleagues, also found that girls tended to think they were too fat, whereas boys tended to think they were too thin. An interesting twist in this study was that the boys' parents and doctors were also interviewed. The researchers found that the boys were more likely to consider themselves either underweight or overweight than their doctors or parents were. In other words, boys may be unhappy with their bodies even when their parents and doctors think they look just fine.

Interestingly, some (though not all) studies have found that boys seem to get even more unhappy with their appearance as they get older. For example, researcher Lori Folk and her colleagues asked ninety students in grades three and six to fill out several questionnaires, including a body image questionnaire. The sixth-grade boys were more dissatisfied with their bodies than the third-grade boys. Why does body dissatisfaction seem to increase with age? Possibly because the older boys have had more exposure to our society's powerful messages about the male body and how men should look. Dan Moore has speculated that "increase of body shape dissatisfaction with age may be related to longer exposure to societal and media ideals of male body shape. . . ." As you know from our own theories in Chapter 2, we strongly agree.

Body shape dissatisfaction isn't the only form of the Adonis Complex that boys develop as they grow older. For example, one study found that a majority of fourth-grade boys want to be taller. And in a community study of 780 adolescent boys, 23 percent considered acne an important health problem that they wanted solved. Interestingly, concern about acne was more frequent among the boys than the girls. Another community-based study of 1,000 adolescents from Canada found that acne was the most common health concern, with nearly 50 percent of adolescent boys saying that they worried about it "some" or "a lot." It is striking that these boys considered an appearance-related problem more important than many health-related problems, reflecting the importance of appearance during the adolescent years.

Body image dissatisfaction of all types among boys has almost certainly increased over the last twenty or thirty years, just as it has among adult men. A survey from the early 1970s found that only 5 percent of male adolescents worried about being overweight, whereas one done in the 1980s yielded a figure of 32 percent. Or consider our own findings with forty-three adolescent boys using the Adonis Complex Questionnaire at a private prep school, as shown in the scattergram on page 81 near the end of Chapter 3. Seven of these boys, or about 15 percent of the group, scored 10 or above on the ACQ—indicating significant concerns about body appearance. These numbers must be taken very seriously—because body image is very closely tied to self-esteem, particularly when it comes to boys. For example, Folk and her colleagues found that the more dissatisfied a boy was with his appearance, the poorer his self-concept was likely to be.

Other studies have come out with the same news. One study found that children who underrated their facial attractiveness tended to have lower self-esteem. Another study found that boys with a more negative body image tended to be more depressed. Researcher Dale Blyth and colleagues similarly found that seventh-grade boys who disliked their appearance tended to be more self-conscious and have lower self-esteem than boys who liked how they looked. The group with poorer self-esteem included particularly the short boys, the late developers, and boys dissatisfied with their muscularity. The study authors speculated that the higher self-esteem of the early developers reflected satisfaction with their greater muscularity and loss of "baby fat." Other researchers have also found that late-maturing boys are less satisfied with their appearance. Indeed, body image has been shown to be the greatest single predictor of self-esteem for adolescents. According to one study, feeling good about appearance is more important for adolescents than scholastic competence, athletic competence, or acceptance by peers.

Jim, now in his forties, feels pretty secure about his body appearance today. But his memories of his teenage years underscore these study results. "When I was a teenager I was late to develop," he reminisced, "and I felt extremely self-conscious about it. I was always very aware of every detail of the development of my body. I especially remember being embarrassed by not having enough muscles, not having hair on my legs or other parts of my body, and especially not having pubic hair. I was always really self-conscious, especially when I was taking a shower in the locker room. It was one of those gang showers with about ten showerheads in one big room, and there was just no way to escape the eyes of all the other boys around me.

"I especially remember September of 1969. I guess I was fourteen. That year, as soon as I took my first shower, some of the other boys made fun of me because I had been so slow to develop. I was still boyish and the other boys weren't. When I flexed my arm, I couldn't see any bicep there—just a hunk of baby fat. I felt left out and really bad about myself, and I didn't play sports for the whole next year just because I wanted to avoid ridicule."

In the thirty years since Jim was a young teenager, body self-consciousness among boys may have reached even greater heights. "In my high school, they just installed a brand-new locker room," said Alex, a teenager in an affluent suburban community in Connecticut. There's a huge open shower area with about twenty-five showers all in a row in one big room. But I've hardly ever seen a kid in my class actually take a shower. Once in a while, you'll see some old faculty member or some other middle-aged guy in there, taking a shower all by himself. But me and my friends would never strip down and take a shower in public like that."

"So all those expensive new shower facilities just go to waste?" we asked.

"Oh no," Alex responded. "It's a great lacrosse practicing area on rainy days. It's a big long open space, so we always use it for throwing a lacrosse ball back and forth."

DANGEROUS RITES OF MUSCLE

As the above studies and anecdotes demonstrate, the Adonis Complex has infected adolescent boys throughout America. As adolescent girls become preoccupied with waistlines and dieting, and comparing themselves to the models in teen magazines, their brothers begin to eye the models in bodybuilding and fitness magazines, and surreptitiously begin examining their chests and biceps in the secrecy of the bathroom mirror.

We suspect that boys have always dreamed of being bigger and stronger, and have compared their developing bodies with those of other boys of their age. Muscular bodies are strong, and they symbolize power, virility, and masculinity. But why would so many young boys today want a body bigger than they could attain without drugs?

We've asked boys this question. Many are at a loss for an answer; others have some possible explanations. Greg, one of the boys in our local gym, felt his drive for weightlifting arose from being the youngest kid in his class for many years. "I was always a little behind the other boys athletically," he said. "When I was in elementary school, they could catch a ball better than I could, throw more accurately than I could, and fight better than I could. I never felt very good about myself. When I started lifting weights in high school, it opened a whole new world for me. When I saw I was getting bigger, my self-confidence went up incredibly." Greg now spends two hours a day, six days a week, at the gym, and he doesn't regret a minute of it.

Greg's weightlifting partner, Wesley, thinks that some of his drive to work out came from having no father in his household. His father left the home when he was two years old, and he was raised entirely by his mother. Now, the gym helps define his masculinity; he has no regrets either. But childhood and family experiences can't possibly account for all of the high school boys flocking to the gym nowadays. In response to our questions, Greg and Wesley both estimated that 50 percent of the high school boys in their working-class town engaged in some form of weight training to get bigger. They also guessed that close to half of the boys in their class were dieting, using food supplements, or using other nutritional techniques to gain muscle or lose body fat. We've heard similar estimates from other boys in communities at all socioeconomic levels. By any reckoning, these forms of the Adonis Complex are far more common than they were thirty years ago—another sign that society's messages have made today's boys increasingly anxious about their appearance.

Mothers and even fathers rarely glimpse the full extent of their sons' body image concerns. We remember one mother's account: "It's quite a contrast, having both a daughter and a son in high school. When I take my daughter and her friends in the car, I'll hear one talking in the back seat, saying, 'I had only three lettuce leaves with a quarter of a teaspoonful of salad dressing for lunch!' And then another will say, 'I only had two Diet Cokes, with one calorie apiece, for my lunch.' Then, two hours later, I'll have my son and his friends in the back seat of the car, and one of them will be saying, 'You should try this new protein supplement powder I bought. It has three thousand calories per serving!' Then the other will say, 'My new weight-gainer powder is even better. It has forty-five hundred calories per serving!' I don't know who's crazier, the girls or the boys!"

Once in a while, a boy allows us to get a closer look at his body image concerns. One of these was Jerry, whom you may recall from the scene at the Olympic Gym. Jerry is nineteen. He can't say exactly when he first became interested in getting more muscular, although he can remember admiring muscular bodies on television and in magazines even when he was very young. By the time he was thirteen, the summer before starting high school, he had already started lifting weights in the basement of his house, following the example of several of his friends. Once in high school, he quickly sought out the advice of the older boys, and soon began to devour weightlifting and fitness magazines. His mother noted that his bedroom was filling up with worn copies of *Muscle and*

Fitness, Muscular Development, Flex, Ironman, and many others. She didn't take much interest in this new development, figuring it was a normal stage of growing up.

Protein supplements and weight-gainer powders, however, were only the beginning of Jerry's experiments in getting bigger. Soon he was purchasing all manner of other "food supplements" and "herbal extracts" in his local "health" store: amino acids that were supposed to increase growth hormone levels, plant substances that were supposed to triple blood levels of testosterone, potions purporting to prevent muscle breakdown and maximize muscle growth, and many others. When he heard that baseball star Mark McGwire had used androstenedione, he bought a large supply and used three times the dose recommended on the bottle.

Jerry had seen many of these supplements advertised in bodybuilding magazines. Often the advertisements showed pictures of a flabby-looking man on the left, side by side with the same man sporting a highly muscular and sculpted body on the right. The pictures were labeled "before" and "after"—implying that the advertised supplement had caused the transformation. But upon reading the fine print, this claim was not actually made; instead, many of the men had almost certainly taken substantial doses of anabolic steroids in between the times the two photographs were taken.

Jerry thought he benefited from many of the supplements, but in reality he spent a lot of money and didn't gain any muscle. After a couple of years of trying supplements, it was only a small step for Jerry to start his first cycle of anabolic steroids.

Jerry was careful to get a good deal of advice from his older friends who had already used drugs. They counseled him to use a combination of both steroids in pill form—"orals"—and injectable steroids—"injectables"—to optimally stimulate the testosterone receptors in his muscles—a technique known in the underground as "receptor mapping." Although he was initially scared to give himself injections, Jerry's thirst for muscle quickly overrode his anxieties. He secured a hundred 3-cc syringes from a friend at the gym, and practiced his injection technique on an orange borrowed from his mother's refrigerator. As soon as he had learned to jab the syringe in a single swift motion, he filled it with testosterone cypionate and tried it on himself.

Usually, the injections went well, but once Jerry aimed the syringe badly and hit the sciatic nerve in his buttock. Fortunately, no one was in the house at the time to hear him scream, and he didn't damage the nerve to the point where his gait was affected. On another occasion, he developed an infection in his left buttock from a contaminated syringe. For days, he feared that he would be forced to see a doctor and reveal the cause of the infection, but finally it cleared spontaneously.

These were minor inconveniences, however, in comparison to the enormous rewards that Jerry perceived. Within less than a year, he had put on nearly thirty pounds of solid muscle. He enjoyed new status among his friends, and a feeling of self-confidence he'd never known before.

"I'm going to go on another cycle of steroids in eight weeks," Jerry once told us, "and I'm counting the days 'til I can start."

Jerry's mother still took little interest in her son's bodybuilding. She regarded it as a little idiosyncratic, perhaps—but at least she felt reassured her son was pursuing a healthy lifestyle. As far as we know, it never dawned on her that he was taking illegal drugs.

Although Jerry felt better about himself, his newfound self-esteem had a fragile basis—the use of illegal and dangerous drugs. What will happen to Jerry thirty years from now? Having invested himself so heavily in the appearance of his body, he may become depressed as he ages, with no other sources of self-worth. If he continues to take high doses of steroids for many years, he might fall victim to heart disease, prostate cancer, or some other medical problem.

LOSING FAT FAST

Many boys, like Jerry, become focused on gaining muscle. But others, particularly those who were slightly chubby as children, become equally obsessed with losing fat. Like the boy on the Internet, quoted at the beginning of this chapter, many boys spend a lot of time wishing that they could have a flat stomach with the six-pack of abdominal muscles that they see on the front covers of magazines every time they go to the supermarket or the drugstore.

Studies show that these boys aren't rare or isolated cases. One study of boys as young as eight to twelve found that approximately one-quarter had tried to lose weight. Another found that 36 *percent of third-grade boys* had tried to lose weight. And a recent study by Susan Paxton and colleagues, looking at more than two hundred high school boys, found that 26 percent had used an extreme weight-loss method at least occasionally, and 9 percent at least weekly. Even though some of the individual percentages might not sound high, the total figure of 26 percent of high school boys translates into close to *a million boys* presently in high school in the United States alone who are risking their health in various extreme and dangerous ways to lose fat. These findings are particularly alarming because restricted food intake at a young age can interfere with the ability to concentrate and learn, and thus affects school performance. It may also retard growth and delay puberty. And dieting during childhood for cosmetic reasons may be associated with an increased risk of developing an eating disorder during adolescence. In fact, eating disorders in males usually begin during the teenage years.

Wrestlers are a group of boys at especially high risk for unhealthy—and potentially dangerous—weight-control and eating behaviors, although boys who participate in other types of sports may also be at risk. Wrestlers often restrict food and fluid intake to "make weight"—in other words, to qualify for a certain weight class. The goal is to get into a weight class with smaller and weaker opponents, who can be beaten in the ring. These boys become very focused on their bodies. Is their weight optimal? Are they strong and muscular enough? In some cases, the Adonis Complex drives boys to wrestling—it's a vehicle to becoming fitter and more muscular, a way to achieve a magazine-cover body. But sometimes it's the other way around: wrestling can foster and amplify the Adonis Complex by making boys focus excessively on their weight and body fat. As one high school wrestler told us, "If you do wrestling, you're going to see a lot of other wrestlers looking really muscular and really good with their bodies exposed in their wrestling uniforms—it's going to make you start thinking a lot about your own appearance."

Percentage of 221 High School Boys Who Reported Having Used Various Extreme Weight-Loss Behaviors

Behaviors	Frequency, %
Fasting	17
Crash dieting	10
Cigarette smoking	8
Vomiting	6
Fluid tablets (diuretics)	5
Diet pills	4
Laxatives	4

In one study of this problem, researcher Charles Tipton and his colleagues looked at weight-loss methods in 747 high school wrestlers in Iowa in 1970. During the seventeen days before certification for their weight class, the boys lost an average of nearly 7 pounds, or close to 5 percent of their initial body weight. To lose weight, they fasted, severely restricted their fluid intake, and exercised in a hot environment. A more recent study by researchers Suzanne Steen and Kelly Brownell from the University of Pennsylvania reported similarly alarming findings in high school and college wrestlers: nearly half of the boys fasted at least once a week, and some reported weekly weight fluctuations of more than 20 pounds! These practices can cause a wide range of unhealthy, even dangerous, effects on kidney function, muscle strength, testosterone levels, and other bodily functions. In addition, many wrestlers report that when trying to make weight, they feel fatigued, angry, anxious, depressed, and isolated.

Aaron, now in his thirties, reminisced with us about some of the extreme weight-loss strategies he used while a wrestler in high school. "I was desperate to lose weight," he told us. "So were all my friends. Even though I was underweight to begin with, I went down one weight category, thinking I'd win more matches by wrestling smaller and weaker guys. In retrospect, it was pretty dangerous."

"What kinds of things did you do to lose weight?" we asked.

"I didn't eat all day, I made myself vomit, I kept spitting into cups, thinking I'd lose a few pounds. We'd also put on rubber suits and roll ourselves up in the wrestling mats till we were sweating bullets—we'd stay wrapped up for like an hour, until we were miserable and screaming to get out. Sometimes I got so tired and weak from doing these things I ended up losing the match. I wish my coach had told us it wasn't a good idea, but he just let us do it. And my parents were clueless."

These weight-loss strategies can be even more dangerous than Aaron now realizes. In late 1997, many people were shocked to hear that three young wrestlers died within a month of one another, all apparently from complications of aggressive weight loss. The first was nineteen-year-old Billy Saylor, from North Carolina's Campbell University, who died apparently from cardiorespiratory arrest while trying to lose weight. Less than two weeks later, twenty-two-year-old Joseph LaRosa from the University of Wisconsin–La Crosse also died. He was wearing a rubber suit and riding a stationary bicycle, trying to shed a few more pounds. His body temperature reportedly reached an incredible 108 degrees. Then, just two weeks after that, a twenty-one-year-old college wrestler at the University of Michigan named Jeff Reese died while trying to lose another 12 to 17 pounds to wrestle in the 150-pound class. He wore a rubberized wet suit during a two-hour workout in a 92-degree room. The reported cause of death was rhabdomyolysis—a massive cellular breakdown of skeletal muscle. That, combined with excessive exercise and dehydration, caused kidney failure and heart problems.

In the wake of these deaths, the National Collegiate Athletic Association has implemented safeguards in competitive wrestling. Among these changes, they have banned the use of diuretics (drugs that induce water loss), laxatives, emetics (drugs that induce vomiting), and excessive food and fluid restriction. They have also banned vapor-impermeable suits and workouts in a room warmer than 79 degrees Fahrenheit. But despite these efforts, dangerous weight-loss practices undoubtedly continue among boys and young men, sometimes even with the knowledge of their coaches. Indeed, the previously mentioned study by Suzanne Steen and Kelly Brownell documents that this is the case. One former competitive college wrestler, Patric Charest, has stated that "weight loss is such a major part of wrestling that I don't think that actions such as banning rubber suits will make a substantial difference. Wrestlers will always find other means of losing weight. . . . I honestly don't see it changing either way." Even Mike Moyer, the chair of the NCAA wrestling committee, admitted: ". . . it's difficult to change 100 years of tradition in 100 days."

Even if these policies are successful in preventing the most dangerous methods of weight loss, they still cannot prevent all of the complications of aggressive dieting in boys who must "make weight" for various athletic competitions. These complications can include fatigue, fainting, nausea, impairment of short-term memory, and abrupt mood changes. And to an unknown extent, weight preoccupation and drastic dieting practices may set the stage for various forms of the Adonis Complex, including the eventual development of outright eating disorders such as anorexia nervosa and bulimia nervosa, described in Chapter 6.

Hundreds of thousands of boys may face these risks. A 1998 survey by the National Federation of State High School Associations found that wrestling was the eighth-most-popular boys' sports program in the United States, and that 8,900 schools had active wrestling programs with a total of more than a quarter of a million participants. And remember that these numbers are for high school wrestlers alone; in other sports as well, boys may strive to abruptly increase or decrease their weight to meet the demands of competition. These pressures may extend even down into elementary school. In the study by M. Elizabeth Collins, a second-grade boy volunteered that he needed to "lose two pounds to make the wrestling team," hinting that even very young wrestlers feel pressures to maintain a certain weight.

In our studies, we've seen several men who described both eating disorders and body image disorders associated with their wrestling experience. For example, Miles, a man in our study of college men with eating disorders, was the captain of his wrestling team at a New England community college. But he was bulimic. And remarkably, much of this bulimic behavior was endorsed by his coach and other teammates. "It started with simple dehydration techniques: saunas, spitting in a cup, constant exercising," he described. "Then it got pretty obsessive. I would fast for days, exercise in sweatsuits in saunas, make myself vomit, and eat a package of chocolate laxatives within three to four days. I've fainted several times during these periods."

After Miles was weighed in, he was free to eat or, rather, binge: "After the weigh-in, I felt so excited to eat. The first thing I did was drink a glass of water, because I was so dehydrated. This is kind of sick, but I would look in a mirror while I was drinking and actually see the tissues in my cheeks start to hydrate and puff up. It was pretty bad. After that I would binge on tons of pasta and bread until I passed out. Then I would weight-train the next couple of days until the meet."

"Did others on the team also do this?"

"Yeah. Our coach told us in so many words that this was really the only way to do it. He said he did it when he was a college wrestler and that's how he won so many championships. I'm one of the few guys who got addicted to it, meaning most guys only do this stuff during the season. For me and two other guys, at least that I know of, the fasting and binge eating just kept right on going. I couldn't stop, even out of season."

"Were your parents aware of this?"

"Sometimes they noticed that I gained or lost a lot of weight in a short period of time, but they never asked any questions. Only my coach knew the whole story."

THE SUPPLEMENT BUSINESS

As boys strive to develop the lean and muscular bodies to which they aspire, they often fall prey to the growing, multibillion-dollar supplement industry. Just as girls begin to spend large portions of their allowance on beauty products, boys often begin investing in protein powders, "fat burners," and dozens of other agents advertised to improve their physiques.

We talked to one young man who works at a small suburban store that specializes in supplements for bodybuilding and dieting. He estimated that this one outlet sells something like $20,000 per week of various types of supplements, the vast majority of these to males, and a substantial portion of that to teenagers and even younger boys. "I see lots of kids age fourteen, fifteen, or sixteen who regularly spend fifty dollars, even a hundred dollars, per week on all kinds of supplements," he says. "They're always asking me for advice on the best things to take to gain muscle or lose fat."

His four biggest sellers are protein powders and bars, creatine, supplements containing ephedrine, and adrenal hormones such as DHEA, androstenedione, and their relatives. Creatine is a substance that occurs naturally in meats like beef or chicken. But when taken daily in doses much larger than the amount present in a normal diet, it appears to increase body weight without increasing fat. It's not completely clear, however, what portion of this increase is due to water and what portion to an actual increase in muscle protein. Nevertheless, creatine has accumulated a huge following: its use is epidemic among high school and college athletes, and we've heard of coaches who have put whole sports teams on creatine supplementation.

Creatine is simply a food substance, but the other two best sellers—ephedrine and adrenal hormones—are actual drugs. Ephedrine is a powerful stimulant of the nervous system, just like its prescription-only cousins amphetamine and methamphetamine, or "speed." DHEA and androstenedione are potent hormones, but it's perfectly legal to buy them in the United States and most other countries without a prescription. These hormones are normally made in the human body by the adrenal glands, which are located near the kidneys. Adrenal hormones are chemically related to testosterone and can even convert into testosterone to a limited degree inside the body. Thus, thousands of boys and men, seeking a legal alternative to testosterone and other anabolic steroids, hope for similar benefits from these drugs, although there's little research data to prove that they actually work.

Creatine, ephedrine, and adrenal hormones, when taken in small amounts or for a limited period of time, probably aren't dangerous. But when taken in large doses, or over long periods, their dangers are still unknown, as shown in the table on the next page. "Judging from the amount

The Most Commonly Used Nutritional Supplements

Protein supplements
(powders such as Met-Rx, Myoplex, Lean Gainer; bars such as Power Bar, etc.)

Acceptable sources of protein, but little scientific evidence that they are superior to ordinary food such as skim milk or lean meat for muscle gain. Long-term use of very high doses of protein may cause kidney damage.

Creatine
(Phosphagen, Creatine Edge, etc.)

Shown in various double-blind studies to increase lean body mass by a few pounds. However, some of this gain may simply be water. Dangers of long-term use at high doses remain untested.

Ephedrine
(Thermadrine, Dymetadrine, *ma huang*, etc.)

A chemical relative of amphetamine ("speed") derived from a Chinese plant. Promotes fat loss, but weight is quickly regained upon stopping use. In excessive doses may cause addiction, heart problems, and even death.

Adrenal hormones
(DHEA, androstenedione, various androstenedione derivatives)

These hormones are partially metabolized into testosterone in the body, and thus are claimed to promote muscle gains. Recent studies suggest that they may have little value for muscle gains but may increase levels of cholesterol and may promote development of female breast tissue. Long-term dangers in high doses are unknown.

that some of these kids are buying," says our friend from the supplement store, "they've got to be taking a lot more than it says on the label."

We remember a local high school boy named Vernon who became a victim of the supplement racket. Like the thirteen-year-old boy on the Internet quoted at the beginning of this chapter, Vernon got started because he worried that he was "pudgy."

"I always thought I had a lot of baby fat after I started high school," Vernon said. "I would look at myself in the mirror when I was alone, and I could pinch a big roll of fat between my thumb and finger when I grabbed my stomach or my side."

Vernon can't remember where he first heard about supplements containing ephedrine. "I might have seen an ad for them in a magazine or somewhere else," he reflected, "or else I saw them on the shelf in some nutrition store somewhere." He bought a couple of bottles of one of these products; his parents never asked him what it was.

"The bottle said that it contained *ma huang*, which was some kind of a Chinese herb," he said. "I figured that if it was just an herb, and if it was being legally sold in stores all over the place, it couldn't do me any harm."

Once Vernon discovered that he was beginning to lose weight, he started upping his dose. He found that he could buy the raw herb, or even tablets containing straight ephedrine. They were available not just in health and supplement stores, but even in convenience stores and truck stops. Soon his daily dose of ephedrine had climbed from the "recommended" dose of 24 milligrams to more than 300 milligrams per day.

At first he couldn't understand his racing heartbeat, headaches, and chronic insomnia. But he didn't worry too much, because he'd lost more than 10 pounds. But then, one day, he ran out of his supply of ephedrine and became severely depressed and lethargic. That night he slept for thirteen hours.

"It suddenly dawned on me that I'd become an addict," he admitted. "So I finally broke the habit—but I almost immediately gained back about fifteen pounds."

Stories like this are not uncommon. In fact, the United States Centers for Disease Control and Prevention in Atlanta has now received hundreds of reports of adverse medical events from ephedrine use, including even a number of deaths. Among the supplements frequently purchased by boys, ephedrine is perhaps the best-documented hazard. As for the possible dangers of long-term use of massive doses of protein powders, creatine, or adrenal hormones, it's still too early to tell. These supplements and drugs, unlike prescription drugs, are not regulated by the FDA, and their long-term effects in high doses have not been well studied. In effect, hundreds of thousands of today's boys are conducting a large-scale experiment on themselves.

Furthermore, even if the above legal "nutritional supplements" were perfectly safe, we still believe (as do other experts we know) that they may act as "gateways" to the use of anabolic steroids. As illustrated by the story of Jerry earlier in this chapter, many boys begin by experimenting with creatine or androstenedione, and thereby get introduced to the idea of taking substances to increase muscle growth. They also grow increasingly familiar with the weightlifting and bodybuilding subculture, and inevitably learn through this subculture that anabolic steroids can deliver in a way that no supplement can.

It isn't just weightlifters and bodybuilders who may graduate from supplements to steroids. Football players, wrestlers, and boys who do track and field also appear at higher risk for steroid use than other boys. And steroid use isn't limited to athletes; many boys use these drugs simply to look better. Tragically, in addition to the risks already discussed in Chapter 5, steroid use carries the risk, at least in theory, of decreasing boys' height when they reach adulthood. Despite these dangers, many boys graduate to these illegal drugs in search of the body they want.

"I WISH THE WHOLE WORLD WAS BALD"

Boyhood is a vulnerable time for another reason: it's when symptoms of body dysmorphic disorder (BDD) usually begin. As we discussed in Chapter 7, the body image worries of BDD go beyond normal concern, to the point that a boy experiences serious distress or interference with his functioning. The dissatisfaction can focus on any aspect of appearance—not just body build, muscle, or fat. Whereas boys with BDD think that their perceived flaws are obvious to others, parents and friends generally consider them minimal, or can't even see them at all. BDD often strikes at puberty—around age thirteen. Jay was one boy we met who had this problem.

At fifteen, Jay was a star athlete, and an impressive drummer who played in an up-and-coming band. He'd always been popular and a good student—my "golden boy," as his mother, Maria, called him. Maria brought him to see us after he'd been having trouble for about a year.

"I really don't know what's going on with him," she told us. "He's always done great, and never really had any trouble or problems at all. But in the past year, he's been going downhill. He started not going out and staying in the house with the lights turned off. He didn't even want to see his girlfriend, and she started getting really upset. We all got really upset, especially when he started being late for school. Then he missed a band performance at school—that's when it really hit me that something was wrong. He wouldn't miss playing with his band if the world was coming to an end!"

At this point, Maria began to cry.

"Jay, it sounds as though things have been pretty rough for you," we ventured very carefully. "What can you tell us about what's been going on?"

"I don't want to talk about it."

It took a while for us to help Jay feel comfortable enough to confide in us. But finally, he opened up.

"I look really gross. Period. My hair looks really weird, and my skin is all wrinkled. See?"

We really couldn't see what he was referring to, but Jay was convinced that it was obvious. He even wore makeup, he revealed, to cover the wrinkles he perceived. "That's the really embarrassing part," he said. "That's something girls do, and I feel totally fake. But letting people see the wrinkles freaks me out even more."

Slowly, in response to our gentle questioning, more and more pieces of Jay's story emerged. "I really can't be around people because I feel so embarrassed about how I look," he explained. "I even had to break up with my girlfriend because she would put her hand through my hair and mess it up even more, and then she'd get real close to my face, and I'd feel like she was staring at me and thinking how ugly I looked."

"He's always in the mirror," his mother told us. "He'll lock himself up in the bathroom for over an hour, working on his hair. He won't let us in, and we can't get him to come out, no matter how hard we try."

Even though Maria felt as though she didn't know what to do, she had been far more successful than many other mothers in the same situation. She had persuaded her son to open up to her about what was going on, and she talked with him about it for many hours. Finally, she convinced him to see us.

Jay's story has a happy ending. We treated him with the medication Luvox and cognitive-behavioral therapy—two of the same treatment techniques that we've described in previous chapters. We also met with his family, to help them to understand BDD and to cope with Jay's behavior and support his recovery. With this approach, Jay improved dramatically. "The BDD's pretty much gone," his mother told us about four months later. "I have my son back!"

Jay's experience is similar to that of many boys with BDD. We've seen boys as young as five with this troubling disorder. The five-year-old we saw, Alex, was adorable, but he thought he looked hideous. He hated his hair (which he thought "wasn't right"), his teeth (which he thought were "too yellow"), and his stomach (which he thought was "too fat"). His mother estimated that Alex talked about his hair, teeth, and stomach for at least three hours a day. He hated thinking about his hair all the time, but, like other people with BDD, he couldn't stop. As Alex said to us, "I wish the whole world was bald, including me, so I wouldn't have to worry about my hair."

During one study, we carefully interviewed six boys with BDD. All reported social problems, such as not going out with their friends, because they were so embarrassed and ashamed over their appearance. They also had school problems, because they were so focused on their appearance or got caught up in BDD behaviors, such as checking their hair over and over in a compact mirror during class. Gym class was especially hard, and one of them simply refused to go because he was too embarrassed to be seen in gym clothes. A particularly disturbing finding was that two boys had dropped out of school because of their BDD. Another high school boy we treated hadn't dropped out but had missed more than a hundred days of the previous school year because of his appearance concerns. Several of the boys thought about suicide, or had even tried to kill themselves, because they suffered so much.

Of course, the boys we saw in this study were those willing to come to our offices and participate in a research interview. What about the far larger number of boys with BDD who have never discussed their concerns with a professional, or even with their parents? We've often wondered: how many teenage suicides may be caused by underlying body obsessions, silently endured by a boy who doesn't dare reveal his preoccupations to anyone?

RECOGNIZING THE ADONIS COMPLEX IN YOUR SON

Most boys don't get to the point of dropping out of school or becoming suicidal because of their body image. But a huge number suffer, and the signs of their suffering frequently go unrecognized. A recurrent theme, throughout most of the stories of the boys in this chapter, is that their parents often had no idea of what was happening in their sons' minds. In our experience, parents are often quick to recognize their daughters' anxieties about their bodies, especially as these girls enter their teenage years. For example, most mothers nowadays have heard about eating disorders, such as anorexia nervosa and bulimia nervosa. They're usually aware when their daughters become preoccupied with dieting, purchasing beauty products, and reading magazines emphasizing appearance. But parents often ignore or minimize similar signals from their sons. It's widely assumed that boys don't worry all that much about their appearance, so parents don't ask, and boys don't tell.

Many boys are embarrassed and ashamed of their appearance concerns, and keep them a secret. They may feel it's wimpy or "girlish" to worry about their looks. In the absence of feedback from their families, boys listen to other voices. They watch television and look at magazines. They're especially sensitive to society's increasing emphasis on male body appearance and increasingly vulnerable to the advertising messages of the supplement industry and other body image industries eager to capitalize on their anxieties.

To help deal with this problem, we've compiled a list of twelve clues to the Adonis Complex in boys. The list isn't exhaustive, but it highlights some of the most important behaviors that parents, teachers, and coaches should look for. A boy who does these things probably has at least some symptoms of the Adonis Complex, and he might even have a full-fledged body image disorder, such as BDD, muscle dysmorphia, or an eating disorder.

Clues to the Adonis Complex in Boys

1) Does your son work out excessively—for example, more than two hours a day in the gym? Does his time in the gym seem out of proportion to what he needs for his athletic activities at school? Do his workouts constantly take precedence over other important activities, such as studying, hobbies, or other healthy activities with peers?

2) Does your son seem preoccupied with looking like extremely muscular men in bodybuilding magazines, comic books, television, or movies?

3) Does your son use large quantities of dietary supplements, such as creatine or protein powders, hoping to build up his body and become more muscular?

4) Does your son use drugs found in "health" or "nutrition" stores like ephedrine, DHEA, or androstenedione in an attempt to become more muscular?

5) Are there any clues that your son is using steroids? Has he grown more muscular than appears naturally possible, as explained in Chapter 2? Has he developed a physique that raises the suspicion of steroid use, as illustrated by the photographs in Chapter 2? Has he abruptly developed acne or mood changes during a time when he was rapidly gaining muscle size?

6) Does your son have sudden, sharp fluctuations in weight? Does he suddenly gain or lose large amounts of weight?

7) Does your son use dangerous techniques to lose weight? For example, does he fast or go on extreme diets? Does he refuse to eat with the family because he's on a special diet? Does he use laxatives or diuretics?

8) Does your son spend a lot of time examining himself in the mirror or looking at himself in other reflecting surfaces like store windows?

9) Does your son spend a lot of time grooming and still feel he doesn't look good enough? Does he spend a lot of money on appearance-enhancing products (such as hair gel or skin products) or spend lots of time in the bathroom trying to make himself look better?

10) Does your son use any type of body camouflage? For example, does he often wear a baseball cap, even indoors or when it doesn't fit the occasion? Does he wear bulky clothes that cover him up, even in the heat of summer?

11) Does your son frequently ask you or other people if he looks okay? When people tell him that he looks fine, does he still think he doesn't look right?

12) Is your son reluctant to go out and engage in activities for no apparent reason? For example, is he reluctant to go to school or participate in social activities?

Regarding the first several clues, parents often assume that the pursuit of strength, fitness, and muscularity is invariably healthy. In most cases, of course, it is healthy—it's a natural part of male development. But parents are often unaware of the dangers that lurk behind the fitness facade. Few parents recognize that their sons can purchase potent and potentially dangerous drugs, such as ephedrine or adrenal hormones, over the counter in local stores—and then take them in any dose they wish. And few have considered that these legal "supplements" may be gateway drugs from which their sons may progress to illegal anabolic steroids, or to clenbuterol, Nubain, growth hormone, thyroid hormones, and the other dangerous drugs that we described in Chapter 5.

There's a particular irony in this: vast and expensive educational campaigns have admonished parents to ask their kids about drugs and to look for signs of drug use in their children. But it isn't easy to tell whether your child is surreptitiously smoking marijuana or snorting cocaine. Anabolic steroid abuse, on the other hand, may often be recognized simply by glancing at a boy's body—as shown in the pictures in Chapter 2 of this book. But tragically, many parents may be well informed about ordinary drug abuse, yet know almost nothing about steroids. They don't see what is happening to their sons, and they don't talk with them about it before it gets out of hand.

Eating disorders, too, are often easy to recognize in boys, just as they are in girls. If a boy has sudden, sharp fluctuations in weight—whether he's a wrestler, some other type of athlete, or not athletic at all—it's important to ask him what's going on. Again, looking back at the many men in our studies who developed eating disorders during adolescence, or looking at boys who used dangerous techniques to lose weight for athletic competitions, we recall very few whose parents recognized that something was wrong. Many of these parents, we think, just didn't believe that body image concerns could affect their boys so badly.

Of course, even if a boy gains 20 pounds of muscle or loses 20 pounds of fat, the reasons may be benign. His attempts to improve his body appearance may be perfectly healthy and may work wonders for his self-esteem. But if the gain or loss seems to occur too quickly, or seems too extreme, it's time to ask why. If he uses substances such as those mentioned in clues 3, 4, or 5, parents shouldn't be afraid to ask questions. In such cases, open and loving communication between parent and son may prevent dangerous consequences.

Clues 8 through 12 may hint that a boy has body dysmorphic disorder. In milder cases, these clues may be subtle. In boys with full-scale BDD, they are easier to notice—but again, only if a parent or teacher stops to think about them. If a boy isn't going out with his friends, isn't dating, or is missing school, what's the reason? In our experience, parents sometimes miss the significance of these clues, thinking they're just a minor adolescent "phase." But with careful observation, the clues may fall into place: if a boy spends too much time grooming or looking in the mirror, wearing camouflaging clothes, or searching for reassurance about his appearance, parents should stop to ask why.

Finally, if your son fills out the Adonis Complex Questionnaire or takes the computerized Body Image Test in Chapter 3, his answers may alert you that he has some problem with body image. Of course, you must be sure that your son is willing to be honest and open in his answers to these tests. Remember that he may deny even to himself that he has difficulties with body image—and thus he may score seemingly normally on the tests, even though the behavioral clues indicate otherwise.

Just as it's important to recognize body image problems in girls, such as eating disorders, it's important to be alert for the Adonis Complex in boys. More severe forms of the Adonis Complex can seriously interfere with a boy's development. Adolescence is a critically important time for emotional as well as physical growth. Adolescents must negotiate many important developmental tasks, such as becoming more involved with peers, growing more independent of their families, coming to grips with their sexuality and intimacy, and developing a stronger and more cohesive sense of identity and autonomy. When the Adonis Complex begins during boyhood, it can sabotage these important developmental tasks.

Identity formation, one of the central developmental tasks for adolescents, is a fragile process that is particularly vulnerable to the Adonis Complex. A boy's identity includes his personality, character, and sense of self; it also includes the establishment of his anticipated lifestyle and career, and his place in the community and the world. The Adonis Complex may tarnish a boy's identity formation with self-doubt, insecurity, and low self-esteem. A boy with a more severe form of the Adonis Complex may even miss out entirely on critical steps of identity formation, isolating himself because of self-consciousness about how he looks, or avoiding dating and other activities with peers.

In short, parents must learn to recognize the Adonis Complex so that boys won't be alone with their doubts and insecurities. Left alone, their body image fears and worries may escalate, causing significant problems and interfering with healthy development. Recognizing the Adonis Complex is the first essential step to breaking the silence and helping boys feel good about themselves.

WHAT CAN PARENTS DO?

What can you do if you suspect that your son or a boy you know has the Adonis Complex? We often suggest that mothers and fathers integrate these ten basic strategies into their daily family routine:

1) *Educate yourself about the Adonis Complex* in both its milder and more serious forms. In addition to this book, you can consult other sources about body image problems and disorders. Some of these sources are listed in Appendix III.

2) *Look for the Adonis Complex clues* listed above and elsewhere in this book. If you see them, or suspect they're present, pay attention to them. Parents who are involved with their son's athletic activities have a head start here. Don't ignore the clues. It's understandable that parents and other adults would want to ignore them—after all, it's hard to acknowledge that something is wrong with your child. But if you ignore the clues, a boy's body image problems may become even worse.

3) *Listen to your son.* Sometimes boys talk but adults don't listen. Pay attention to what a boy is saying if he ventures something about his appearance concerns. Even if you weren't concerned about your appearance as a youth, remember that a boy's world in the new millennium is very different from what yours was. So

listen and encourage him to explain anything you don't quite understand. While many adults with the Adonis Complex keep their concerns a secret, such secrecy can be even more intense in boys and adolescents, because many are reluctant to confide in and trust adults. Often, a trusting relationship with an adult must be established before they're willing to reveal their worries.

4) *Talk with your son.* Ask your son about his body image concerns. Encourage him to be open, confide in you, and tell you about what worries him. If he hints that he has a problem, ask about the clues in the various chapters in this book. Some parents may worry that talking about the Adonis Complex with a boy will only increase his body image concerns. This is rarely the case. More often, damage is done because these concerns remain unspoken and are allowed to fester.

5) *Express your concern without blaming.* If your son exhibits any Adonis Complex clues, tell him your concerns. Educate him about the potential hazards of anabolic steroids, weight-loss drugs, diuretics, laxatives, fasting, and other risky ways of changing his appearance. One study has found, for example, that boys who used steroids had experienced less parental involvement regarding drugs than those who had not. This study shows that being involved with your son on these issues may make a difference—as long as you don't slip into using "scare tactics."

Of course, you can be supportive of healthy habits of eating, exercise, and grooming—but if you think they're being carried to excess, say so. At the same time, avoid blaming your son for his concerns or behaviors, as this approach may make him even more reluctant to talk with you.

6) *Don't criticize or tease.* Don't criticize boys about how they look. Teasing boys about their appearance can exacerbate or even trigger the Adonis Complex. If a boy you know has an actual health-threatening appearance problem (such as serious obesity), a supportive discussion is far preferable to criticism. Also avoid criticizing boys simply because they express worries about their appearance. If they get up the courage to confide in you about their appearance concerns, it's best to listen sympathetically. Above all, don't call a boy a "sissy" or tell him to stop whining

and be "more of a man." Criticism will only further shame a boy and reinforce the code of silence.

7) *Use reassurance wisely or not at all.* Boys with milder forms of the Adonis Complex may respond well to simple words of reassurance—comments that they look fine and don't need to worry about their body. If you offer a boy such reassurance, ask him if it was helpful, and watch to see if the Adonis Complex clues disappear. If they don't, reassurance isn't enough, and professional help may be needed. For more serious forms of the Adonis Complex, simple reassurance almost certainly won't work, and professional help will be necessary.

A potential hazard of offering reassurance is that some boys won't talk about their appearance again after being reassured. They will still worry, but subsequently keep their concerns to themselves. This can happen because they feel that the reassuring person doesn't "get it"—parents or other adults just don't understand how bad they really look. Some boys suspect the reassuring person is being dishonest or just trying to be "nice."

8) *Encourage your son not to buy into society's unrealistic media images.* Boys are particularly vulnerable to media images. Explain to your son that many of these images are unrealistic, created by photographic touch-ups, or with male models who have used illegal and dangerous drugs. Explain to your son no "real" man can look like G.I. Joe Extreme or Duke Nukem. If you show that you aren't impressed with steroid-pumped male bodies, your son may be less likely to try to emulate them.

9) *Encourage your son to look for other sources of healthy self-esteem.* If you suspect that your son has low self-esteem that may be fueling his body image concerns, encourage him to look for other ways to feel good about himself. Athletic achievement, scholastic skills, mastering a hobby, making friends, and having an appealing personality are all things that should help a boy develop good self-esteem. Show him that you consider these things to be more important than the look of his body.

10) *If the Adonis Complex persists* despite following the above steps, professional help may be necessary. If your son's behaviors are dangerous or threaten his emotional or physical well-being,

or if he has BDD, muscle dysmorphia, or an eating disorder, we definitely recommend professional help, which we will discuss at greater length in Chapter 11.

In these cases, do what Maria did in the story above, and try to persuade your son to see a professional right away. Don't postpone seeking help because you assume that his body image concerns are a "normal stage" or will disappear with the simple passage of time. With modern treatments, it may be possible to arrest a body image disorder in its early stages, before it becomes crippling and sabotages healthy development.

In conclusion, parents should realize that their sons are at risk for the Adonis Complex, in various forms, throughout boyhood and adolescence. Many—perhaps even most—boys experience mild forms of the Adonis Complex that will respond to simple reassurance and understanding. But in its more extreme forms, the problem can derail normal development and even be life-threatening. Even when it's extreme, however, boys may be very reluctant to reveal their body image concerns—probably more so than girls of the same age. An informed parent, sensitive to these issues, and following the recommendations above, can do a lot to ease these burdens in a son as he faces the challenges of growing up.

CHAPTER NINE

Dealing with the Adonis Complex
Women's Voices

Parents of growing boys aren't the only ones who struggle with the consequences of the Adonis Complex. Adult men's body obsessions may profoundly affect their relationships with the women in their lives, undermining intimacy and sexual relationships. Under certain circumstances, the Adonis Complex may even lead to violence toward women. But unfortunately, many women—even those who have known a man intimately for years—have trouble believing that men could be so vulnerable to body image concerns, although they would immediately understand the same concerns in another woman.

Even when a woman recognizes the Adonis Complex in a man close to her, she often finds that his concerns don't respond to simple reassurance. Often, the most heartfelt comments to a man that he "looks just fine" will do little to relieve his worries. Just as women have been subjected for years to society's impossible beauty standards, and have found it hard to be reassured about their bodies, men are now being exposed to similar social forces.

This problem becomes understandable when we look back to our research findings about the striking discrepancies between what men *think* women like and what women *actually* like. As you'll remember from our studies in Europe and the United States with the computerized Body Image Test, college-age men typically estimated that women would prefer a male body about 30 pounds more muscular than themselves, whereas women actually preferred a much more ordinary male body. And note that this figure of 30 pounds is only an *average:* some men estimated that they would need to pack on 40 or even 50 pounds of additional muscle to optimally appeal to the opposite sex. With the big differences between men's and women's perceptions of the ideal male body, it's little wonder that women have trouble convincing men that they look okay as they are.

On the following pages, we offer the voices of some of the women we've met, describing how their lives have been touched by the Adonis Complex. Many of these women found it painful to reveal these stories. Sometimes they felt they must be the only women who had ever encountered such problems in a man, or they felt that they had failed because they couldn't seem to help their men to feel better.

THREATENED INTIMACY

A few months ago, a forty-year-old woman named Eileen arrived at the office, accompanied by her obviously reluctant husband, Ray. "He realizes that he worries about his looks too much," she told us when we met her and Ray. "But getting him to come here was like moving Mount Everest—he was too embarrassed to see you and talk about these things. He thinks they're pretty personal and that no one would understand."

Little by little, we heard about Ray's appearance concerns. Mostly, he disliked his hair, which he thought was thinning noticeably, even though it was barely noticeable to everyone else.

"I do worry about my looks, but it isn't really that much of a problem," Ray interjected, trying to force a smile.

"Don't believe him!" Eileen said, trying to control her pent-up frustrations. "He thinks about his looks constantly, especially his hair. As you can see, it's hardly thinning at all, but he thinks it looks terrible. Sometimes he even refuses to do things with me or the kids because of it. He doesn't like to go out on a windy day because he's afraid the wind will blow his hair and expose his 'bald spot,' as he calls it. He sometimes even refuses to take the kids to Little League games because of his hair. Last week, we actually had to leave a party in our neighborhood because he got so nervous about his looks. You need to understand that his concerns don't affect just him—they affect me and the kids, too! I keep telling him that he looks fine, but it falls on deaf ears. He just won't believe me for more than about five minutes."

Ray's smile had faded, and he looked resigned. "I'm glad Eileen's telling you this stuff," he admitted, "because it's true. I guess I'd just be too embarrassed to talk about all of it myself. Guys aren't supposed to be so self-conscious about the way they look."

Ray had always thought that he must be unique. He was amazed when we told him that we'd seen dozens of other men with similar preoccupations. Gradually, he began to open up about the full depth of his problem.

"It wasn't really a big deal until a few years ago," he continued, "when I started realizing that I was showing signs of aging. The first sign was my hair—it seemed it was falling out a little more and I thought I started looking slightly bald. I hate the thought of getting old—our society is so focused on looking young! You don't get any respect for being old."

"Have you tried any treatments for hair loss?" we asked.

Ray looked sheepishly at Eileen. "I tried all the usual stuff—Rogaine, Propecia, a couple of different consultations at hair-replacement centers. Then there was a program that was advertised on the radio a few months ago. I tried that, too. And I've tried things I found in health food stores, or things that I could send away for. I've lost track of all of them; it's been going on for about five years."

"How much has it cost?"

"God knows how many thousands of dollars," Eileen broke in. "And that doesn't count the price of the off-road vehicle he got last year. I think it's just a way for him to feel young again. The thing has never been off-road in the entire time since we bought it. I think Ray just likes how he looks sitting in it. The ridiculous thing is, he looks really great even without a fancy car. But he can't hear these things when I tell him. And he keeps thinking that his hair is the biggest sign of aging and he's getting flabby. He keeps worrying that his youth is gone."

"What effect is this having on you, Eileen?"

She hesitated and looked warily at Ray. "He's a good father, and he cares a lot about the kids. But he spends too much time at the gym. Sometimes he's working out instead of spending time with us. It's really undermining the closeness of our relationship."

"But it's the only thing I do that really makes me feel better about myself," Ray protested.

Ray isn't alone in his thinking. He speaks for thousands of men of the baby boomer generation whose body insecurities increase with each passing year. As Ray approached middle age, he started worrying about his appearance, developing an exaggerated and distorted view of his minor flaws. At the same time, he started to devalue his many accomplishments and his success as an executive, a husband, and a father. He developed what behavioral psychotherapists call "cognitive distortions"—in other words, a distorted way of thinking about himself. The most striking of these distortions was his narrow focus on small negative details of his appearance, while ignoring the vast array of positive things in his life.

Eileen sensed these distortions even in the early days, when Ray first started worrying about his looks, but she didn't know what to do about them. She thought they would quickly run their course. And when that didn't happen, she thought they'd respond to her own loving reassurance. And when that, too, failed, she thought that at least they'd respond to logical argument. When logic failed as well, she felt lost.

"It was like dealing with a husband who has a problem with gambling, or alcohol, or drug use," she later told us privately. "You come to realize that just talking to him isn't going to work."

Eileen's marriage felt threatened and her frustration mounted. But fortunately, she found out that Ray's body dysmorphic disorder was a recognized and treatable psychiatric condition. She located information about it on the Internet and soon contacted us. Persuading Ray to come with her was a major task, but eventually he conceded. Ray has subsequently responded well to cognitive-behavioral therapy, and the tensions between him and Eileen have declined dramatically.

Not all women succeed in convincing their husbands or boyfriends to talk to a professional. We remember Helen, an impeccably dressed, petite woman who arrived nervously at the office with no advance explanation of her reasons for seeking a consultation. As soon as the door was closed, she pulled her chair close to the desk and whispered, "Can you promise, absolutely promise, that you will never tell my boyfriend I came to visit you?"

Once we had reassured her, she launched immediately into her story, almost as though she had rehearsed it in advance. "I fell in love with Will because he was such a warm and tender guy. But his preoccupation with bodybuilding has just been getting worse and worse. He's constantly asking me if he looks bigger. And it doesn't matter what I say; it just seems to make him angry. He's always checking himself in mirrors. Recently, it's gotten so bad that I just can't stand it anymore."

"Have you tried to discuss it with him?"

"Well, a couple of days ago I finally lost it and I really blew up. I accused him of being a gym addict. He just started laughing at me. He said, 'You women are constantly obsessed with your bodies and what you look like, buying all kinds of cosmetics and spending money on hairdos and stuff. The only thing that I spend money on is four hundred bucks a year for a membership in the gym!' I made the mistake of trying to argue with him. I tried to point out just how many hours a day he spent looking at himself and worrying if he was big enough. But he denied everything. He was just blind to it."

"It sounds like this is really beginning to hurt your relationship."

"It's prevented him from ever committing himself to me in any way. He's married to his body. I exist only to tell him he looks good and that he's muscular. What can I do about it?"

We felt sorry that we couldn't offer Helen any simple formula to mend her relationship with Will. We explained the nature of muscle dysmorphia, and then gave her copies of some of our papers to read. Most important, we counseled her that Will was unlikely to respond simply to an angry confrontation. Asking him to simply shut off his preoccupations with his body, we explained, was like asking somebody with a fear of heights to climb a 40-foot ladder. It wasn't the kind of thing that would go away through a sudden act of sheer willpower.

We made it clear that we'd be happy to talk to Will if he wanted, but only if he was interested in talking to us. If Helen tried to drag him in against his will, we advised, it was almost sure to backfire.

We heard from Helen only once after that, in a brief telephone call. She didn't sound optimistic, and we wondered whether her relationship with Will was going to survive.

POISONED SEXUALITY

Pamela is a twenty-six-year-old Hispanic woman. She has been in a relationship with her fiancé, Orlando, for six years now. "We met during our junior year at college," she told us. "It was really love at first sight. The beginning of the relationship was just magical for both of us. Even the simplest activities, like riding on the subway together, were wonderful. But even looking back to those first months together, there were things . . ."

"What sort of things?"

"Things that should have told me that he was ashamed of his body. He would never want to go swimming. He said that he just wasn't a water person. He never took his shirt off at the beach and didn't like to go to pool parties."

But Pam's concerns were minor until they consummated their relationship. "The first time we had sex was the first time for me. I wanted to wait for the right guy. After three years with Orlando, I knew he was the one. I had lots of expectations in my mind, after talking to friends, and reading *Cosmo*." She laughed nervously and then paused, looking for words. "Instead, I felt like a therapist."

"A therapist?"

"He wanted all the lights off during sex because he didn't feel comfortable with his body. I told him that I loved him regardless of what his chest looked like."

"Was he reassured?"

She paused again. "He didn't believe me. The worst was . . . well . . . this is kind of embarrassing. I've never told anyone about this. He stopped in the middle of sex that first time and many other times because he could feel his body jiggling."

"Jiggling?"

"He said having sex made him more self-conscious about his fat. The thing that kills me is that he wasn't fat. I mean, he was slightly overweight, but not fat. I told him that it really didn't matter much to me. I mean, I'm no Cindy Crawford."

"Has he tried any methods to lose weight?"

"Oh yeah. He went to a gym for a while. But he said that seeing all those muscular guys at the gym bums him out. He's really down on himself." Pamela's eyes began to tear. "It sounds stupid. I thought women were bad about this kind of stuff, but Orlando is worse. I would never tell him that. He already feels awful.

"Anyways, about methods. He also used to take diet pills, but he gave them up. He also told me that he made himself throw up once. But he hated the feeling, so he never did it again. He told me about this years after the fact. He's been feeling this way about himself since he was fourteen."

"How does this affect you?"

"I'm so confused. What can I do to help him? I found out through the grapevine that his last relationship was ruined because his previous girlfriend couldn't deal with this. But I'm sure I can deal with it, somehow. I just need help. He needs help. It's really affected our intimate life. It's not like he's sexless. He has a strong sex drive, but his concerns about his body get in the way. Actually, there was one time his sex drive was affected, because he was fasting. That lasted about two weeks."

"Has Orlando ever discussed this with anyone—like a friend, a family member, or a therapist?"

She laughed. "Are you kidding? First, you're not going to find many guys who will admit this to a soul. Second, being Latino makes it doubly hard."

"What do you mean?"

"Well, Latino men are 'supposed' to be tall, dark, handsome, and macho. The concept of machismo is really big in his family. They are very traditional. Men are supposed to be *the* heads of the household—confident and sure of themselves. They aren't supposed to be 'like women.' I was there once when Orlando passed on a second helping of dinner at his father's house. He explained that he was trying to cut down. Orlando's father said, 'Cut down for what! You're a man. You need to worry about being healthy and strong—not pretty!' "

"How did Orlando react to that?"

"He felt disgraced. Our culture plays a role in this. He feels that being out of shape goes against the suave Lorenzo Lamas image. Yet, pursuing that image and feeling like crap about himself goes against the machismo image that guys are not supposed to care. It's tough on him."

Pamela was one of many women we have spoken to who are con-fused and helpless regarding their mate's appearance concerns. She loved her fiancé and wanted to support him, but she just didn't know how. In-terestingly, a week after we spoke to her, she called us and reported that she had revealed her situation to a friend of hers, who then admitted—very hesitantly—that she was going through a similar experience with her boyfriend.

Orlando and Pamela have stayed together, but Pamela still feels that she cannot reassure Orlando—and she knows he'd refuse to see any type of therapist. "He'll say that everything is okay. But I know that he still doesn't think highly of himself. I've tried my best to encourage him."

Pamela's story is a particularly graphic illustration of how men's body image worries may poison their sexual relationships with women. But other secret cases are everywhere. We've talked with numerous men who have confessed to us that they often failed to enjoy sex, or some-times even deliberately avoided having sex entirely, because they felt un-comfortable about some aspect of their body appearance. In most of these cases, the men told us, their girlfriends or spouses never knew the real reasons behind their sexual difficulties. The Adonis Complex prob-ably undermines more sexual relationships between men and women than anybody suspects.

In men who take anabolic steroids in the hope of improving their body appearance, sexual relationships can be undermined in other, more malignant ways. We remember a twenty-six-year-old woman named Renee who had been happily married for four years, until her husband Luke tried his first cycle of steroids at the gym. At first, his sex drive rose dramatically; he wanted sex three or four times a day, and she obliged faithfully. But then, for some reason, Luke's sex drive wilted, and he became quiet, brooding, and angry.

"He was no longer the man I knew," said Renee. "He became incredibly jealous. One day, we were at the mall, and I was talking innocently to the sales clerk at a clothing store for just a moment, about nothing in particular. And Luke saw me and just got enraged, right in front of everybody in the store. He created a huge scene. For a moment, I thought they were even going to call the security people for the mall and have us kicked out.

"Then it got even worse. If I was away from home for any reason, I would have to account to Luke for every minute that I'd spent out of the house. I remember once I missed a train from New Haven, and I was scared out of my mind because I knew he'd be suspicious when I got home late. I can remember that my hands were shaking and my palms were sweating when I called him on the telephone from the train station to tell him that I'd have to take the next train. I was terrified.

"Also, when we did have sex, he'd always find something wrong with me. No matter what I did, it was always my fault. I wasn't doing the right thing to turn him on, or I had spoiled the sex because of something I said or did.

"I *knew* it was the steroids. He'd never been like that in all the five years I'd known him. I tried, very, very gently, to explain this to him, but it failed completely. If anything, he only got more suspicious. I was afraid he was going to hit me."

She unconsciously tightened her grip on the purse in her hand. "Finally, to make a long, painful story short, I told him it was the steroids or me."

"And what happened?"

"He chose the steroids. He left."

STEROID-INDUCED VIOLENCE

Jealousy, sometimes verging on outright paranoia, is only one of the possible side effects of high doses of steroids. As we've mentioned before, a more dangerous side effect is violence—and the most frequent victims of this violence seem to be wives or girlfriends.

We don't know why steroid users are so prone to take out their anger on women, but we've heard these accounts so often that it can't be a chance association. You'll remember some of our stories from Chapter

5—the steroid user who abducted the lady from a store; the formerly shy teenager who went on testosterone and murdered his fourteen-year-old girlfriend with a kitchen knife.

For every case like this that finds its way into the courts, there must be hundreds, even thousands, in which the woman's plight is never known. As in other types of male-on-female violence, the victim rarely comes forward, and the male often denies or minimizes what has happened. Indeed, when taking steroids, some men perceive their violence as perfectly justified—merely a natural reaction to an aggravating situation. For example, we remember the following interview:

"Have you ever noticed that you're any more irritable or aggressive when you're taking a cycle of steroids?"

"No, not particularly—except that sometimes when I'm on a cycle I get into fights with my girlfriend."

"When on a cycle?"

"Yeah. When I'm on the juice, little things she does are more likely to piss me off."

"Do the fights ever get physical?"

"Not really . . . except maybe a couple of times I threw something at her."

"What did you throw at her?"

"A brick."

This particular story came up in a study that we did in collaboration with Dr. Precilla Choi, one of England's foremost steroid researchers, in which we interviewed a group of steroid users and a comparable group of weightlifters who didn't use steroids. The study focused specifically on violence toward women. All of the men in the study were selected because they had either wives or steady girlfriends. On several different measures of both verbal and physical aggression toward women, the steroid users scored much higher during the periods when they were taking the drugs as compared to when they were not. When off drugs, the steroid users didn't show any more aggression toward women than the comparison group of nonusers. Thus, the violence toward women among the steroid users was not attributable to some aspect of their personalities; it was specifically triggered by the drugs they were taking to increase their muscularity.

The "brick" story was only one of several frightening accounts that we heard during this study. Another man, while on steroids, picked up his girlfriend and flung her across a hotel room. Another fractured several bones in his girlfriend's hand by deliberately crushing it with his grip. Another reported that when on steroids, "I was always at my girl-friend's throat."

Significantly, most of these men continued to take further cycles of steroids despite such experiences. The promise of a bigger and more muscular body, in effect, outweighed the risk of becoming uncontrollably violent toward a woman they cared about.

Dr. Choi tells us that steroid-induced violence toward women is widely recognized in her home country. In March 1991, a British women's magazine published an article in which a woman described living with her bodybuilder husband whose "personality had changed when taking steroids." According to the article, this woman started the Steroid Abusers' Wives Association. The magazine invited other women who were in the same situation to contact her. She soon was inundated with hundreds of letters and telephone calls from other women who had also been victims of violence by boyfriends and husbands taking steroids. In practically all of these cases, prior to using steroids, these boyfriends and husbands had never physically hurt a woman.

We've heard similar stories from women in the United States. Anna, a woman in her early twenties, told us that her husband, Joe, had always been a gentle, loving man, and a wonderful father to their two-year-old son, Jason. Joe lifted weights regularly, but this had never been any big deal. Then, for no apparent reason, Joe started getting into "funny moods."

"I told him something was wrong," Anna said, "but he got angry and denied that he had any problem."

In addition, Joe began to get tight for money. Anna didn't know at the time that he had spent hundreds of dollars to buy steroids.

"One day I complained to him that we didn't seem to have enough money anymore," she went on. "He flew into a rage. He yelled, 'If you didn't buy so many fucking clothes, we'd have more fucking money,' and he started grabbing my clothes out of the drawers of the bureau and throwing them out the windows of the apartment into the street. He'd never done anything like that before.

"This rage went on for weeks," she continued. "Looking back on it, it's amazing that I went for so long without even thinking about the possibility that he might be taking steroids. Finally, it dawned on me that he must be on some kind of drug. When he was out of the house one day, I searched through his things and found a bottle of pills. There was nothing on the label to say what they were. I asked him when he got home, just in passing, very low-key, pretending that I had just noticed the pills by accident. He told me that they were just some kind of proteins, or something like that, that he was taking to make sure his nutrition was good for weightlifting.

"I didn't believe him. I kept one of the pills that I found, and I took it to a guy I knew who had worked at a gym. He took one look at the pill, listened to the story, and immediately told me it was steroids.

"When Joe got home that night, I confronted him. He got a look in his eye that I'd never seen before, and he grabbed me by the throat. Hard. I couldn't breathe. Joe had never laid a hand on me before that time.

"Then we both heard a sound. We looked and we saw Jason standing at the bottom of the stairs. The commotion had awakened him, and he'd come down from his bedroom. He just looked at us and asked, 'Daddy, what's going on?'

"I think if that hadn't happened, Joe might actually have physically hurt me. I mean it. But seeing his little boy standing there, it must have stopped him."

"What happened?"

"Well, we had a long talk. Joe admitted that he had actually done steroids twice before, but not such a large amount. After he told me that, everything started falling into place. I remembered him complaining that he wasn't making enough muscle gains at the gym or something like that, and then a little later he suddenly started to get bigger. And I can remember he just felt different. He made love differently. His body was hotter and sweatier than normal when I felt him in bed. His sweat even smelled different. Everything was different. But I never stopped to think it could be drugs.

"Then there was another time that he had taken steroids, a couple of months before Jason turned two. He finished taking them about a week before Jason's second birthday. I remembered how he seemed really sluggish, and how I had to get him out of bed right in the middle of the afternoon for Jason's birthday party. And he'd forgotten to get Jason a present, even though he'd promised him that he would. Jason cried. Looking back on it, the whole thing was caused by his reaction to coming off the drugs.

"I went through all of those memories with Joe over the next few weeks. I was careful. I was still pretty scared, actually. But Joe started to admit that these things were true. I made him promise that he'd never take steroids again. It was hard. But so far, he's kept that promise. If he broke his promise and went back on the drugs, I swear I'd be able to tell instantly."

WHAT CAN WOMEN DO?

In our experiences talking to women of all ages, we've been impressed by the many ways in which the Adonis Complex can scar their relationships with the men they love. Its effects may range from a subtle erosion of intimacy to the extremes of anabolic-steroid-induced violence. Women in such relationships, we have found, are often slow to recognize that their men are suffering from a body obsession. Most women are simply not expecting it. It doesn't occur to them that a man could have such hang-ups. And even when women recognize the problem for what it is, they still often think that it will go away with just a few words of reassurance.

Typically, these women were surprised to discover that simple reassurance didn't work. Many of their boyfriends or husbands, like Eileen's husband, Ray, denied or minimized their preoccupations with body image. Ray eventually agreed to come with his wife to see us. But we suspect that for every man willing to come for professional help, many others refuse to even consider such a thing, no matter how much their wives or girlfriends plead with them.

Tragically, at this point, many women think that they are all alone. Since, after all, men aren't supposed to have problems with body image, these women often think that their husbands or boyfriends are rare exceptions. Not knowing where to turn, some women grow frustrated, impatient, and hurt. Often they exacerbate the problem by getting angry.

One of the things we'd like to accomplish with this book is to alert women everywhere to the Adonis Complex in the men around them. We want to help women to recognize that men can be affected by unrealistic societal standards of appearance in the same way that women themselves are. Men's appearance concerns, in one form or another, may injure millions of relationships. It is our hope that women in such situations can learn that the man they love is not strange or unique. His problem is readily understandable against the cultural and social backdrop of our age. If a woman understands the Adonis Complex, and can talk about it compassionately with the man she loves, the wounds in many a relationship might be healed.

CHAPTER TEN

Straights and Gays
Not So Different After All

No discussion of the Adonis Complex would be complete without addressing the concerns of gay men. If you're gay, are you more likely to suffer from body obsessions? Are you at greater risk for developing an eating disorder or some form of body dysmorphic disorder like muscle dysmorphia? Conventional wisdom would say yes: gay men are widely believed to have more hang-ups about their appearance than straight men. In fact, many gay men themselves have assured us that this is true. They've told us to take a look at the Gay Pride Parade on Eighth Avenue in New York City or on Santa Monica Boulevard in West Hollywood. Where in the straight world would you find such a fixation on the male body?

On the surface, the conventional wisdom sounds reasonable, but is there hard scientific evidence to support it? Looking carefully, it turns out that, in their susceptibility to the Adonis Complex, gay and straight men may differ less than one would think.

ARE GAY MEN AT HIGHER RISK
FOR THE ADONIS COMPLEX?

Few good studies have looked at body image in gay men—and, of those available, many were conducted on gay men attending a clinic or a hospital. Obviously, it's hazardous to generalize from men attending clinics to men in the community as a whole. Take the case of eating disorders. Studies of men in eating disorder clinics have reported that as many as 34 to 42 percent were gay or bisexual. But in our two studies of college men with eating disorders out in the community, as described in Chapter 6, the overall percentage of bisexual or gay men was only 14 percent.

This percentage is still higher than the prevalence of gay men in our society, but it indicates that the association between homosexuality and eating disorders in men may be much less clear than studies in clinical settings would have us believe.

Furthermore, even if researchers go out of the clinic and into the community, they still face other methodological problems that may bias their findings about the attitudes of gay men. For example, one study of Yale University college students found that homosexual men had more body dissatisfaction than heterosexual men. For example, when asked why they exercised, the gay men most often responded "to improve appearance," while straight men emphasized "health" and "enjoyment." Also, when presented with a sequence of nine figure drawings, ranging from a very thin male to a very big one, gay men preferred a thinner ideal than straight men. The authors concluded that the gay subculture, because of its overemphasis on appearance, was at increased risk for eating disorders.

But can we be sure? Take the "exercise" question. Maybe the straight men in the Yale study wanted to improve their appearance just as badly as the gay men but were less willing to admit this motivation to the interviewers. They may have felt that exercising for appearance was too "vain" or "feminine." We're reminded here of the words of Daryl, a twenty-three-year-old heterosexual graduate student, who privately told us: "Of course I work out for looks. Let's face it. I wouldn't be doing this if I didn't think it would attract girls. Any guy who tells you different is lying."

As Daryl's comments illustrate, there's nothing abnormal about working out because you want to look sexually attractive. This applies regardless of whether you're a heterosexual man who wants to be sexually attractive to women, or a homosexual man who wants to be sexually attractive to other men. You have the Adonis Complex only if your need to work out interferes with other aspects of your life, or if in spite of working out, you're still chronically dissatisfied or unhappy with your body. Using this latter criterion, it's not obvious that the homosexual Yale college students were any more impaired than the heterosexual ones.

Admittedly, a number of studies have suggested that gay men are more dissatisfied with their bodies than straight men. For example, the previously mentioned *Psychology Today* survey found that gay men were somewhat more unhappy with their bodies than straight men: 57 percent of the straight men said that they were "extremely satisfied" or "somewhat satisfied" with their bodies, as opposed to 44 percent of the gay men. Also, more gay men than straight men reported dieting—70 percent versus 58 percent. These findings indicate some differences between the two groups, but still the differences are modest.

Using our computerized Body Image Test, we examined attitudes toward body image among forty-nine gay men in Innsbruck, Austria, recruited from gay clubs around the city. When asked to choose the body they'd ideally like to have, these men didn't choose a thinner image than the heterosexual men. Instead, just like straight men who had taken the same test, the gay men chose an image with about the same level of body fat that they had themselves, but with substantially more muscle. Interestingly, however, the average discrepancy between the gay men's actual muscularity and the muscularity of their ideal body was smaller than for the straight Austrian men described in Chapter 3. In other words, the gay men were *closer* to their own body ideal, suggesting that they were more satisfied with the way they looked than the straight men. Although another study using figure drawings did not find this, our study, which has a number of advantages over previous studies, casts doubt on the stereotyped notion that gay men are much more neurotic than straight men about their levels of fat and muscularity.

SEXUAL PREFERENCE VERSUS GENDER IDENTITY

Many people, gay or straight, would still argue that gay men are at increased risk of developing the Adonis Complex. Why? One standard theory is that gay men are more likely to have a "feminine gender identity," which is to say that they're more likely to be effeminate and to relate to people and situations the way a woman would. Therefore, the argument runs, gay men pursue thinness in the same way that women do. The problem with this theory is that "sexual orientation" and "gender identity" are very different things. Gay men may prefer other men sexually, but they don't necessarily have a feminine gender identity, just as heterosexual men don't necessarily have a masculine gender identity. Of course, a certain percentage of gay men are effeminate; these men may be more recognizable to a casual observer, and they may be over-represented in research studies of gay men. But in fact, a majority of gay men show little or no evidence of feminine gender identity at all.

Even though most gay men don't have a feminine gender identity, it's reasonable to suspect that some might still feel that their masculine identity is in peril. For example, gay activist Michelangelo Signorile has suggested that "internalized homophobia" may prompt gay men to value a hypermasculine body. Being gay, in other words, so violates their perception of masculinity that they seek out a large, muscular body to compensate for their perceived lack of manliness. Therefore, they hit the gym and may take steroids.

Some of our observations favor this theory. We remember several gay men from our studies who stated flatly that weightlifting and getting muscular had done wonders for their sense of masculinity. Some admitted that they had started lifting weights explicitly for this purpose. But then, a roughly equal proportion of the heterosexual men in our studies have reported exactly the same motivations.

Now consider another typical research finding: twenty years ago, a study of body image found that the gay men displayed lower self-esteem and body esteem than their straight counterparts. Once again, one might be tempted to conclude that homosexuality is a risk factor for body dissatisfaction. But consider the following: boys who grow up gay in our culture are subjected to many psychosocial stressors. In particular, studies have shown that as boys, gay men were more likely to have been teased about their behavior and appearance. And if you're chronically teased or harassed about the way you look as a child or adolescent, you may very well become more concerned about the way you look as an adult. So, being gay, in and of itself, may not have caused your body image problem; teasing may have been the major factor.

Peter, a college man in our study of eating disorders, easily identified with this point. "I was teased a lot as a kid. They used to call me a 'faggot' and a 'weakling.'"

"Why did they call you a weakling?"

"I don't know. I was just as big and strong as any other kid at my school. But it was obvious, even when I was quite young, that I was gay. I mean, I didn't specifically realize in junior high school that I was attracted to men, but there was definitely something noticeably different about me even at that time. I sensed it, and the other kids sensed it. They didn't have the words to describe what was different about me, so instead they disparaged my body—even though my body was just as good as theirs."

"How do you think this affected you?"

"Well, I guess I just began to disparage my body, too."

Even if gay men are secure about their bodies and their gender identity, they might still be prone to the Adonis Complex because they're being scrutinized by other gay men who may be potential sexual part-

ners. "In the gay world, your body is the only currency you've got to negotiate with," said Kyle, a thirty-year-old gay man. "With a woman, it's
going to matter whether you show up in a '00 Porsche or an '87 Ford.
But to a gay guy, that's not going to make much difference in comparison to what you look like."

We'll grant Kyle's point, but we'd note that as we said in Chapter
2, men's bodies now appear to be growing increasingly important to
women as well. As we demonstrated in our survey of undressed men in
magazine advertising, the male body seems to have acquired a higher
"currency" value for women than it had thirty years ago. So if you're a
heterosexual man in the new millennium, it may help to show up in a '00
Porsche, but you'd better have a good body, too.

AN ADVANTAGE FOR GAYS?

As indicated above, many people have suggested that gay men are more
at risk for body obsessions than straight men, and we'll admit that this
is intuitively reasonable. Gay men, on average, probably do suffer more
teasing about their bodies when growing up, they may be more insecure
about masculine gender identity, and body appearance is more important in the gay world. But on any of these measures, the difference between gays and straights is narrower than most people would think.
New evidence, including many of the studies described in this book, suggests that heterosexual men are almost equally at risk for body obsessions. The Adonis Complex may just be more *announced* in the gay
community, not necessarily more *pronounced*.

As a result of this openness, gay men may actually have an advantage over straight men in their ability to talk about body image concerns.
Indeed, straight men often don't reveal their body image problems,
specifically because they're afraid they'll be labeled as gay. This theme
has emerged over and over again in our conversations with college men
who had eating disorders, when we asked why they had never come forward and disclosed their problems to a professional:

- "I was so embarrassed about having a female disease."
- "I was afraid someone would think I was gay."
- "I thought I was the only guy who had this."
- "People would see me as a vain woman."
- "Are you kidding? I would be announcing myself as a fairy."

How often does our cultural homophobia shame heterosexual men into hiding their body obsessions? As we've noted before, "real" (read "heterosexual") men in our society aren't supposed to fuss about their appearance, and they're certainly not supposed to check out other men's bodies in comparison. If they do, they fear—realistically—that they'll be called "feminine," "vain," or, worse, "gay." As a result, many heterosexual men become disconnected from what is sometimes called their "body consciousness." These men may deny even to themselves that appearance matters to them, while in their psyches they are troubled by these conscious or semiconscious preoccupations.

Many gay men, in contrast, have confronted these issues openly for years. They often can talk comfortably about their appearance concerns with their friends, their sexual partners, or professionals. This is not to say that they're liberated from the effects of media images or the male body image industries hawking food supplements or body treatments. Creatine and protein powders are big sellers among gay men, as are liposuction and hair transplants. But at least some gays are more equipped with the awareness and the language to express how they feel about their bodies.

AIDS AND THE PURSUIT OF MUSCLE

The AIDS epidemic has particularly heightened gay men's sensitivity and awareness about body appearance. The frightening image of the wasting syndrome of AIDS—the severe loss of weight and muscle with advancing disease—has left an indelible mark on the gay consciousness. Now, gay men routinely tell us, thinness is ugly, because it speaks of sickness and death. Muscles equal health.

An additional factor in this equation is the availability of anabolic steroids. Anabolic steroids, especially testosterone injections, are very effective for treating or preventing the wasting syndrome in HIV-infected men. But if a little is good, wouldn't more be better? Many HIV-positive men, following this line of reasoning, are using more than the prescribed amount of testosterone to bulk up. And HIV-negative men, not to be outdone, have discovered that testosterone and other steroids can make them more muscular as well. As a result, steroid use is catching on among gay men.

Aldo, an HIV-negative twenty-two-year-old gay man in one of our studies, felt this pressure. "I haven't done juice yet, but give me a year. There's no question I'm gonna do it eventually."

"Why are you so certain you're going to take steroids?"

"I've watched what steroids have done for my friends. My friend Gary has gotten huge, and he's HIV-positive! He's put on all that extra muscle on his shoulders and chest, and he looks hot. I'll be damned if someone with HIV looks healthier than I do."

Some of our older gay subjects, from the baby boomer generation, can reminisce about the role of body image in the gay world both before and after the advent of AIDS. Jeff, a man in his late forties, told us a story that illustrated many aspects of growing up gay and its effect on body image through the years. Jeff, in our opinion, does not suffer from the Adonis Complex. We tell his story here to illustrate one of the central points of this chapter—that gay men may have strong and lifelong concerns about their body image *without* necessarily exhibiting any serious pathology.

Jeff was born in a small town in upstate New York. His stable, loving family could have been a prototypical American household; his father worked nine to five as an officer at the local bank; his mother volunteered for a Lutheran Church group but spent most of her time managing the home. Jeff's two older sisters both went to the local high school, married their high school sweethearts, and settled not far away.

On the surface, Jeff's childhood and adolescence seemed equally ordinary. But as a teenager in the 1960s, he sensed that something was different. "Of course, I hadn't figured out I was gay," he remembered. "But I always felt there was something wrong with me, especially in athletics. The other kids seemed to understand team sports in a way that I didn't. For instance, I remember that when I was in junior high school, we played football as part of gym class. At one point, a kid asked, 'Where's the line of scrimmage?' All of the other boys immediately seemed to know what a 'line of scrimmage' was, but I didn't. I just couldn't talk the talk. There were many little incidents like that that made me feel excluded from sports."

In high school, Jeff gradually withdrew from athletics almost entirely. "It was a shame," he reflected, "because in fact I was stronger and more muscular than most of the other kids, and I would have been a damn good athlete. But instead, I ended up watching sports from the sidelines. I remember getting attracted to the guys on the high school football team, watching them come in sweaty from the field. I just figured I wasn't muscular enough or athletic enough to be able to be in there with them."

Jeff left his hometown to come to college in the Northeast in 1970, falsely convinced by years of peer feedback that his body didn't measure up to the bodies of other boys. But his vantage point was soon to change: in his sophomore year, Jeff found himself in bed for the first time with one of the young men from his class.

"Bill was very good to me," Jeff recalled. "He dragged me, screaming and kicking, to Sporter's, which was the best bar for gay college men in Boston at the time. At first, I was really nervous, but I quickly found that I was in my element. After that, I went back to Sporter's regularly. It was so nice, after feeling completely left out among the boys at high school, to find myself in a group of men where I felt comfortable. And good-looking men, too. I went wild in those days. I cut a swath through the men of Sporter's like Sherman cut through Georgia."

"How important was body appearance to you at that point?" we asked.

"Well, of course it was important, but I never worried a great deal about it in those days. I was careful to stay thin, but I never particularly worried about whether I was muscular or not. I was young and good-looking enough that I could get almost any hot little number I wanted. It probably wasn't until several years after college, when I moved to New York in the late 1970s, that I first started to think about muscularity. It may have been because I was getting a little bit older, and I noticed that I wasn't attracting the younger guys quite as much as I had before. I started thinking more about my body. When you're dancing with your shirt open at a club, nobody cares where you got your college degree. It's what your chest looks like."

"Did you try working out at a gym?"

"No. There weren't many gyms in the late 1970s. I don't think I knew any other gay guys in New York City at that time who went regularly to a gym. I thought about working out, and I thought it would be nice to be more muscular, but I didn't really know where to start.

"Then I met Shawn. He was a big blond guy I met one Saturday night—actually, more like 4 A.M. on a Sunday morning—at the Mine Shaft. He looked like a surfer. He'd been working out for a year or two. I remember, holding him, I could feel his triceps flexing against my hands, and suddenly I got really turned on. I could feel the outline of his chest muscles along the bottom and in the groove between them in the center. When I felt them, he would instinctively flex them, and that turned me on even more. I remember thinking how much I really, really wanted to look like that.

"The next morning, I asked Shawn to take me to his gym. It was a little Nautilus place in the basement of a building on Twenty-third Street, with no windows and a torn-up carpet and a bunch of old Nautilus machines. Shawn walked me through the machines that he used— the leg extension, leg curl, chest machine, shoulder machine, super pullover. I was surprised to see how much stronger he was than I, and I resolved that I was going to get that strong myself."

"Then what happened?"

"Shawn and I worked out together a few times, and gradually I started going sporadically by myself. By the mid-1980s, I had a more flexible job in the advertising firm where I was working, and I got to the gym practically every day after work. And of course, I started to get reinforcement from other guys I met. They'd say, 'Boy, are you built!' or something like that. And also I started to notice that other gay guys were beginning to work out more as well."

"By this point the AIDS epidemic had started?"

"Yes. I was lucky. When the blood test finally came out, I took it and found out that I was negative. But I had several friends who died. Most of all, I remember in June of '87 I decided to call Shawn, the man who had introduced me to lifting, because I hadn't seen him in two or three years. Some guy picked up the phone and I asked, 'Is Shawn there?' There was a long pause, and the guy carefully asked me my name, and I got this sick feeling in my gut because I knew what was going to come next. It turned out Shawn had died six months earlier. The guy on the phone had taken care of him until the time of his death, and was still living in the apartment."

Jeff continued, "It was pretty scary to think that I had probably been sleeping with Shawn while he was positive for HIV. I guess it made me even more thankful that I still had my health, and made me even more conscious of my body and of being in shape. So I worked out even more. I can remember several occasions that I happened to weigh myself and found that for some reason I had lost a few pounds. I'd immediately start thinking, in spite of my negative blood test, that it might be an early sign of AIDS. But then at the gym I'd satisfy myself that I could do the same number of repetitions as usual with two hundred twenty-five pounds on the bench press, and I'd be reassured that I was okay."

The gym rewarded Jeff in many other ways. "There was just no doubt that it made a difference in my ability to attract other guys," he said. "I also began to notice how other gay guys my age, who didn't work out, were beginning to look old and flabby in comparison to me. I pitied them because I knew they weren't getting any ass. And I myself became more critical of their appearance. It got so that pretty boys, if they didn't have any muscle, didn't turn me on as much anymore. I started to prefer guys who were as muscular as myself, or preferably more so."

Over the last seven years, Jeff has lifted weights regularly at a predominantly gay gym in New York. "But I don't mind lifting in straight gyms, either," he said. "In fact, being more muscular has made me feel a lot more comfortable around straight guys. Lifting has made up for all those years of my having felt inferior back in high school. Now, I can look at some other guy who works with me in the office and think, 'Look at that couch potato. I could knock him over with one jab of my elbow.' That same guy might well have been one of those hot football jocks that I envied when I was a teenager. But now the tables are turned. There's a lot of satisfaction in that."

Several of the men in Jeff's gym have taken steroids, and Jeff has debated trying them himself. "So far, I still do pretty well in the marketplace just with my natural body," he said. "But if I start slipping, I wouldn't hesitate to do a cycle or two."

"Since you've been an adult, would you say that you've had any problems with your body image? In other words, have you had concerns about your appearance that affected your life in some adverse way?"

"Not at all. I'm very concerned about my appearance, and I go to the gym faithfully, but I know exactly why I do it. I want to look good in the gay marketplace, and I've been handsomely rewarded for the time I've put in the gym. I don't have any problems with that at all."

REPRESSED HOMOSEXUALITY IN THE GYM?

Jeff's story reminds us of a question we're often asked: how many weightlifters are gay? And—to anticipate a related question—how many weightlifters are superficially straight, but harbor repressed homosexual urges? Some writers have seemed to imply this possibility by arguing that bodybuilding and weightlifting are inherently "homoerotic." They hypothesize that half-nude men, posing and displaying their muscles, exhibit a form of disguised homosexuality. Bodybuilding, so the theory goes, provides a means for men to gaze at and desire other men in an environment where they will not be judged for doing so. We've heard similar theories about men who watch World Wrestling Federation matches or other sporting events where men's bodies are prominently featured.

Although these theories may apply to some men, we're somewhat skeptical of this idea. Certainly, we'll admit that in every big city there are gyms like Jeff's with predominantly gay memberships. But we believe that Jeff represents a minority. In talking to hundreds of weightlifters and bodybuilders, we haven't noticed a higher prevalence of gay men in these sports or hobbies than in the general population. The majority of gyms we've seen appear predominantly heterosexual. Men in these gyms may quite naturally talk to one another about muscle and body fat, but it does not necessarily follow that there is an unconscious homoerotic theme running through these conversations.

In short, there's nothing inherently gay about going to the gym, any more than there's anything inherently gay about being concerned with body appearance, or even having an outright body image disorder. The Adonis Complex can strike gay men and straight men in very similar ways. Certainly, many gay men like Peter and Jeff faced greater disparagement of their bodies and their masculinity as they were growing up—and this may leave its scars. But on the other side of the equation, many gay men are more in touch with their feelings about body image, and less afraid to talk about these feelings, than their straight counterparts.

HELPING GAY MEN WITH THE ADONIS COMPLEX

Treatment of gay men with body image disorders isn't fundamentally different from that of straight men. The odds of successful treatment appear equally good regardless of a man's sexual orientation. Some aspects of therapy, however, are unique to gay men. If we had to highlight just one of these, it would be the issue of self-acceptance. We have often encountered men who were clearly gay but had never admitted this to a single person and had tried to hide it even from themselves. Such a man must first overcome the problem of hating himself because of his sexual orientation—so-called "internalized homophobia." Once he's addressed this problem, he's in a better position to move on to address the issue of hating the appearance of his body.

Enrique, a twenty-four-year-old Hispanic man, exemplified this dilemma. For several years, he had suffered from many of the symptoms of muscle dysmorphia. He was a college graduate but had taken a job working in construction. "I had to have a job that gave me physical exercise," he explained. "If I had a desk job, I'd get too fat and flabby."

Fat and flab were certainly the least of Enrique's problems. His body fat measured only 5 percent—close to the lower limit theoretically attainable by a healthy man. To keep his fat at that level, while maintaining muscularity, he lifted weights for a good two hours every day and ran seven mornings a week on the beach near his house, regardless of the weather. Running in the deep sand was much more strenuous than ordinary running, and he liked it because it burned more calories. But even though he had a well-defined body, he had no girlfriend and had gone on only a few dates with girls in the last couple of years.

"How come you haven't had a girlfriend in the last few years?" we asked.

"Oh, I've just been too busy," he said. "I get a lot of girls who almost throw themselves at me, wanting me to invite them out, but I just don't have the time."

Not wanting to be too confrontational, we let this answer pass. But Enrique himself quickly seemed to recognize that it wasn't an adequate explanation. "Also," he added, "I'm usually just too tired. After busting my ass at work and then pumping iron for two hours at the gym, I just don't have the energy or the interest to hang out with some chick. It's not that I'm gay or anything. Seriously. I'm just too busy."

We didn't want to challenge Enrique's defenses too aggressively during the first meeting. But during several subsequent meetings, with some gentle questioning, a much clearer picture emerged. Enrique was clearly attracted to men. Deep down, he knew this. But he was still engaged in a lifelong campaign to deny this reality. Even when he had come to trust us after many weeks of therapy, he would still skirt only briefly around the issue. During one of these brief moments of candor, he remarked, "You don't know what it's like coming from a family in my culture. I came from a *very* Catholic family. I mean. . . . I remember my mother watching *Oprah* or something and wondering if scientists could one day come up with a cure for homosexuality. If my dad thought that I had even one gay bone in my body, he'd shoot me." Then, almost immediately, Enrique changed the subject.

We remember another candid moment when Enrique said something about masturbating, and we tried probing a little deeper with our questions: "What sexual things do you fantasize about when you masturbate?"

"Nothing."

"Nothing at all?"

"That's right. I just try to get it over with as quickly as possible."

As time went on, a coherent picture emerged. Enrique's compulsive exercising served several purposes for him. First, it made him big and muscular, and that provided him with some reassurance about his masculinity. Second, it kept him occupied. Between the hours he spent lifting at the gym, running on the beach, counting his calories and protein consumption, and doing all of his other exercise-related activities, he had little time left to dwell on the possibility that he was gay. And third, by keeping his body fat extremely low through very heavy exercise, he kept his own sex drive biologically suppressed. In the same way that girls with anorexia nervosa lose their menstrual periods, Enrique's extreme fat loss suppressed his own sexual hormonal function. By keeping his sexual urges low, he didn't have to worry so much about what they were telling him.

Eventually, Enrique dropped out of therapy. He thanked us greatly for our help, but explained that going to and from the therapy, plus the time spent in the office, was just too much, and it was eating into his workout schedule. We urged him to call back any time he wished, but we haven't heard from him since.

In telling Enrique's story, we don't mean to imply that most men with muscle dysmorphia are secretly gay. In fact, the great majority of men with muscle dysmorphia are clearly heterosexual. But Enrique's lonely life illustrates how homophobia can profoundly affect gay men, just as it can affect men who are straight. In both cases, the net effect of homophobia is to prevent men from talking openly about their body image concerns or learning to understand the reasons behind them.

Our impression, then, is that homosexuality and body image problems are linked, but not nearly as strongly as many believe. The core features of the Adonis Complex, such as body dissatisfaction and insecure masculinity, can affect men whether they're gay or straight. Gay men like Jeff may be very concerned about their body appearance, but that doesn't necessarily mean that they're unhappy with their bodies or that body preoccupations hamper their lives. Straight men, conversely, may appear superficially unconcerned about their body appearance—because they don't want to appear "gay"—yet privately suffer from body loathing or body obsessions. So in the final analysis, straight men and gay men may be similarly vulnerable to the Adonis Complex. Of course, straights and gays may differ in many of their attitudes, behaviors, and lifestyles. But in their private feelings about the appearance of their bodies, they may not be so different after all.

CHAPTER ELEVEN

Rx for the Adonis Complex
A Guide for Men and Their Loved Ones

The Adonis Complex, in various forms, afflicts millions of boys and men. Sometimes it manifests itself as a serious condition, such as muscle dysmorphia, anabolic steroid abuse, an eating disorder, or body dysmorphic disorder. In a much larger number of cases, it causes milder appearance-related problems but still robs millions of boys and men of potential pleasure and fulfillment in their lives. However, much can be done to help men with the Adonis Complex—and to change society's attitudes about men's bodies.

Before we go on, we should first emphasize what we are *not* saying. We're not claiming that there's anything pathological about wanting to look good. We're definitely not implying that there's anything wrong with working out regularly at the gym, being a dedicated athlete, striving to eat a low-fat diet, or trying to maintain a healthy weight. Ordinary activities to improve body appearance are perfectly normal and justified. They pay off in the positive responses that they may generate from people around you. They become pathological only when they get out of hand—when the need to change your appearance begins to cause emotional distress, undermines social relationships, or impairs school or work performance. Remember our earlier analogy to hand washing. If you wash your hands five times per day, that's healthy. But if you wash your hands two hundred times a day, you very likely have a problem.

If you're a man reading this book, or if you're someone thinking about a boy or man you love, you must first decide where normal appearance-related behaviors leave off and abnormal ones begin. If you've read this far, the answer to this question may already be fairly obvious. If not, you might want to turn back and look at the specific clues presented in various chapters or at the more general Adonis Complex Questionnaire in Chapter 3. As you may remember, we've provided representative scores on this questionnaire from several hundred men in many different groups, and we've also given numerical guidelines to help you interpret the meaning of different scores. Keep in mind that the scores are only a rough guideline; you'll want to consider other information you have about yourself or someone you care about. Also remember that if you're a man taking the questionnaire yourself, your score is only as accurate as your ability to rate yourself honestly. Some men with the Adonis Complex have become so accustomed to their lifestyles that they don't notice anything wrong; they assume that their distress, or their preoccupations with working out, dieting, or grooming, are simply normal. In cases like this, insight from a loved one or close friend can make a big difference.

BARRIERS TO GETTING HELP

To confront their problems, boys and men with the Adonis Complex often need the help of someone close to them. Maybe you're a parent thinking about your son, a wife thinking about your husband, or possibly a gay man thinking about your partner. If so, we would reiterate what we've said in the last three chapters: victims of the Adonis Complex rarely come forward spontaneously to complain about it. Many deny it even to themselves. They might emphatically answer "a" to all of the questions on the Adonis Complex Questionnaire—in other words, claiming that nothing really bothers them—even though it may be obvious to you that the true answer to many of the questions is "b" or "c."

We're not being critical of men who display this sort of denial. It's completely understandable. It's tough to admit to other people, or even to yourself, that you have a problem with appearance concerns, especially if you're a man. As we've pointed out throughout this book, our society puts up a lot of barriers to self-revelation. Here are a few of them.

The Feeling and Talking Taboo

As we've mentioned before, men in our society aren't supposed to fuss about how they look. Women are allowed, even expected, to talk about their beauty concerns—even on televised talk shows in front of millions of viewers. But if a man in our culture confesses to others that he's preoccupied with his muscle mass, or his love handles, or—perish the thought—his penis size, he's often considered weird. Men just aren't supposed to get hung up about such things. And so, if a man suffers from the Adonis Complex, what can he do? The embarrassment of revealing his concerns to his friends, or even to loved ones, may be greater than the pain of keeping his feelings bottled up inside.

There's a curious paradox in this: On the one hand, everywhere we look we're surrounded with messages about the importance of appearance. But if a man gets up the courage to voice his concerns about appearance, he may be criticized for doing so.

Feeling You're the Only One

Partly because of the talking and feeling taboo, few people recognize how common the Adonis Complex really is. Men with problems like muscle dysmorphia, eating disorders, and body dysmorphic disorder often think that they're the only ones in the world with such symptoms. Often, they're both astonished and relieved to hear from us that so many other men have experienced the same problems as themselves. If you're one of these men, thinking your problem is rare or unique, we hope that this book has already given you some relief. Once you know you're not alone, it may be a lot easier to share your concerns with others.

Thinking You Deserve It

Another problem for some men is that they think it's normal to suffer from the Adonis Complex. Some have been teased about their appearance since boyhood. And all have been bombarded throughout their lives with advertisements showing lean and muscular bodies. These advertisements subtly imply that if you don't look like the man in the picture, you *should* be worrying about how you look. This illusion of course is just what the advertisers would like; if all men realized that it was okay to look ordinary, then the advertisers would never be able to sell their products. Men need to be liberated from this myth.

These barriers to self-disclosure remind us of the old parable of the guy who buys an expensive videocassette recorder—one of those machines with a fifty-page instruction manual full of complicated programming options. The buyer never really figures out how to program his VCR, but he doesn't dare admit this to his friends, because he assumes that they all know how to program their VCRs perfectly. In fact, his friends can't program their VCRs either, but they're equally afraid to admit it, because each secretly thinks he's the only one too dumb to figure it out.

Like the "VCR complex," the Adonis Complex often remains secret even between people who are close to one another. This is where the help and support of a loved one can make a huge difference. If you're a parent, and you sense that your son may have some of the problems we've described in this book, or if you're someone who sees these problems in your boyfriend or husband or lover, then your sympathy and understanding may be crucial. To start with, you'll have to decide how best to raise this issue with the boy or man who is close to you. Even if he seems reluctant to talk to you, or denies that he has any problem at all, he may still be willing to consider reading some of the chapters of this book. And if he acknowledges that body image concerns truly are bothering him, he may be willing to consider getting some type of help.

But remember, you must be sensitive and realistic in talking to any man about this subject. If you are too confrontational, it's only going to backfire. For example, we periodically get telephone calls like the following:

"I want to make an appointment to bring my boyfriend in to see you. I just found out that he's been taking steroids, and he doesn't want to get off them."

"Okay, but does your boyfriend want to see us?"

"I haven't talked to him yet about it, but someone has to tell him about the dangers of what he's doing."

"Of course we'd be happy to see both of you, but it sounds like first you really need to talk to him about it."

As you may guess, the boyfriend in this scenario did not take kindly to the fact that his girlfriend had surreptitiously called a mental health professional about him, wanting him to become a patient. In fact, he was very well informed about the dangers of taking steroids, and he had no interest in paying money to hear about this from somebody else. Instead, his main concern was that he wasn't big enough, and he wanted to get bigger.

Now perhaps if his girlfriend had begun differently, and first asked him to explain why he had originally decided to take the steroids, she might have fared better. She might have discovered that his concerns about body image ran much deeper than she imagined, and that his drug use was a consequence of this underlying problem. Possibly, with her support and encouragement, he would have grown gradually more comfortable with his body image and less tempted to use steroids. Or alternatively, he might have agreed to talk about these issues with a knowledgeable professional.

The point here is simply that you must first *listen* to the boy or man whom you think suffers from the Adonis Complex. Are body image concerns affecting his life or his relationship with you? If so, is he running up against some of the barriers to treatment that we've just described? For example, does he acknowledge that he has a problem in the first place? Does he realize that he isn't it alone with this problem? Can he recognize that his body image ideals may be unrealistic? Is he locked into the endless pursuit of an unreasonable and unattainable goal? Questions like these are not likely to be answered in the space of a single discussion. Too many questions, all at the same time, often don't work well. It's better to be patient and to seek the answers more slowly, over the course of many conversations.

Your sympathetic listening, in and of itself, may be very helpful. For men with mild appearance concerns—say, scores ranging from roughly 5 to 11 on our Adonis Complex Questionnaire—your insight and reassurance may be all that he really needs. But for certain men, those with more serious body image preoccupations, professional help may be necessary and invaluable. And here, fortunately, there are several good options.

THINGS THAT DON'T WORK FOR
THE ADONIS COMPLEX

Before we discuss effective treatments for the Adonis Complex, let's go through a few things that *don't* work. For starters, men with the Adonis Complex are not likely to be cured by any technique that is supposed to make their body look perfect. We've seen bodybuilders who swore that they would at last be satisfied if only they could just do one more cycle of steroids and put on five more pounds of muscle. We've treated men with eating disorders who claimed that all their problems would be solved if only they could lose a few more pounds of fat. Men who have undergone several cosmetic surgeries come in and protest that just one more operation would do the trick. Needless to say, in cases like this, no amount of body manipulation is ever quite enough. Unless we can get at the roots of the discontent itself, little progress will be made.

There's no scientific evidence that body image problems will respond to "alternative" therapies like herbal medicines, acupuncture, nutritional therapies, or the like. Maybe someday there will be a methodologically sound scientific study showing that one of these techniques is effective for the Adonis Complex, but as scientists, we remain skeptical. You can waste a lot of time and money on untested therapies that may be completely valueless for your condition. Some, despite being natural, are potentially dangerous, even life-threatening.

We're also skeptical of the effectiveness of conventional Freudian therapy for the Adonis Complex. This is the sort of treatment in which you explore issues such as your childhood memories, your feelings about your mother, or your family problems. We're not denying, of course, that childhood experiences can profoundly affect body image—as some of the personal accounts in this book have poignantly illustrated. In fact, we've argued throughout this book that childhood exposure to unrealistic male body images—from action toys to television shows to magazine advertisements—undoubtedly contributes to the Adonis Complex. More personal, individual experiences may sometimes contribute as well. But lying on a couch and searching for repressed memories of childhood trauma is not going to make the Adonis Complex go away.

We're not saying that all "talking therapy" is valueless; it may be helpful for other problems. And a session with a knowledgeable counselor may work wonders for a man with mild body image concerns. But the key word here is "mild." Talking therapy alone, in our experience, is rarely effective for men with more severe body image problems. If you have muscle dysmorphia, steroid use, an eating disorder, or body dysmorphic disorder, you need someone who is experienced with these conditions, and you need more than conventional talking therapy.

TREATMENTS FOR MORE SERIOUS BODY IMAGE DISORDERS: COGNITIVE-BEHAVIORAL THERAPY

If you have a more serious form of the Adonis Complex, how can you find someone who is experienced? Unfortunately, we can't offer any simple formula for picking an ideal doctor or other professional. Your best bet will probably be to get a referral from a knowledgeable professional in your area. You may also be able to get advice from the department of psychiatry at a local medical school or the department of psychology at a local university. Also, in Appendix III of this book, we provide several additional leads to Web sites, foundations, and associations that may be able to provide treatment or help you with a referral.

Don't underestimate your ability to distinguish between a treatment professional who is knowledgeable and someone who isn't. If your instinct tells you, in the first meeting or two, that a particular individual isn't well suited for you, you're probably right. If necessary, try scheduling an appointment with a different person for comparison. You may even want to check out several different people before you decide who is the best "match" for you. And we recommend that you specifically ask any professional whether he or she is experienced in treating men with body image issues. In particular, if you suffer from one of the more serious body image problems described in this book, you should strongly consider a professional who is experienced with two well-tested treatments: cognitive-behavioral therapy and antidepressant medications.

Cognitive-behavioral therapy, or CBT, has been demonstrated to be very effective in clinical studies for eating disorders; preliminary data suggest that it is also often effective for body dysmorphic disorder. The basic premise behind CBT is that your thoughts have a significant impact on your behavior and mood. For example, if you say to yourself repeatedly, "I'm a failure," you'll most likely feel down on yourself and develop a negative attitude about new activities or relationships. You'll become convinced that you'll just botch them up. CBT focuses on challenging and changing such thoughts, so as to alter your negative behavioral patterns.

All of us have automatic thoughts in various situations. We can't control them. For example, when you walk into a cocktail party, you may be thinking, "I'm somebody people will want to meet." Or you could be thinking, "Everyone will think I'm boring." These two different thoughts may lead to very different behaviors when you're at the party.

People who struggle with depression, eating disorders, and other body image disorders are masters at negative thoughts. We hear these beliefs in our sessions all the time.

- "If I gain one pound, I'll be obese."
- "No girl will find me attractive unless I'm more muscular."
- "Everyone who looks at my ugly nose must be wondering why I haven't gotten a nose job."

Thoughts like these can cause men significant distress, while baffling and frustrating their partners, friends, or parents. Men with these thoughts may know that they're being irrational, but that knowledge doesn't really help. The Adonis Complex is set firmly in place.

Can you change such entrenched thoughts? In many cases, yes. The first step is to recognize the cognitive distortions in your thinking. For example, don't take your thoughts at face value. Question them. After discussing them in the course of CBT, you may be surprised to find how far you have drifted from the truth. Here are a few examples of cognitive distortions commonly seen in men with the Adonis Complex.

Filtering

Filtering is the process by which we ignore all of the positive aspects of a situation and attend only to the negative. This was the case with B.J., who had muscle dysmorphia. Although he had a body that many men envied, B.J. didn't see it. He was too focused on the small "love handles" around his waist.

"I need to get rid of this fat."

"But is there anything about your body that you like?" we asked.

"I'm not sure. All I know is that these love handles have to go!"

By overly focusing on the one thing that he disliked about himself, B.J. lost sight of all of the positive aspects of his physique. If he attended to these, he might be less distraught over the one part of his body that wasn't perfect.

Black and White Thinking

Black and white thinking is the thought process by which people see a situation as all or nothing—they can't see the more realistic, in-between shades of gray. Nicholas, a twenty-two-year-old man with anorexia nervosa, exemplified this.

"If I eat something sweet, I'll never stop eating and I'll become so fat."

"Would this be the case even if you ate just one bite of something sweet?"

"Absolutely. It's either no calories or tons of calories."

Nicholas could not imagine that there were options in between these two extremes.

"Should" Statements

"Should" statements are cognitive distortions in which people expect that they "should" be a certain way. Often these statements are so unrealistic that they merely breed anxiety, because the victim of this kind of thinking can never reach his goal. For instance, Hank employed "should" statements daily when it came to his body.

"I should be bigger."

"Who says?"

"I don't know. I just know that I should be bigger than I am now."

Mind Reading

Mind reading is the thought process by which people make assumptions about what others think. Rodney, who suffers from BDD, often used mind reading.

"I know people are looking at my ears and thinking they're too big."

"Has anyone ever told you this?"

"No. They don't have to. I can tell by the way they're looking at me. They're probably wondering why I haven't done something about them."

In CBT, we work with our patients to search for these and other cognitive distortions. Then, we work to replace the irrational thought with a more rational one. For example, we examine the evidence for and against a particular cognitive belief. In Rodney's case, for example, we would explore with him the evidence that "proves" that people are looking at his ears and the evidence that argues against it.

We also teach our patients to monitor their feelings—as we described in the case of Christopher in Chapter 6. For many men, depression and anxiety can trigger body image preoccupations or make small preoccupations grow into overwhelming ones. But if you are in touch with your depression or anxiety, you'll be better prepared for the cognitive distortions they may create. Thus, it's important to monitor your mood throughout the day. Marcus described success with this method:

"I noticed yesterday that my thoughts about my body were getting really out of control. But then I noticed that I was going through a period of anxiety at that point in the day, for no particular reason. Whenever I get anxious, the first thing that my mind does is to start focusing on my appearance. So, I was able to step back and realize that my mind was just playing tricks on me, so to speak, and that my body didn't look any different than it did an hour before."

Even after working on their cognitive distortions, many men still suffer from body obsessions. In such cases, exposure plus response prevention treatment (EPRP) can help. This is a technique in which a person is exposed to an anxiety-provoking situation or to his problem behavior but is then prevented from responding to his obsessions. For example, we used this method to treat Mario, a man with bulimia nervosa. We allowed him to have an eating binge in the office but then encouraged him to wait for longer and longer periods before making himself vomit afterward. With the help of relaxation techniques, and the chance to talk about his anxiety, Mario was able to greatly reduce his urge to vomit. That, in turn, helped him to reduce his urge to binge. He became increasingly skilled at finding alternative ways to control his anxiety.

You may recall that we also used this approach successfully with Pete, the man with body dysmorphic disorder whom we described in Chapter 7. We had him "expose" his supposedly flawed skin to others and helped him to avoid his excessive behaviors, such as mirror checking. Gradually, his anxiety declined.

ANTIDEPRESSANT MEDICATIONS: ANOTHER EFFECTIVE TREATMENT FOR MORE SERIOUS BODY IMAGE PROBLEMS

Cognitive-behavioral therapy isn't the only option. For men with some of the serious body image disorders described in this book, certain antidepressant medications can be dramatically effective. For bulimia nervosa, a wide range of antidepressants have been shown to be effective. In binge-eating disorder, and also in body dysmorphic disorder, fewer studies have been conducted, but these conditions appear to respond particularly well to antidepressants called "selective serotonin reuptake inhibitors" or "SSRIs." In the United States, these drugs currently include Prozac, Paxil, Luvox, Zoloft, and Celexa. Another effective antidepressant from a different chemical family is Anafranil. For men with prominent depression or suicidality as a result of severe appearance preoccupations, antidepressant medications like these may be lifesaving.

We remember one man named Sam who was chronically preoccupied that his hair was getting thinner. Every day, he would feel compelled to stand in front of the mirror for fifteen or twenty minutes, meticulously examining his head to see if he had lost any hair in the last twenty-four hours. Often during the course of the day, he would have to interrupt what he was doing to go and find a mirror to reexamine his head. He realized that his worries and compulsive behavior were excessive, but he couldn't turn them off. He had seen several therapists of different types over the years, but none seemed to have helped. In fact, his obsessions about hair loss had been growing steadily worse, and he admitted that on a bad day his "mirror time" could approach two hours.

After evaluating Sam, we recommended that he try Zoloft, the chemical name of which is sertraline. We explained to him that in people with BDD, the beneficial effects of Zoloft and other antidepressants typically don't appear for four to twelve weeks, so he would have to be patient and not expect much at first.

When Sam came to the office two weeks later, he was quite discouraged because he hadn't noticed any improvement at all. He was even debating whether it was worth continuing to take the medication, and twice he asked us anxiously if there were any possibility that Zoloft might cause hair loss as one of its side effects. We reminded him that two weeks was too soon to expect any benefit and did our best to reassure him that we had never seen anybody lose hair from antidepressants of this type. Somewhat reluctantly, he agreed to continue the medication for a little longer.

Then, just after the six-week mark, we saw Sam in the office again. From his expression as he walked in the door, it was obvious that he was feeling better.

"I can't believe it," he exclaimed. "Over the last couple of weeks, practically all of my preoccupations with my hair have gone away. They've just lifted—like a cloud. It used to be that when I opened my eyes in the morning, the first thought in my head would be about my hair, and the thoughts would continue like that all day long until the last minute that I closed my eyes at night. But now those thoughts are almost gone! I can actually think about how it's a nice day outside, and think about things I want to do that morning. In fact, until now I never even realized just how much my hair thoughts had dominated my life. Why didn't somebody give me this stuff before?"

At first, accounts like this may seem too good to be true, but we've seen many men like Sam with body image preoccupations whose symptoms almost evaporated after several months of antidepressant treatment. But we hasten to add that treatment is not always so simple. With some men, the first antidepressant may fail entirely, and it may be necessary to try a second one, or even a third.

In a word, treatment with the proper antidepressant can sometimes be easy and very effective, but at other times it can become a complicated affair, requiring the skills of an experienced psychopharmacologist familiar with treating body image disorders. As you might expect, numerous scientific studies have examined the beneficial effects and side effects of many different antidepressant medications in many different conditions—not just depression, but also eating disorders and body dysmorphic disorder. A detailed discussion of this topic would go far beyond the scope of this book. Therefore, to properly inform yourself, we would strongly advise that you get a referral to someone who is experienced with the use of these medications and who is familiar with various forms of the Adonis Complex. Again, the advice of a local general practitioner, a telephone call to the department of psychiatry at a local medical school, or one of the sources listed in Appendix III may provide you with the best leads.

But how do you know whether you should consider a medication consult in the first place? Basically, if you're experiencing significant distress or impairment of your day-to-day functioning, you owe it to yourself to at least explore the possibility of a medication. If your score on the Adonis Complex Questionnaire in Chapter 3 is 20 or higher, we'd strongly recommend that you seek a professional opinion about antidepressant treatment. And if you're severely depressed or feeling suicidal about your appearance, medication is a must.

It's a pity, but many men who might really benefit from antidepressants don't even consider this treatment because of various misconceptions. Let's clear up a few of these:

Misconception No. 1:   *Antidepressants work only for people who are depressed.*

Reality: The word "antidepressant" is really a misnomer; these medications work for many different types of symptoms, whether or not you are depressed. For example, in studies of people with the eating disorder bulimia nervosa, antidepressants have been found to work equally well to treat bulimic symptoms regardless of whether the person is depressed. Similarly, in studies of people with various types of obsessive-compulsive symptoms, including body dysmorphic disorder, antidepressants counteract the obsessions and compulsions whether or not the person is depressed. However, if a person is depressed, the antidepressant is also likely to be effective for the depressive symptoms.

Misconception Number 2:   *Antidepressants just create a false sense of happiness.*

Reality: Antidepressants have little effect unless you have a psychiatric condition to start with. If you're already happy, antidepressants won't make you artificially happier. Admittedly, there has been some legitimate scientific debate about this question recently, but there is little hard evidence that antidepressants benefit people who don't have any psychiatric illness. In other words, giving antidepressants to an asymptomatic individual is like giving penicillin to someone with no signs of infection: it probably won't do any harm, but it won't do much good either.

In fact, recent data show that when antidepressants are successful for a person with a psychiatric disorder, such as depression or obsessive-compulsive disorder, the function of the brain actually becomes more normal, not abnormal. These findings suggest that the antidepressants work by correcting a "chemical imbalance" in the brain that causes people to get depressed or to obsess in the first place. In other words, antidepressants do not create a "false" happiness at all; they simply restore the brain to a healthy balance.

Misconception No. 3:   *Antidepressants are habit-forming; once you get on them, you can't ever get off them.*

Reality: Although you may have some mild withdrawal effects if you stop certain antidepressants abruptly, they're not addictive. As a result, you can try an antidepressant, and then if you don't like it, you can simply taper and stop it—in consultation with your doctor, of course. It's important to remember this fact; people are sometimes very apprehensive about trying an antidepressant, because they seem to feel as if they were committing themselves to an irreversible decision, like having surgery. But in fact, you're not locked into any commitment by trying an antidepressant; you can change your mind, stop the medication, and go back to where you started.

Misconception No. 4:   *Antidepressants simply drug you into a state of not caring about your symptoms anymore.*

Reality: Most antidepressants, especially the modern ones, don't make you feel "doped up." Many people hardly notice side effects, or have none at all, and it's very rare that people on antidepressants say that they feel "drugged" or "like a zombie" in the way that patients used to complain about old-time heavy-duty antipsychotic drugs like Thorazine or Haldol. Furthermore, if for some reason you do feel unpleasantly sedated, or get some other undesirable side effect from an antidepressant, you can simply tell your doctor that you want to stop taking it and perhaps consider an alternative medication. After all, you haven't signed a contract to stay on the medicine.

If you're a man with serious body image problems, make sure that you understand these four points; you'll feel a lot more comfortable about exploring the possibility of medication. It's a tragedy, as illustrated in Sam's case above, to see people who've gone for years without antidepressant treatment—often because they labored under one of the misconceptions above—when such medications could have transformed their lives.

RX FOR ORDINARY BODY IMAGE CONCERNS:
A NEW VISION FOR MEN

Over the last several pages, we've talked primarily about psychiatric treatment for serious body image disorders—muscle dysmorphia, major eating disorders, and body dysmorphic disorder. But what about the milder and much more common forms of the Adonis Complex described in so many of the stories throughout this book? What about the millions of men who don't need to see a therapist or take medication, but who still are haunted by doubts about some aspect of their appearance or are spending too much time exercising, dieting, or grooming? What can we offer to these men and to those who love them?

In answer to this question, we feel that men need to acknowledge and confront the pervasive and powerful forces that have kindled the Adonis Complex in today's society. We need to see a fundamental cultural change in the way that men think about their bodies. If we could speak to all men today, to summarize everything we've learned from our research in the last fifteen years, we'd try to communicate five basic points:

1. Don't Buy Into the Media Images Around You

As we've emphasized throughout these pages, if you're a boy or man in any contemporary Western society, you've been bombarded throughout your lifetime with thousands of media messages constantly telling you that the ideal male body is handsome, spectacularly lean, and muscular. These messages have become so ubiquitous that you probably don't even think about them anymore. They've become so much a part of daily life that they go almost unnoticed.

To appreciate just how much these images have infiltrated our consciousness, you have to go back, as we did in Chapter 2, to the 1950s or '60s, and compare the images of that time with the images of today. In those days, even the most masculine of men had perfectly ordinary bodies. Stars of the screen like Gregory Peck, Humphrey Bogart, and Clark Gable didn't have to go to the gym every day to be appealing to their many admirers. The Vietnam-era G.I. Joe, the heroes of old-time boys' comic strips, the men in magazine advertisements and television shows of the fifties and sixties—almost all were ordinary-looking guys. But nowadays, boys and men are fed an ideal of masculinity that is virtually unattainable. Modern action toy figures sport huge shoulders and biceps; muscle-bound characters in boys' computer games, like Duke Nukem, take steroids to power themselves up for a shooting spree. Male heroes from comic strips to magazines, from television to movie screens, display sharply defined chests and chiseled abdominal muscles. The vast majority of boys and men can't hope to look like the images they see. As a matter of fact, 89 percent of the men in one survey responded that they wanted models in magazines to look more like normal men; this statistic hints at the discomfort that these images have created.

As we've noted earlier, men now seem to be getting a dose of the same medicine that women have had to swallow for decades—seeing pictures of impossibly beautiful bodies, portrayed as if this were the standard to which everybody should aspire. In recent years, commentators have called women's attention to this phenomenon, and, as a result, women have begun to learn, slowly, that they *don't* have to buy in to the media images that they see, and that it's okay for them to look ordinary rather than to pursue a forever unattainable ideal.

So our first message to men is take a lesson from what many women have so painfully learned. Don't fall for the media images.

2. Remember That Many of the Supermuscular Male Bodies You're Seeing Are Just Products of Drugs

Although both men and women are besieged with images of unattainably beautiful bodies, there's an extra twist for men—namely that anabolic steroids can make men far bigger than they could naturally be. Of course, female models can also use various drugs and cosmetic techniques to look better. But women really have no equivalent of anabolic steroids—a chemical that can blast them far beyond the outer limits of what Mother Nature intended.

What makes matters worse is that many boys and men, looking at the spectacular bodies of these supposed role models, still don't realize that many of these bodies got to look that way through chemicals. As we've pointed out many times in this book, steroids have remained a well-kept secret among those who have used them over the last few decades. The public still fails to recognize that a surprising number of the sports stars, advertising models, and actors that they see are simply using black market drugs.

As we stated earlier in this book, we think the only real answer to this problem is to make the public aware of what's going on. If everyone knew that these men had taken steroids, much of their glamour would fade. That's why we've taken pains in the text and pictures of this book to emphasize that research shows a fairly sharp upper limit to muscularity that can be attained without using drugs. We believe that most men who get bigger than that limit, and claim they did it "naturally," are lying. So don't fall for the steroid hoax. Unless you want to be a drug user, you're not going to look like these men, and you don't have to.

3. Remember That a Vast Industry Profits from Making You Feel Insecure About Your Body

As we've repeatedly pointed out, billions of dollars are made annually by manufacturers of all sorts of products that are supposed to improve the appearance of the male body. These range from food supplements billed to make you more muscular or more lean, to hair replacements, penis-enlargement procedures, or full-scale surgical overhauls. We're not saying that all of these techniques are ineffective or valueless, or that the purveyors of these techniques are all evil barons driven by the profit motive—although in some cases, unfortunately, that's true. Even though these techniques can sometimes be helpful for men, the fact remains that body image industries make money off of your bodily insecurities, and they're not going to make a profit by telling you that you look fine already.

Again, the parallel to women is obvious. For decades, even centuries, beauty industries of every description have preyed upon the insecurities of women, tempting them to buy often valueless products and procedures in an endless quest for a more beautiful body. But only in recent decades have the same industries begun to scout out the other 50 percent of the market—men who could be convinced to spend money for a supposedly more handsome appearance. Huge chains of stores now hawk proteins and herbal supplements, and even, as we've seen, potent drugs and hormones. Most of this business didn't even exist twenty or thirty years ago. Surgical techniques, hair-growth and hair-replacement methods, and other cosmetic methods for men have also blossomed from a few small enterprises twenty years ago to big business today.

So, when you see advertisements for any of these products or services, consider how much money they're making off your insecurities. Sometimes advertisements for such products—especially those promoted to add muscle or burn fat—will feature a male model who has almost certainly used steroids. Don't be foolish enough to think that the product will make you look like him.

4. Masculinity Isn't Defined Just by the Way You Look

We're not sure why so many of today's men have forgotten this simple fact. Perhaps, as we've speculated in Chapter 2, the rise of feminism has caused men to focus increasingly on their bodies as the defining feature of masculinity. We've also presented research findings, using our computerized Body Image Test, showing that boys and men in Western societies believe that women want them to be far more muscular than they actually are. But as these studies also showed, most women don't actually want a supermuscular male body; instead, most women choose a fairly ordinary-looking male body. So if you're a heterosexual man, relax. You don't have to look like a bodybuilder to appeal to the opposite sex. If you're a gay man, then admittedly the situation is a little different, because a muscular body may be more appealing to other gay men around you. But regardless of your sexual orientation, you shouldn't fall prey to the illusion that your masculinity is measured by your appearance. Muscularity is not masculinity.

In today's world, this illusion has become more and more pervasive. With our ability to place an image in front of the eyes of a billion people at a time, the superficial appearance of the face and the body have grown increasingly commercialized. The "appearance byte," like its cousin the "sound byte," has become valuable and negotiable currency throughout the world media. But real masculinity, and real femininity, are not measured in bytes, and feelings of self-worth and confidence in one's gender identity are not built on appearance alone.

5. It's Okay to Look Okay

The essence of all these points is that the boys and men of today need to learn what their grandfathers knew all along—that it's okay to look ordinary. Naturally, it's good to be healthy and fit, and it's fine to try to look your best. But it's time for men to liberate themselves from the artificial and unattainable standards that Western society and the media have imposed upon them in the last twenty or thirty years. It's time for men to stop getting taken in by the pervasive messages that there's something inadequate about how they look. Only with such awareness will today's men cast off the Adonis Complex, with all of the unhappiness it has bred, and regain the comfortable acceptance of their bodies that earlier generations took for granted.

The Fat-Free Mass Index (FFMI) and How to Calculate It

The formula for fat-free mass index in a male is:

$$FFMI = \frac{LBM}{H^2} + 6.1 \times (1.8 - H)$$

where LBM is lean body mass in kilograms and H is height in meters. Lean body mass is your total body weight minus the percentage of your body weight that is fat. Body fat can be estimated by various methods, such as measuring the thickness of body skin folds with calipers, weighing an individual under water, or various electrical impedance measuring techniques. To get a rough estimate of the appearance of the various levels of body fat, see the drawings of male bodies with different levels of fat shown in the self-test on pages 68–70. To see how the calculation of FFMI works, here are three examples:

Example 1: Suppose that you're a man who is 5 feet 10 inches tall, weighs 173 pounds, and has 20 percent body fat. To convert your height into meters, multiply your height in inches by 0.0254, which makes you 1.78 meters tall. To convert your weight into kilograms, divide your weight in pounds by 2.2, which gives you a body weight of 78.6 kilograms. However, since 20 percent of your body mass is from fat, then your lean body mass is 80 percent of 78.6 kilograms, or 62.9 kilograms. Therefore, your fat-free mass index is

$$\frac{62.9}{(1.78)^2} + 6.1 \times (1.8 - 1.78) = 20.0$$

On the basis of our studies to date, this figure of 20.0 would make you just about average for a thirty-year-old American man.

Example 2: Suppose that you're a man who does a lot of weightlifting and is very muscular. This time we'll assume that you are only 67 inches tall, weigh 154 pounds, and have only 4.5 percent body fat. In that case, your height comes out to 1.70 meters, your body weight is 70.0 kilograms, and your lean body weight is 95.5 percent of that weight, or 66.9 kilograms. Your fat-free mass index is:

$$\frac{66.9}{(1.70)^2} + 6.1 \times (1.8 - 1.70) = 23.7$$

This man is close to the upper limit of muscularity that we believe can be attained without the use of anabolic steroids or other drugs. Even with maximal weightlifting, we would predict that he will be able to add at most about 8 to 10 pounds more muscle without chemicals (unless he gets considerably fatter). The measurements used in this example are taken from an actual man: he is the non-drug-using bodybuilder in the first set of photographs in Chapter 2.

Example 3: Suppose that another man is 67 inches tall, has 7 percent body fat, but weighs 213 pounds. His FFMI would be:

$$\frac{90.0}{(1.70)^2} + 6.1 \times (1.8 - 1.70) = 31.7$$

These are the measurements of the steroid-using bodybuilder in the first set of photographs in Chapter 2. An FFMI in this range (with this degree of body fat), in our opinion, would be impossible to attain without using anabolic steroids.

For a full presentation of the FFMI formula and how we developed it, see: E. M. Kouri et al., "Fat-Free Mass Index in Users and Nonusers of Anabolic-Androgenic Steroids," *Clinical Journal of Sports Medicine* 5 (1995):223–28.

Diagnostic Criteria for Body Image Disorders

Mental health professionals generally use so-called operational diagnostic criteria to diagnose major psychiatric disorders. The most widely used operational diagnostic criteria are those published in the American Psychiatric Association's *Diagnostic and Statistical Manual of Mental Disorders, 4th Edition* (Washington, D.C.: American Psychiatric Association, 1994). This manual is generally known as DSM-IV.

These criteria, as shown below, provide concrete guidelines for making a particular diagnosis. Thus, professionals using these criteria can be sure that they agree among themselves when they speak of a particular disorder. This is known in science as "a high level of inter-rater reliability." In other words, when a professional in New York diagnoses a patient as having, say, "body dysmorphic disorder" using the operational diagnostic criteria shown below, he or she can be reasonably sure that a professional from San Francisco, if presented with the same patient, would make the same diagnosis. Scientists publishing research studies, including ourselves, routinely use the operational diagnostic criteria of DSM-IV to maximize diagnostic reliability among themselves and other scientists.

Presented below are operational diagnostic criteria for five of the major body image disorders discussed in this book: muscle dysmorphia, anorexia nervosa, bulimia nervosa, binge-eating disorder, and body dysmorphic disorder. The criteria for the last four of these disorders are taken directly from DSM-IV. However, muscle dysmorphia is not included as a specific diagnosis in DSM-IV, and therefore we ourselves have drafted and published operational diagnostic criteria for this particular condition, using the same style as DSM-IV. In each case, to meet the full criteria for a given diagnosis, an individual must have all of the attributes indicated by letters of the alphabet in the list of criteria. For example, for a diagnosis of anorexia nervosa, an individual must display all of the three attributes in the list from "A" to "C."

Remember that the criteria below are used by mental health professionals to make formal diagnoses in clinical and research settings. If you have body image problems, but do not meet the full diagnostic criteria for one of the disorders below, you may still be suffering and still benefit from treatment.

Diagnostic Criteria for Muscle Dysmorphia

A. Preoccupation with the idea that one's body is not sufficiently lean and muscular. Characteristic associated behaviors include long hours of lifting weights and excessive attention to diet.

B. The preoccupation is manifested by at least two of the following four criteria:

1. The individual frequently gives up important social, occupational, or recreational activities because of a compulsive need to maintain his or her workout and diet schedule.

2. The individual avoids situations where his or her body is exposed to others, or endures such situations only with marked distress or intense anxiety.

3. The preoccupation about the inadequacy of body size or musculature causes clinically significant distress or impairment in social, occupational, or other important areas of functioning.

4. The individual continues to work out, diet, or use ergogenic (performance-enhancing) substances despite knowledge of adverse physical or psychological consequences.

C. The primary focus of the preoccupation and behaviors is on being too small or inadequately muscular, as distinguished from fear of being fat as in anorexia nervosa, or a primary preoccupation only with other aspects of appearance as in other forms of body dysmorphic disorder.

Diagnostic Criteria for Anorexia Nervosa

A. Refusal to maintain body weight at or above a minimally normal weight for age and height (e.g., weight loss leading to maintenance of body weight less than 85% of that expected; or failure to make expected weight gain during period of growth, leading to body weight less than 85% of that expected).

B. Intense fear of gaining weight or becoming fat, even though underweight.

C. Disturbance in the way in which one's body weight or shape is experienced, undue influence of body weight or shape on self-evaluation, or denial of the seriousness of the current low body weight.

(For women, DSM-IV also has a requirement of amenorrhea, namely the absence of menstrual cycles. This criterion of course does not apply to men.)

Diagnostic Criteria for Bulimia Nervosa

A. Recurrent episodes of binge eating. An episode of binge eating is characterized by both of the following:

1. eating, in a discrete period of time (e.g., within any 2-hour period), an amount of food that is definitely larger than most people would eat during a similar period of time and under similar circumstances

2. a sense of lack of control over eating during the episode (e.g., a feeling that one cannot stop eating or control what or how much one is eating)

B. Recurrent inappropriate compensatory behavior in order to prevent weight gain, such as self-induced vomiting; misuse of laxatives, diuretics, enemas, or other medications; fasting; or excessive exercise.

C. The binge eating and inappropriate compensatory behaviors both occur, on average, at least twice a week for 3 months.

D. Self-evaluation is unduly influenced by body shape and weight.

E. The disturbance does not occur exclusively during episodes of Anorexia Nervosa.

Diagnostic Criteria for Binge-Eating Disorder

A. Recurrent episodes of binge eating. An episode of binge eating is characterized by both of the following:

1. eating, in a discrete period of time (e.g., within any 2-hour period), an amount of food that is definitely larger than most people would eat in a similar period of time under similar circumstances

2. a sense of lack of control over eating during the episode (e.g., a feeling that one cannot stop eating or control what or how much one is eating)

B. The binge-eating episodes are associated with three (or more) of the following:

   1. eating much more rapidly than normal

   2. eating until feeling uncomfortably full

   3. eating large amounts of food when not feeling physically hungry

   4. eating alone because of being embarrassed by how much one is eating

   5. feeling disgusted with oneself, depressed, or very guilty after overeating

C. Marked distress regarding binge eating is present.

D. The binge eating occurs, on average, at least 2 days a week for 6 months.

E. The binge eating is not associated with the regular use of inappropriate compensatory behaviors (e.g., purging, fasting, excessive exercise) and does not occur exclusively during the course of Anorexia Nervosa or Bulimia Nervosa.

Diagnostic Criteria for Body Dysmorphic Disorder

A. Preoccupation with an imagined defect in appearance. If a slight physical anomaly is present, the person's concern is markedly excessive.

B. The preoccupation causes clinically significant distress or impairment in social, occupational, or other important areas of functioning.

C. The preoccupation is not better accounted for by another mental disorder (e.g., dissatisfaction with body shape and size in Anorexia Nervosa).

Where to Get Help

National Organizations

If you or someone you know has a serious body image disorder (especially body dysmorphic disorder or an eating disorder), several national organizations may be helpful in providing referrals to treatment professionals in your area:

1. The Body Image Program at Butler Hospital/Brown University in Providence, Rhode Island, provides information on body dysmorphic disorder and its treatment, including free study treatment that we are providing for male and female adults and/or adolescents in the Providence–Boston area, the New York City area, and the Cincinnati area. You can call us at 401-455-6466, e-mail us at Katharine_Phillips@brown.edu, or write to Dr. Phillips at the Body Image Program, Butler Hospital, 345 Blackstone Boulevard, Providence, RI 02906. To get information on free study treatment for male and female adolescents with body dysmorphic disorder in the New York City area, you can directly contact Dr. Eric Hollander (212-241-3623); in the Cincinnati area, you can contact Dr. Brian McConville (513-558-5512).

2. The Obsessive Compulsive Foundation, Inc., P.O. Box 9573, New Haven, CT 06535 (tel: 203-315-2190; fax 203-315-2196), can provide treatment referrals for both medication and cognitive-behavioral therapy for body dysmorphic disorder.

3. If you are interested in trying cognitive-behavioral therapy for a body image disorder, you may be able to get a referral from the Association for Advancement of Behavior Therapy, 305 Seventh Avenue, New York, NY 10001 (tel: 212-647-1890; fax: 212-647-1865).

4. If you have symptoms of anorexia nervosa, bulimia nervosa, or binge-eating disorder, you may be able to obtain referrals from the National Association of Anorexia Nervosa and Associated Disorders (ANAD), P.O. Box 7, Highland Park, IL 60035 (tel: 847-831-3438; fax: 847-433-4632).

5. The Center for Education on Anabolic Steroid Effects (CEASE), P.O. Box 720280, Atlanta, GA 30358 (tel: 770-393-1665 or 1-877-STEROID), can provide information on steroid dependence and the psychiatric effects of steroids.

Web Pages

There are many Web sites on the Internet that you may find helpful if you have body obsessions. In particular, try the following addresses:

1. http://www.adoniscomplex.com. On this Web site, we provide up-to-the-minute information about scientific findings on body image, studies of body image disorders in progress, and referral organizations.

2. http://www.butler.org/bdd.html. This Web site of the Butler Hospital Body Image Program (see no. 1 above) provides information on body dysmorphic disorder and its treatment, including free treatment that we're providing in the Providence, Rhode Island, area for adults and adolescents. If you live in the Northeast, you can call us at 401-455-6466 or write to us at the Body Image Program, Butler Hospital, 345 Blackstone Boulevard, Providence, RI 02906.

3. http://www.steroidsinfo.com. This Web site, maintained by our laboratory in collaboration with CEASE (see above) provides information about anabolic steroids, including especially their psychiatric effects, together with links to many other steroid-associated sites.

4. http://eatingdisorders.mentalhelp.net. This site provides links to online resources and information about eating disorders and treatment.

5. http://www.headdocs.com. Provides information on body image.

Books

The Broken Mirror: Understanding and Treating Body Dysmorphic Disorder, by Katharine A. Phillips, M.D., published by Oxford University Press in 1996, is written for both the public and professionals. It is the most comprehensive source on body dysmorphic disorder.

Notes

Chapter I   Secrets of the Men at the Olympic Gym

PAGE

3   *All of these displays convey:* A substantial scientific literature has shown that comparing oneself to images like these tends to increase body dissatisfaction and decrease self-esteem. J. K. Thompson et al., *Exacting Beauty: Theory, Assessment, and Treatment of Body Image Disturbance* (Washington, D.C.: American Psychological Association, 1999).

6   *In Greek mythology, Adonis:* There are many versions of the Adonis myth. See, for example, online, http://has.brown.edu/~maicar/adonis.html. We should note that we aren't the first authors to use the term the Adonis Complex. Anthropologist David Gilmore also uses this term in his article "The Beauty and the Beast: Male Body Imagery in Anthropological Perspective," in M. G. Winkler and L. B. Cole, eds., *The Good Body* (New Haven: Yale University Press, 1994). Mr. Gilmore doesn't define the Adonis Complex but implies that it refers to a cultural preoccupation with male beauty. Our definition of the term includes this notion, but also embraces a broader range of male body image concerns, including body dissatisfaction and body image disorders.

10   *We call it "muscle dysmorphia":* H. G. Pope, Jr., et al., "Muscle Dysmorphia: An Underrecognized Form of Body Dysmorphic Disorder," *Psychosomatics* 38 (1997):548–557.

11   *A recent study of ours illustrates:* R. Olivardia, H. G. Pope, Jr., and J. I. Hudson, "Muscle Dysmorphia in Male Weightlifters: A Case-Control Study," *American Journal of Psychiatry,* in press.

11   *First, there's almost certainly a genetic:* See K. A. Phillips et al., "Body Dysmorphic Disorder: An Obsessive-Compulsive Spectrum Disorder, a Form of Affective Spectrum Disorder, or Both?" *Journal of Clinical Psychiatry* 56 (suppl. 4) (1995): 41–51; Pope et al., "Muscle Dysmorphia," and Olivardia et al., "'Muscle Dysmorphia' in Male Weightlifters."

12   *such as being teased:* Thompson et al., *Exacting Beauty.*

12   *For example, a 1997 study:* D. M. Garner, "Body Image Survey," *Psychology Today* 30 (January-February 1997): 1, 30–84. This body image survey, published by *Psychology Today* in 1997, reported results of a questionnaire survey developed by experts in body image.

12   *figures unmatched by any previous television series:* See online, for example, http://www.geocities.com/Hollywood/Screen/9442/index.html.

18   *a ratio of about 40 percent male:* See R. L. Spitzer et al., "Binge Eating Disor-
      der: A Multisite Field Trial of the Diagnostic Criteria," *International Journal
      of Eating Disorders* 11 (1992): 191–203.

21   *almost all of his savings:* On the size of the underground steroid economy, see
      E. Kouri, H. G. Pope, Jr., and D. Katz, "Use of Anabolic-Androgenic Steroids:
      We are Talking Prevalence Rates," *Journal of the American Medical Associa-
      tion* 271 (1994): 347.

21   *steroids decrease the proportion of "good" cholesterol:* See discussion in E. M.
      Kouri, H. G. Pope, Jr., and P. S. Oliva, "Changes in Lipoprotein-Lipid Levels
      in Normal Men Following Administration of Increasing Doses of Testosterone
      Cypionate," *Clinical Journal of Sports Medicine,* 6 (1996): 152–157.

Chapter 2   The Rise of the Adonis Complex: Roots of Male Body Obsession

27   *a landmark national survey:* Garner, "Body Image Survey." In this survey, the
      first 4,000 responses (3,452 women and 548 men) were analyzed. How repre-
      sentative the men in this study are of men in the general population is unclear,
      and it is unknown to what extent the reported numbers would apply to all
      men. Nonetheless, the findings suggest that body image dissatisfaction in men
      is rapidly rising and approaching rates in women.

27   *These numbers have risen sharply from those in earlier surveys:* T. F. Cash,
      B. A. Winstead, and L. H. Janda, "The Great American Shape-up: Body Image
      Survey Report," *Psychology Today* 20 (1986): 30–37. E. Berscheid, E. Wal-
      ster, and G. Bohrnstedt, "The Happy American Body: A Survey Report," *Psy-
      chology Today* 7 (1973):119–131.

29   *In a study of undergraduate students:* M. McCaulay, L. Mintz, and A. A.
      Glenn, "Body Image, Self-esteem, and Depression-Proneness: Closing the
      Gender Gap," *Sex Roles* 18 (1988): 381–390.

29   *in a nationwide survey published in 1986:* Cash et al., "The Great American
      Shape-up."

29   *In fact, one study found that men:* S. H. Murray, S. W. Touyz, and P. J. V.
      Beaumont, "The Influence of Personal Relationships on Women's Eating and
      Body Satisfaction," *Eating Disorders: The Journal of Treatment and Preven-
      tion* 3 (1995): 243–252.

29   *And a recent poll found that:* "Lifeline," *USA Today,* October 26, 1999.

29   *body image experts Marc Mishkind:* M. E. Mishkind et al., "Embodiment of
      Masculinity," *American Behavioral Scientist* 29 (1986): 545–562.

29   *Men consistently express the greatest:* Ibid.; E. Berscheid et al., "The Happy
      American Body"; T. M. Muller, J. G. Coffman, and R. A. Linke, "Survey on
      Body Image, Weight, and Diet of College Students," *Journal of the American
      Dietetic Association* 77 (1980): 561–566.

29   *Older men are particularly dissatisfied:* S.L. Franzoi, V. Koehler, "Age and
      Gender Differences in Body Attitudes: A Comparison of Young and Elderly
      Adults," *International Journal of Aging and Human Development* 47 (1998):
      1–10.

30 *Recent studies have also found:* L. R. Silberstein et al., "Behavioral and Psychological Implications of Body Dissatisfaction: Do Men and Women Differ?" *Sex Roles* 19 (1988): 219–232; A. Drewnowski, D. K. Yee, "Men and Body Image: Are Males Satisfied with Their Body Weight?" *Psychosomatic Medicine* 49 (1987): 626–634; C. Davis and M. Cowles, "Body Image and Exercise: A Study of Relationships and Comparisons Between Physically Active Men and Women," *Sex Roles* 25 (1991): 33–44.

30 *This same preference is also expressed:* R. M. Lerner and E. Gellert, "Body Build Identifications, Preference, and Aversion in Children," *Developmental Psychopathology* 1 (1969): 456–462.

30 *Several studies found that men:* L. A. Tucker, "Relationship Between Perceived Somatotype and Body Cathexis of College Males," *Perceptual and Motor Skills* 54 (1982): 1055–1061; J. K. Thompson and S. Tantleff, "Female and Male Ratings of Upper Torso: Actual, Ideal, and Stereotypical Conceptions," *Journal of Social Behavior and Personality* 7 (1992): 345–354.

30 *many men are just as unhappy:* H. M. Mable, W. D. G. Balance, and R. J. Galgan, "Body Image Distortion and Dissatisfaction in University Students," *Perceptual and Motor Skills* 63 (1986): 907–911; Silberstein et al., "Behavioral and Psychological Implications of Body Dissatisfaction; G. M. Dummer et al., "Pathogenic Weight Control Behaviors of Young Competitive Swimmers," *Physician and Sportsmedicine* 15 (1987): 75–84; Davis and Cowles, "Body Image and Exercise; T. F. Cash, and T. A. Brown, "Gender and Body Images: Stereotypes and Realities, *Sex Roles* 21 (1989): 361–373; Mishkind et al., "Embodiment of Masculinity"; Berscheid et al., "The Happy American Body"; T. M. Miller, J. G. Coffman, and R. A. Linke, "Survey on Body Image, Weight, and Diet of College Students," *Journal of the American Dietetic Association* 77 (1980): 561–566. S. C. Abell and M. H. Richards, "The Relationship Between Body Shape Satisfaction and Self-esteem: An Investigation of Gender and Class Differences," *Journal of Youth and Adolescence* 25 (1996): 691–703.

30 *they may also have a* distorted *body image:* McCaulay et al., "Body Image, Self-esteem, and Depression-Proneness."

30 *obsession breeds discontent:* Mishkind et al., "Embodiment of Masculinity"; K. D. Brownell and J. Rodin, "The Prevalence of Eating Disorders in Athletes," in K. D. Brownell, J. Rodin, and J. H. Wilmore, eds., *Eating, Body Weight, and Performance in Athletes: Disorders of Modern Society* (Philadelphia: Lea & Febiger, 1992).

30 *they tend to have lower self-esteem:* L. B. Mintz and N. E. Betz, "Sex Differences in the Nature, Realism, and Correlates of Body Image," *Sex Roles* 15 (1986): 185–195; R. M. Lerner, S. A. Karabenick, and J. L. Stuart, "Relations Among Physical Attractiveness, Body Attitudes, and Self-Concept in Male and Female College Students," *Journal of Psychology* 85 (1973): 119–129.

30 *some recent studies have indicated:* McCaulay et al., "Body Image, Self-esteem, and Depression-Proneness"; Silberstein et al., "Behavioral and Psychological Implications of Body Dissatisfaction"; S. L. Franzoi and S. A.

Shields, "The Body Esteem Scale: A Convergent and Discriminant Validity Study," *Journal of Personality Assessment* 50 (1986): 24–31.

30 *in McCaulay's survey of college undergraduate men:* McCaulay et al., "Body Image, Self-esteem, and Depression-Proneness."

31 *In the last year alone:* Pope et al., "Muscle Dysmorphia."

31 *The paid circulation of* Men's Health: M. Cottle, "Turning Boys into Girls," *Washington Monthly,* May 1998, 32–36.

31 *several billion dollars that men are now spending:* See C. Kalb, "Our Quest to Be Perfect," *Newsweek,* August 9, 1999, 52–59; A. Farnham, "You're So Vain," *Fortune,* September 9, 1966, 66–82. Also see online, http://www.plasticsurgery.org, and especially, http://cosmeticsurgeryonline.com.

31 *Growing numbers of men:* B. Handy, "That Deadpan Look," *Time,* July 13, 1998, 72.

31 *and a growing number of men: Inside Edition,* August 8, 1999.

31 *men in the United States spent:* M. Cottle, "Turning Boys into Girls."

31 *And a 1996 survey in* Men's Health: Ibid.

32 *Another survey found:* Ibid.

32 *One company has even started:* Ibid.

32 *Many biological, psychological, and sociocultural:* Thompson et al., "Exacting Beauty."

32 *a French doctor named Charles-Édouard Brown-Séquard:* C.-E. Brown-Séquard. "Des effets produits chez l'homme par des injections souscutanées d'un liquide retiré des testicules frais de cobaye et de chien," *Comptes Rendus des Séances de la Societé de Biologie* (1889): 415–422, 429–431.

32 *By the 1930s, German scientists:* K. David et al., "Über Krystallinisches männliches Hormon Hoden (Testosteron), wirksamer als aus Harn oder aus Cholesterin Bereitetes Androsteron," *Zeitschrift für Physiologische Chemie* 233 (1935): 281–282; A. Wettstein, "Uber die künstliche Herstellung des Testikelhormons Testosteron," *Schweizerische Medizinische Wochenschrift* 16 (1935): 912.

32 *Hitler's troops were given steroids:* N. Wade, "Anabolic Steroids: Doctors Denounce Them, but Athletes Aren't Listening," *Science* 176 (1972): 1399.

33 *The drug clearly had antidepressant effects:* M. D. Altschule, and K. J. Tillotson: "The Use of Testosterone in the Treatment of Depressions," *New England Journal of Medicine* 239:1036–1038; H. G. Pope, Jr., and D. L. Katz, "Psychiatric Effects of Exogenous Anabolic-Androgenic Steroids," in O. M. Wolkowitz and A. J. Rothschild, eds., *Psychoneuroendocrinology for the Clinician* (Washington, D.C.: American Psychiatric Association Press), in press.

33 *It started with the Russians:* Wade, "Anabolic Steroids."

34 *forfeited his gold medal:* V. Alabiso, "Johnson Hints at Innocence, Looks Beyond Loss of Gold Medal," *Boston Globe,* September 28, 1988, *Sports,* p. 1.

34 *a 1988 study found that more:* W. A. Buckley et al., "Estimated Prevalence of Anabolic Steroid Use Among Male High School Seniors," *Journal of the American Medical Association* (hereafter *JAMA*) 260 (1988): 3441–3445.

35 *using a mathematical formula that we have published:* E. M. Kouri et al., "Fat-Free Mass Index in Users and Non-Users of Anabolic-Androgenic Steroids," *Clinical Journal of Sports Medicine* 5 (1995): 223–228.

36 *let's take a look at some pictures:* A similar picture appears in H. G. Pope, Jr., and K. J. Brower, "Psychiatric Effects of Anabolic-Androgenic Steroid Use," in H. I. Kaplan and B. J. Sadock, eds. *Comprehensive Textbook of Psychiatry,* 7th ed. (Baltimore: Williams & Wilkins), in press.

40 *studies of the popular girls' doll Barbie:* K. D. Brownell and M. A. Napolitano, "Distorting Reality for Children: Body Size Proportions of Barbie and Ken Dolls," *International Journal of Eating Disorders* 18 (1995):295–298; and K. I. Norton et al., "Ken and Barbie at Life Size," *Sex Roles* 34 (1996): 287–294.

40 *G.I. Joe is undoubtedly the most famous:* V. Santelmo, *The Complete Encyclopedia to G.I. Joe,* 2nd ed. (Iola, Wis: Krause Publications, 1997).

40 *sales surveys in* Playthings *magazine:* Playthings (New York: Geyer-McAllister Publications), 1983–1997.

41 *The pictures on the next pages:* H. G. Pope, Jr., et al., "Evolving Ideals of Male Body Image as Seen Through Action Toys," *International Journal of Eating Disorders* 26 (1999): 65–72.

44 *each year, the sales of male action toys:* "Action Figures Duke It Out," *Playthings* 93 (1995): 26–28.

44 *For example, professional wrestling:* L. Rosellini, "Lords of the Ring," *U.S. News & World Report,* May 17, 1999, 52–58.

44 *Vince McMahon, Jr., who owned the business:* Ibid.

44 *His biggest star, Hulk Hogan:* Associated Press, "Jury Acquits WWF Chief," *Winnipeg Free Press,* July 23, 1994.

45 *Now, professional wrestling is watched:* http://www.wwf.com/bios/mcmahon.html.

45 *One example is Sexual Chocolate:* http://www.wwf.com/bios/henry.html.

46 *a clever group of investigators in Canada:* D. M. Garner et al., "Cultural Expectations of Thinness in Women," *Psychological Reports* 47 (1980): 483–491. See also C. V. Wiseman et al., "Cultural Expectations of Thinness in Women: An Update," *International Journal of Eating Disorders* 11 (1992): 85–89.

47 *The results were just as we had predicted:* R. A. Leit, H. G. Pope, Jr., and J. J. Gray, "Cultural Expectations of Muscularity in Men: The Evolution of *Playgirl* Centerfolds," *International Journal of Eating Disorders,* in press. A similar finding has also appeared from another research group: B. A. Spitzer, K. A. Henderson, and M. T. Zivian, "Gender Differences in Population versus Media Body Sizes: A Comparison over Four Decades," *Sex Roles* 40 (1999): 545–565.

48 *in an excellent article, "The Beauty of the Beast":* D. D. Gilmore, "The Beauty of the Beast: Male Body Imagery in Anthropological Perspective," in Winkler and Cole, eds., *The Good Body.*

49 *are partly biologically:* N. Etcoff, *Survival of the Prettiest: The Science of Beauty* (Garden City, N.Y.: Doubleday & Co., 1999).

49 *to a certain extent to be innate:* J. H. Langlois, L. A. Roggman, and L. A. Rieser-Danner, "Infants' Differential Social Response to Attractive and Unattractive Faces," *Developmental Psychology* 26 (1990): 153–159.

49   *they seem to signify health:* Etcoff, *Survival of the Prettiest.*

49   *get the most mates:* R. Thornhill, "Female Preference of Males with Low Fluctuating Asymmetry in the Japanese Scorpionfly (*Panorpa japonica:* Mecoptera)," *Behaviorial Ecology* 3 (1992): 277–283.

50   *body size confers particular advantages:* F. B. Bercovitch and P. Nürnberg, "Genetic Determination of Paternity and Variation in Male Reproductive Success in Two Populations of Rhesus Macaques," *Electrophoresis* 18 (1997): 1701–1705.

50   *tending to be the most dominant:* Etcoff, *Survival of the Prettiest.*

50   *several authors have noted:* J. L. Dubbert, "Progressivism and the Masculinity Crisis," in E. Pleck and J. Pleck, eds., *The American Man* (Englewood Cliffs, N.J.: Prentice-Hall, 1980). J. Hantover, "The Boy Scouts and the Validation of Masculinity," in Pleck and Pleck, *The American Man*; A. J. Randall, S. F. Hall, and M. F. Rogers, "Masculinity on Stage: Competitive Male Bodybuilders," *Studies in Popular Culture* 14 (1992): 57–69.

50   *one commentator pointed out:* Hantover, "The Boy Scouts and the Validation of Masculinity."

50   *This period saw the rise:* Randall et al., "Masculinity on Stage."

51   *Macfadden is said:* B. Glassner, "Men and Muscles," in M. S. Kimmel and M. A. Messner, eds., *Men's Lives* (New York: Macmillan, 1989).

51   *As body image researchers Marc Mishkind:* Mishkind et al., "Embodiment of Masculinity."

51   *research has shown that well-proportioned muscular men:* E. Darden, "Masculinity and Femininity: Body Rankings by Males and Females," *Journal of Psychology* 80 (1972):205–212; L. B. Hendry and P. Gillies, "Body Type, Body Esteem, School, and Leisure: A Study of Overweight, Average, and Underweight Adolescents," *Journal of Youth and Adolescence* 7 (1978): 181–195; R. M. Ryckman et al., "Social Perceptions of Male and Female Extreme Mesomorphs," *Journal of Social Psychology* 132 (1992): 615–627; R. F. Guy, B. A. Rankin, and M. J. Norvell, "The Relation of Sex Role Stereotyping to Body Image," *Journal of Psychology* 105 (1980): 167–173.

51   *authors James Gillett and Philip White have suggested:* J. Gillett and P. G. White, "Male Bodybuilding and the Reassertion of Hegemonic Masculinity: A Critical Feminist Perspective," *Play & Culture* 5 (1992): 358–369.

51   *Aaron Randall and his colleagues, similarly, have written:* Randall et al., "Masculinity on Stage."

53   *As Barry Glassner writes:* Glassner, "Men and Muscles."

53   *Randall and his colleagues argue:* Randall et al., "Masculinity on Stage."

53   *Gillett and White, similarly:* Gillett and White, "Male Bodybuilding and the Reassertion of Hegemonic Masculinity."

53   *Sociologist Michael Kimmel:* M. Kimmel, *Manhood in America* (New York: Free Press, 1996).

53   *feminist author Susan Faludi has argued:* S. Faludi, *Stiffed* (New York: William Morrow & Co., 1999).

53   *Journalist Michelle Cottle:* Cottle, "Turning Boys into Girls."

53 *Alan Klein, an anthropologist, has documented:* A. Klein, *Little Big Men: Bodybuilding Subculture and Gender Construction* (Albany: State University of New York Press, 1993); A. M. Klein, "Of Muscles and Men," *The Sciences,* November-December, 1993.

54 *one of the most famous male strip shows, Chippendales:* See online, http://www.chippendales.com/menu/chippendales/body.html.

56 *Our predictions were confirmed:* H. G. Pope, Jr., et al., "The Growing Relative Value of the Male Body as Seen Through Advertisements in Women's Magazines," submitted for publication.

56 *In the first three pictures:* Antonio Sabato in Calvin Klein advertisement for underwear (*Entertainment Weekly,* June 28–July 5, 1996). Jockey shorts "firemen" (see http://www.richonthenet.com/cool_ads/underwear/jockey/JOCKEYFIRE. JPG). "Fake It" advertisement for tanning lotion (courtesy of the Body Shop, Burlingame, Calif.). Advertisement for Target Stores (*New York Times Magazine,* March 8, 1998). Advertisement for Samsung telephones (*New York Times Magazine,* July 25, 1999). Advertisement for Kahlúa liqueur (*Cosmopolitan,* November 1999).

56 *As journalist Michelle Cottle has noted:* Cottle, "Turning Boys into Girls."

60 *A recent article in the* New York Times: J. Sharkey, "Lose That Plumber Look and Bulk Up, Beautiful," *New York Times,* June 27, 1999.

60 *The origins of the Adonis Complex:* Thompson et al., *Exacting Beauty.*

60 *Research shows that sociocultural:* Ibid.

60 *suggest the same is true for men:* J. Ogden and K. Mundray, "The Effect of the Media on Body Satisfaction: The Role of Gender and Size," *European Eating Disorders Review* 4 (1996): 171–182; H. Lavine, D. Sweeney, and S. H. Wagner, "Depicting Woman as Sex Objects in Television Advertising: Effects on Body Dissatisfaction," *Personality and Social Psychology Bulletin* 25 (1999): 1049–1058.

60 *As one advertising executive stated:* A. Potter, "Mirror Image," *Boston Phoenix,* December 5, 1997.

Chapter 3   Do You Have the Adonis Complex? Two Tests and Their Astonishing Results

62 *But most of these previous studies:* L. D. Cohn and N. E. Adler, "Female and Male Perceptions of Ideal Body Shapes," *Psychology of Women Quarterly* 16 (1992):69–79; C. Davis et al., "Personality and Other Correlates of Dietary Restraint: An Age by Sex Comparison," *Personality and Individual Differences* 14 (1993): 297–305; L. Jacobi and T. F. Cash, "In Pursuit of the Perfect Appearance: Discrepancies Among Self-Ideal Percepts of Multiple Physical Attributes," *Journal of Applied Social Psychology* 24 (1994): 379–396. For a general review of this topic, see J. K. Thompson, "Assessing Body Image Disturbance: Measures, Methodology, and Implementation," in J. D. Thompson, ed., *Body Image, Eating Disorders, and Obesity: An Integrative Guide For Assessment and Treatment* (Washington, D.C.: American Psychiatric Association Press, 1996), 49–81.

63 *in collaboration with our colleague, Dr. Amanda Gruber:* For details on the development of the somatomorphic matrix, see A. J. Gruber et al., "The De-

velopment of the Somatomorphic Matrix: A Bi-axial Instrument for Measuring Body Image in Men and Women," in T. S. Olds, J. Dollman, and K. I. Norton, eds., *Kinanthropometry VI* (Sydney: International Society for the Advancement of Kinanthropometry, 1999).

67 *we took it down to a local gym for a trial run:* These findings are presented in Gruber et al., "The Development of the Somatomorphic Matrix."

72 *We were dead wrong on both predictions:* H. G. Pope, Jr., et al., "Body Image Perception Among Men in Three Countries," *American Journal of Psychiatry,* in press.

73 *Other researchers have also found:* S. Tantleff-Dunn and J. K. Thompson, "Romantic Partners and Body Image Disturbance: Further Evidence for the Role of Perceived-Actual Disparities," *Sex Roles* 33 (1995): 589–604; A. E. Fallon and P. Rozin, "Sex Differences in Perceptions of Desirable Body Shape," *Journal of Abnormal Psychology* 94 (1985): 102–105; L. Jacobi and T. Cash, "In Pursuit of the Perfect Appearance: Discrepancies Among Self-Ideal Percepts of Multiple Physical Attributes," *Journal of Applied Social Psychology* 24 (1994): 379–396.

73 *In earlier studies using figure drawings:* Fallon and Rozin, "Sex Differences in Perceptions of Desirable Body Shape"; D. B. Herzog, K. L. Newman, and M. Warshaw, "Body Image Dissatisfaction in Homosexual and Heterosexual Males," *Journal of Nervous and Mental Disease* 179 (1991): 356–359.

73 *In fact, men overestimate:* Tantleff-Dunn and Thompson, "Romantic Partners and Body Image Disturbance."

73 *94 percent of women ranked photographs of bodybuilders:* A. M. Klein, "Little Big Man: Hustling, Gender, Narcissism, and Bodybuilding Subculture," in M. A. Messner and D. F. Sabo, eds. *Sport, Men, and the Gender Order: Critical Feminist Perspectives* (Champaign, Ill.: Human Kinetics Books, 1990), p. 131.

73 *researchers Shawn Lynch and Debra Zellner:* S. M. Lynch and D. A. Zellner, "Figure Preferences in Two Generations of Men: The Use of Figure Drawings Illustrating Differences in Muscle Mass," *Sex Roles* 40 (1999): 833–843.

73 *Lynch and Zellner then tried their figure drawings:* Lynch and Zellner, "Figure Preferences in Two Generations of Men."

Chapter 4   Muscle Dysmorphia: Muscularity Run Amok

85 *we wrote a small scientific paper:* H. G. Pope, Jr., D. L. Katz, and J. I. Hudson, "Anorexia Nervosa and 'Reverse Anorexia' Among 108 Male Bodybuilders," *Comprehensive Psychiatry* 34 (1993): 406–409.

85 *The word "bigorexia" was even selected by Oxford Dictionaries:* M. Quinion, *World Wide Words.* Available online at http://www.quinion.demon.co.uk/words/articles/wordsof97.htm.

87 *We found 16 men:* H. G. Pope, Jr., and D. L. Katz, "Psychiatric and Medical Effects of Anabolic-Androgenic Steroids: A Controlled Study of 160 Athletes," *Archives of General Psychiatry* 51 (1994): 375–382.

87 *we decided to change its name once again:* Pope et al., "Muscle Dysmorphia."

87 *a more general condition:* K. A. Phillips, "Body Dysmorphic Disorder: The Distress of Imagined Ugliness," *American Journal of Psychiatry* 148 (1991): 1138–1149; and E. Hollander, L. J. Cohen, and D. Simeon, "Body Dysmorphic Disorder," *Psychiatric Annals* 23 (1993): 359–364.

89 *we've conducted a new "controlled" study:* R. Olivardia, H. G. Pope, Jr., and J. I. Hudson, " 'Muscle Dysmorphia' in Male Weightlifters: A Case-Control Study," *American Journal of Psychiatry,* in press.

97 *The 1997 Psychology Today survey:* Garner, "Body Image Survey."

97 *we think that it may be related to a condition:* See discussions in the following: S. L. McElroy, K. A. Phillips, and P. E. Keck, Jr., "Obsessive-Compulsive Spectrum Disorders," *Journal of Clinical Psychiatry* 55(S) (1994): 33–51; K. A. Phillips et al., "Body Dysmorphic Disorder: An Obsessive-Compulsive Spectrum Disorder, a Form of Affective Spectrum Disorder, or Both?" *Journal of Clinical Psychiatry* 56(S) (1995): 41–52. Also see E. Hollander, ed., *Obsessive Compulsive-Related Disorders* (Washington, D.C.: American Psychiatric Association Press, 1992).

100 *we often recommend cognitive behavioral therapy:* For reviews, see A. T. Beck, *Cognitive Therapy and the Emotional Disorders* (New York: Meridien, 1976); and L. W. Craighead et al., eds., *Cognitive and Behavioral Interventions: An Empirical Approach to Mental Health Problems* (New York: Allyn & Bacon, 1994).

Chapter 5   Anabolic Steroids: Dangerous Fuel for the Adonis Complex

102 *Duke Nukem, a muscle-bound warrior:* See, for example, *Duke Nukem: Total Meltdown.* Available from GT Interactive Software, 417 5th Avenue, New York, NY 10016. Descriptions of Duke's sources of steroids are available at many online sites, such as http://www.gamunday.demon.co.uk/cheat/duke3d.html.

102 *at least 5 million boys have guided Duke:* For estimates of the numbers of Duke Nukem players, see, for example, online, http://www.3dportal.com/features/articles/ascent.

103 *is the most powerful driving force:* E. M. Komoroski and V. I. Rickert, "Adolescent Body Image and Attitudes to Anabolic Steroid Use," *American Journal of Diseases of Children* 146 (1992): 823–828.

103 *researchers Arthur Blouin and Gary Goldfield:* A. G. Blouin and G. S. Goldfield, "Body Image and Steroid Use in Male Bodybuilders," *International Journal of Eating Disorders* 18 (1995): 159–165.

103 *Kirk Brower, another steroid expert:* K. J. Brower et al., "Symptoms and Correlates of Anabolic-Androgenic Steroid Dependence," *British Journal of Addictions* 86 (1991): 759–768. K. J. Brower, F. C. Blow, and E. M. Hill, "Risk Factors for Anabolic-Androgenic Steroid Use in Men," *Journal of Psychiatric Research* 28 (1994): 369–380.

103 *a study in the prestigious* Journal: Buckley et al., "Estimated Prevalence of Anabolic Steroid Use Among Male High School Seniors."

104 *In 1993, in the equally prestigious:* R. H. Durant et al., "Use of Multiple Drugs Among Adolescents Who Use Anabolic Steroids," *New England Journal of Medicine* 328 (1993): 922–926. For other studies on the prevalence of steroid use, see: M. D. Johnson, "Anabolic Steroid Use in Adolescent Males," *Pediatrics* 83 (1989): 921–924; J. Ross et al., *1988–89 Survey of Substance Abuse Among Maryland Adolescents* (Baltimore: Maryland Department of Health and Mental Hygiene, Alcohol and Drug Abuse Administration; 1989); R. Terney, and L. McLain, "The Use of Anabolic Steroids in High School Students," *American Journal of Diseases of Children* 144 (1990): 99–103. C. E. Yesalis et al., "Anabolic-Androgenic Steroid Use in the United States," *JAMA* 270 (1993): 1217–1221; J. Radokovich, P. Broderick, and G. Pickell, "Rates of Anabolic-Androgenic Steroid Abuse Among Students in Junior High School," *Journal of the American Board of Family Practice* 6 (1993): 341–345; C. E. Yesalis et al., "Trends in Anabolic-Androgenic Steroid Use Among Adolescents," *Archives of Pediatrics and Adolescent Medicine* 151 (1997): 1197–1206. Another recent study is A. D. Faigenbaum et al., "Anabolic Steroid Use by Male and Female Middle School Students," *Pediatrics* 101 (1998), available on the Internet at http://www.pediatrics.org/cgi/content/full/101/5/e6. The authors reported that nearly 3 percent of boys in the fifth through seventh grades had used steroids.

105 *Taken in large doses:* See, for example, G. B. Forbes, "The Effect of Anabolic Steroids on Lean Body Mass: The Dose Response Curve," *Metabolism* 34 (1985): 571–573; H. G. Pope, Jr., and D. L. Katz, "Affective and Psychotic Symptoms Associated with Anabolic Steroid Use," *American Journal of Psychiatry* 145 (1988): 487–490; G. B. Forbes et al., "Sequence of Changes in Body Composition Induced by Testosterone and Reversal of Changes After Drug Is Stopped," *JAMA* 267 (1992): 397–399; Kouri et al., "Fat-Free Mass Index in Users and Non-Users of Anabolic-Androgenic Steroids; and H. G. Pope, Jr., and K. J. Brower, "Anabolic-Androgenic Steroid Abuse," in B. J. Sadock and V. A. Sadock, eds., *Comprehensive Textbook of Psychiatry,* 7th ed. (Philadelphia: Lippincott, Williams & Wilkins), (2000), 1085–1095.

106 *the 2000 edition:* Medical Economics Company, *Physicians' Desk Reference* (Montvale, N.J.: Medical Economics Company, 1999).

106 *the* New England Journal of Medicine *published:* S. Bhasin et al., "The Effect of Supraphysiologic Doses of Testosterone on Muscle Size and Strength in Normal Men," *New England Journal of Medicine* 335 (1996): 1–7.

107 *For example, there are more than a dozen studies:* For reviews, see H. A. Haupt and G. D. Rovere, "Anabolic Steroids: A Review of the Literature," *American Journal of Sports Medicine* 12 (1984): 469–484; J. A. Lombardo and R. T. Sickles, "Medical and Performance-Enhancing Effects of Anabolic Steroids," *Psychiatric Annals* 22 (1992): 19–23; and C. E. Yesalis, ed., *Anabolic Steroids in Sport and Exercise* (Champaign, Ill.: Human Kinetics, 1993).

109 *drug-testing laboratories can successfully detect steroids:* For reviews of testing procedures, see D. H. Catlin, "Analytical Chemistry at the Games of the XXIIIrd Olympiad in Los Angeles, 1984," *Clinical Chemistry* 33 (1987):

319–327; Yesalis, *Anabolic Steroids in Sport and Exercise;* and R. Aguilera et al., "Improved Method of Detection of Testosterone Abuse by Gas Chromatography/Combusion/Isotope Ratio Mass Spectrometry Analysis of Urinary Steroids," *Journal of Mass Spectrometry* 31 (1996): 169–176.

111   *especially because of their psychiatric effects:* For a review, see Pope and Katz, "Psychiatric Effects of Exogenous Anabolic-Androgenic Steroids."

112   *we published the first reported case series:* H. G. Pope, Jr., and D. L. Katz, "Bodybuilder's Psychosis," *Lancet* 1 (1987): 863. A more detailed discussion of these findings appears in Pope and Katz, "Affective and Psychotic Symptoms Associated with Anabolic Steroid Use."

112   *One of our first cases was a man:* For a description of several cases of steroid-induced violence, see H. G. Pope, Jr., and D. L. Katz, "Homicide and Near-Homicide by Anabolic Steroid Users," *Journal of Clinical Psychiatry* 51 (1990): 28–31. See also: *State v. Woolstrum,* no. A39981, Court of Appeals of Oregon, 83 Ore. App. 274.730 P. 2d627; 1986 Ore. App. Lexis 4543, Dec. 29, 1986, filed; *State v. Woolstrum,* no. S33670, Supreme Court of Oregon, 303 Ore. 332; 736 P. 2d 566; 1987 Ore. Lexis 1457, Apr. 28, 1987, filed; *Woolstrum v. Oregon State Board of Parole,* no. 88–5116, Supreme Court of the United States, 488 U.S. 861; 109 S. Ct. 157; 1988 U.S. Lexis 3520, 102 L.Ed. 2d 128; 57 U.S.L.W. 3234.

113   *In another case:* B. Lefavi, "Cops on 'Roids," *Muscular Development,* July 1998, p. 144.

113   *One of the most sensational:* For a description of this case, see H. G. Pope, Jr., et al., "Anabolic-Androgenic Steroid Use Among 133 Prisoners," *Comprehensive Psychiatry* 37 (1996): 322–327; A. Reid, "Use of Steroids Seen as Defense Focus in Beverly Slaying Trial," *Boston Globe,* October 12, 1992, Metro/Region, p. 17; A. Reid, "Specialist Tells Jury of Effects of Steroid," *Boston Globe,* October 21, 1992, Metro/Region, p. 31; A. Reid, "Fuller Is Guilty of Murder: Carnevale's Killer Gets Life, No Parole," *Boston Globe,* October 24, 1992, Metro/Region, p. 1.

114   *In more than a dozen studies:* See review in Pope and Katz, "Psychiatric Effects of Exogenous Anabolic-Androgenic Steroids."

114   *In four of the studies:* These are T-P. Su et al., "Neuropsychiatric Effects of Anabolic Steroids in Male Normal Volunteers," *JAMA* 269 (1993): 2760-2764; W. R. Yates et al., "Psychosexual Effects of Three Doses of Testosterone in Cycling and Normal Men," *Biological Psychiatry,* 45 (1999): 254–260; R. Tricker et al., "The Effect of Supraphysiological Doses of Testosterone on Angry Behavior in Healthy Eugonadal Men," *Journal of Clinical Endocrinology and Metabolism* 81 (1996): 3754–3758; and H. G. Pope, Jr., E. M. Kouri, and J. I. Hudson, "The Effects of Supraphysiologic Doses of Testosterone on Mood and Aggression in Normal Men," *Archives of General Psychiatry,* 57 (2000): 133–140.

117   *depressive reactions while coming off steroids:* See review in Pope and Katz, "Psychiatric Effects of Exogenous Anabolic-Androgenic Steroids"; and K. J. Brower et al., "Anabolic Androgenic Steroids and Suicide," *American Journal of Psychiatry* 146 (1989): 1075; S. Allnut and G. Chaimowitz, "Anabolic

Steroid Withdrawal Depression: A Case Report," *Canadian Journal of Psychiatry* 39 (1994): 317–318; G. Elofson and S. Elofson, "Steroids Claimed Our Son's Life," *Physician and Sportsmedicine* 18 (1990): 15–16; H. G. Pope, Jr.: "Anabolic-Andogenic Steroid Use and Suicide," *Physician and Sportsmedicine* 18 (1990): 16; I. Thiblin, B. Runeson, J. Rajs, "Anabolic-Androgenic Steroids and Suicide," *Journal of Clinical Psychiatry* 11 (1999): 223–231.

117   *in one study in Ohio:* D. A. Malone, Jr., et al., "Psychiatric Effects and Psychoactive Substance Use in Anabolic-Androgenic Steroid Users," *Clinical Journal of Sports Medicine* 5 (1995): 25–31.

117   *provoke a syndrome of dependence on steroids:* See, for example, K. B. Kashkin and H. D. Kleber, "Hooked on Hormones? An Anabolic Steroid Addiction Hypothesis," *JAMA* 262 (1989): 3166–3170; K. J. Brower et al., "Anabolic-Androgenic Steroid Dependence," *Journal of Clinical Psychiatry* 50 (1989): 31–33; K. J. Brower, "Addictive Potential of Anabolic Steroids," *Psychiatric Annals* 22 (1992): 30–34; and K. J. Brower, "Withdrawal from Anabolic Steroids," *Current Therapy in Endocrinology and Metabolism* 6 (1997): 338.

118   *Steroids can also drastically alter the ratio:* See, among many studies, J. W. M. Lenders et al., "Deleterious Effects of Anabolic Steroids on Serum Lipoproteins, Blood Pressure, and Liver Function in Amateur Bodybuilders," *International Journal of Sports Medicine* 9 (1988): 19–23; G. Glazer, "Atherogenic Effects of Anabolic Steroids on Serum Lipid Levels," *Archives of Internal Medicine* 151 (1991): 1925–1933; and Kouri et al., "Changes in Lipoprotein-Lipid Levels in Normal Men Following Administration of Increasing Doses of Testosterone Cypionate," *Clinical Journal of Sports Medicine* 6 (1996): 152–157.

118   *We already know of two reports in the medical literature:* J. T. Roberts and D. M. Essenhigh, "Adenocarcinoma of Prostate in 40-Year-Old Bodybuilder," *Lancet* 2 (1986): 742; and G. L. Larkin, "Carcinoma of the Prostate," *New England Journal of Medicine* 324 (1991): 1892.

119   *In the gym, the most popular:* A. J. McBride, K. Williamson, and T. Petersen, "Three Cases of Nalbuphine Hydrochloride Dependence Associated with Anabolic Steroid Abuse," *British Journal of Sports Medicine* 30 (1996): 69–70; J. D. Wines, Jr., et al., "Nalbuphine Hydrochloride Dependence in Anabolic Steroid Users," *The American Journal on Addictions* 8 (1999): 161–164.

120   *Medical complications of ephedrine:* A. M. Whitehouse and J. M. Duncan, "Ephedrine Psychosis Rediscovered," *British Journal of Psychiatry* 150 (1987): 258–261; A. Bruno, K. B. Nolte, and J. Chapin, "Stroke Associated with Ephedrine Use," *Neurology* 43 (1993): 1313–1316; A. J. Gruber and H. G. Pope, Jr., "Ephedrine Abuse Among 36 Female Weightlifters," *The American Journal on Addictions* 7 (1998): 256–261.

120   *the Food and Drug Administration has recently:* Centers for Disease Control and Prevention, "Adverse Events Associated with Ephedrine-Containing Products—Texas, December 1993–September 1995," *Morbidity and Mortal-*

ity Weekly Report 45 (1996): 689–693; Food and Drug Administration, *Dietary Supplements Containing Ephedrine Alkaloids,* Document no. 21, CFR, Part III. (Washington DC: United States Department of Health and Human Services, June 4, 1997.)

120 *over-the-counter drugs, like pseudoephedrine:* See T. D. Noakes and H. Gillies, "Drugs in Sport," *South African Medical Journal* 84 (1994): 364; G. I. Wadler and B. Hainline, "Phenylpropanolamine, Ephedrine, and the 'Look-Alikes,'" in *Drugs and the Athlete* (Philadelphia: F. A. Davis, 1989), 101–106; S. L. Nightingale, "From the Food and Drug Administration," *JAMA* 275 (1996): 1534.

120 *amphetamine and methamphetamine:* V. G. Laties and B. Weiss, "The Amphetamine Margin in Sports," *Federation Proceedings* 40 (1981): 2689–2692; G. I. Wadler and B. Hainline, "Amphetamine," in *Drugs and the Athlete* (Philadelphia: F. A. Davis, 1989): 75–86. C. R. Lake and R. S. Quirk, "CNS Stimulants and the Look-alike Drugs." *Psychiatric Clinics of North America* 7 (1984): 689–701; M. S. Miller, R. B. Millman, and M. S. Gold, "Amphetamines: Pharmacology, Abuse, and Addiction," *Advances in Alcohol and Substance Abuse* 8 (1989): 53–69.

120 *Then there are thyroid hormones:* See for example D. Duchaine, *Underground Body Opus: Militant Weight Loss & Recomposition* (Carson City, NV: XIPE Press, 1996); P. Grunding and M. Bachmann, *World Anabolic Review 1996* (Houston, TX: MB Muscle Books, 1995).

120 *Clenbuterol, a drug used largely for veterinary purposes:* C. T. Elliott, et al., "Monitoring for Clenbuterol Abuse in Northern Ireland, 1989–1994," *Veterinary Quarterly* 18 (June 1996): 41–44; editorial, "Muscling in on Clenbuterol," *Lancet* 340 (1992): 1165; H. Perry, "Clenbuterol: A Medal in Tablet Form?" (letter), *British Journal of Sports Medicine,* June 1993, 141; F. T. Delbeke, N. Desmet, and M. Debackere, "The Abuse of Doping Agents in Competing Bodybuilders in Flanders (1988–1993)," *International Journal of Sports Medicine* 16 (1995): 66–70; I. D. Prather et al., "Clenbuterol: A Substitute for Anabolic Steroids?" *Medicine and Science in Sports and Exercise* 27 (1995): 1118–1121.

120 *Another potentially nasty category:* S. M. Kleiner, T. I. Bazzarre, and M. D. Litchford, "Metabolic Profiles, Diet and Health Practices of Championship Male and Female Bodybuilders," *Journal of the American Dietetic Association* 90 (1990): 962–967; J. F. Hickson et al., "Nutrition and Prospect Preparations of Male Bodybuilders," *Journal of the American Dietetic Association* 90 (1990): 264–267; M. Appleby, M. Fisher, and M. Martin, "Myocardial Infarction, Hyperkalemia and Ventricular Tachycardia in a Young Male Bodybuilder," *International Journal of Cardiology* 44 (1994): 171–174; P. Croyle, R. Place, and A. Hilgenberg, "Massive Pulmonary Embolism in a High School Wrestler," *JAMA* 241 (1979): 827–828; T. Al-Zaki and J. Talbot-Stern, "A Bodybuilder with Diuretic Abuse Presenting with Symptomatic Hypotension and Hyperkalemia," *American Journal of Emergency Medicine* 14 (1996): 96–98.

122 *education seems like an obvious technique:* The most successful steroid education program to be reported is the ATLAS program. See L. Goldberg et al., "Effects of a Multidimensional Anabolic Steroid Prevention Intervention: The Adolescents Training and Learning to Avoid Steroids (ATLAS) Program," *JAMA* 276 (1996): 1555–1562.

123 *One specialized program in Oregon:* L. Goldberg et al., "Anabolic Steroid Education and Adolescents: Do Scare Tactics Work?" *Pediatrics* 87 (1991): 283–286.

123 *But another steroid prevention program:* L. Goldberg et al., "The Adolescents Training and Learning to Avoid Steroids (ATLAS) Prevention Program," *Archives of Pediatrics and Adolescent Medicine* 150 (1996): 713–721.

123 *the Steroid Trafficking Act in January of 1991:* Committee on the Judiciary, United States Senate. Hearings before the Committee on the Judiciary, United States Senate, 101st Congress, 1st Sess., on the steroid abuse problem in America, focusing on the use of steroids in college and professional football today (Washington: U.S. Government Printing Office, 1990); and 101st Congress, *The Steroid Trafficking Act of 1990* (Washington: U.S. Government Printing Office).

Chapter 6   Fear of Fat: Men and Eating Disorders

129 *are generally called "eating disorders":* See diagnostic criteria for the various eating disorders in American Psychatric Association, *Diagnostic and Statistical Manual of Mental Disorders,* 4th ed. (hereafter, DSM-IV), and in Appendix II of this book.

129 *excessive preoccupation with his body:* See H. G. Pope, Jr., and J. I. Hudson, *New Hope for Binge Eaters: Advances in the Understanding and Treatment of Bulimia* (New York: Harper & Row, 1984); and K. A. Halmi, "Eating Disorders," in B. K. Sadock and V. A. Sadock, eds., *Comprehensive Textbook of Psychiatry,* 7th ed. (Philadelphia: Lippincott, Williams & Wilkins: 2000), 1663–1676.

129 *Part of this increase, we think:* M. M. Fichter and C. Daser, "Symptomatology, Psychosocial Development, and Gender Identity in 42 Anorexic Males," *Psychological Medicine* 17 (1987): 409–418.

130 *Earlier statistics:* A. R. Lucas, "50-Year Trends in the Incidence of Anorexia Nervosa in Rochester, Minnesota: A Population-Based Study, *American Journal of Psychiatry* 148 (1991): 917–922.

130 *Imagine our surprise:* Pope and Katz. "Psychiatric and Medical Effects of Anabolic-Androgenic Steroids."

130 *One man from New Hampshire:* Pope et al., "Anorexia Nervosa and 'Reverse Anorexia' Among 108 Male Bodybuilders."

131 *Another man named Geoff:* Ibid.

134 *Bodybuilders and runners:* Ibid.; G. S. Goldfield, D. W. Harper, and A. G. Blouin, "Are Bodybuilders at Higher Risk for an Eating Disorder?" *Eating Disorders* 6 (1998): 133–157; R. E. Anderson et al., "Weight Loss, Psychological, and Nutritional Patterns in Competitive Male Bodybuilders," *International Journal of Eating Disorders* 18 (1995): 49–57.

134 *The National Runner's Survey:* K. D. Brownell, J. Rodin, and J. H. Wilmore, "Eat Drink and Be Worried," *Runner's World,* August 1988, 28–34.

134 *Another study found that male runners:* L. Pasman and J. K. Thompson, "Body Image and Eating Disturbance in Obligatory Runners, Obligatory Weightlifters, and Sedentary Individuals," *International Journal of Eating Disorders* 7 (1988): 759–769.

134 *We recruited twenty-five men:* R. Olivardia et al., "Eating Disorders in College Men," *American Journal of Psychiatry* 152 (1995): 1279–1285.

138 *an almost identical controlled study:* B. Mangweth et al., "Eating Disorders in Austrian Men: An Intracultural and Cross-Cultural Comparison Study," *Psychotherapy and Psychosomatics* 66 (1997): 214–221.

139 *But in the community at large:* A. E. Andersen, "Eating Disorders in Gay Males," *Psychiatric Annals* 29 (1999): 206–212.

140 *is simple uncontrolled binge eating:* DSM-IV.

140 *Paul Garfinkel and his colleagues:* P. E. Garfinkel et al., "Bulimia Nervosa in a Canadian Community Sample: Prevalence, and Comparison of Subgroups," *American Journal of Psychiatry* 152 (1995): 1052–1058.

140 *when we studied an antidepressant:* J. I. Hudson et al., "Fluvoxamine in the Treatment of Binge-Eating Disorder: A Multicenter Placebo-Controlled Double-Blind Trial," *American Journal of Psychiatry* 155 (1998): 1756–1762.

141 *there are other men who are seriously overweight:* See, for example, M. Rothschild, "Depression in Obese Men," *International Journal of Obesity* 13 (1989): 479–485; K. Raikkonen, "Association of Stress and Depression with Regional Fat Distribution in Healthy Middle-Aged Men," *Journal of Behavioral Medicine* 17 (1994): 605–616; R. Rosmond, "Mental Distress, Obesity, and Body Fat Distribution in Middle-Aged Men," *Obesity Resarch* 4 (1996): 245–252. There are also important reviews of this area in many leading textbooks, such as T. A. Wadden and S. T. Bell, "Obesity," in A. E. Kazdin, M. Hersen, and S. Bellack, eds., *International Handbook of Behavior Modification and Therapy* (New York: Plenum Press, 1990), 449–473; and the entire section on obesity in D. J. Goldstein, ed., *The Management of Eating Disorders and Obesity* (Totowa, N.J.: Humana Press, 1999).

141 *it's estimated that up to a third of patients with obesity:* M. Fitzgibbon, M. Stolley, and D. Kirschenbaum, "Obese People Who Seek Treatment Have Different Characteristics Than Those Who Do Not Seek Treatment," *Health Psychology* 12 (1993): 342–345.

144 *we've found few differences:* R. Olivardia and H. G. Pope Jr., "Eating Disorders in Men: Prevalence, Recognition, and Treatment," *Directions in Psychiatry* 17 (1997): 41–51.

145 *the widespread publicity about eating disorders:* S. Reed et al., "Di's Private Battle," *People,* August 3, 1992, 60–70.

148 *"setpoint"—the level of body fat:* For an excellent review of this topic for laypersons, see W. Bennett and J. Gurin, *The Dieter's Dilemma: Eating Less and Weighing More* (New York: Basic Books, 1982).

148 *which actually impedes weight loss:* J. Garrow, "The Regulation of Energy Expenditure," in E. A. Bray, ed., *Recent Advances in Obesity Research,* vol. 2 (London: Newman, 1978); Mishkind et al., "Embodiment of Masculinity."

Chapter 7 Beyond Muscle and Fat: Hair, Breasts, Genitals, and Other Body Obsessions

152 *worry about parts of their bodies:* K. A. Phillips et al., "Body Dysmorphic Disorder: 30 Cases of Imagined Ugliness," *American Journal of Psychiatry* 150 (1993): 302–308. See also K. A. Phillips and S. Diaz, "Gender Differences in Body Dysmorphic Disorder," *Journal of Nervous and Mental Disease* 185 (1997): 570–577. See also G. Perugi et al., "Gender-Related Differences in Body Dysmorphic Disorder (Dysmorphophobia)," *Journal of Nervous and Mental Disease* 185 (1997): 578–582.

152 *shouldn't seem surprising in light of the study results:* Garner, "Body Image Survey."

152 *Probably the biggest secret fear is penis size:* K. A. Phillips, *The Broken Mirror: Understanding and Treating Body Dysmorphic Disorder* (New York: Oxford University Press, 1996). See also Phillips and Diaz, "Gender Differences in Body Dysmorphic Disorder."

153 *serious, full-scale psychiatric condition:* Phillips, "Body Dysmorphic Disorder: The Distress of Imagined Ugliness." See also Phillips, *The Broken Mirror.*

154 *the official diagnostic criteria for BDD:* DSM-IV.

154 *People with BDD suffer:* L. M. DeMarco et al., "Perceived Stress in Body Dysmorphic Disorder," *Journal of Nervous and Mental Disease* 186 (1998): 724–726.

154 *shows the percentage of these men:* These percentages are taken from the largest published series of men with BDD: Phillips and Diaz, "Gender Differences in Body Dysmorphic Disorder."

158 *BDD is as common in men as in women:* Phillips and Diaz, "Gender Differences in Body Dysmorphic Disorder." See also G. Perugi et al., "Gender-Related Differences in Body Dysmorphic Disorder (Dysmorphophobia)"; and E. Hollander, L. J. Cohen, and D. Simeon, "Body Dysmorphic Disorder," *Psychiatric Annals* 23 (1993): 359–364.

158 *affecting an estimated 1 to 2 percent:* Phillips, *The Broken Mirror.*

158 *In one study that looked at this:* J. Ishigooka et al., "Demographic Features of Patients Seeking Cosmetic Surgery," *Psychiatry and Clinical Neuroscience* 52 (1998): 283–287.

158 *we've developed a list:* Adapted from Phillips, *The Broken Mirror.*

160 *Men with severe BDD:* Phillips, "Body Dysmorphic Disorder: The Distress of Imagined Ugliness." See also Phillips, *The Broken Mirror.*

161 *What we've found brings home:* Phillips et al., "Body Dysmorphic Disorder: 30 Cases of Imagined Ugliness." See also Phillips and Diaz, "Gender Differences in Body Dysmorphic Disorder." Some of the data presented has not yet been published.

161 *mental health-related quality of life:* We assessed quality of life using a widely used scale known as the SF-36 (J. E. Ware, Jr., *SF-36 Health Survey Manual*

and Interpretation Guide [Boston: Health Institute, New England Medical Center, 1993]). Mental-health-related quality of life is a measure of (1) mental health, a measure of psychological distress and well-being; (2) role limitations due to emotional problems; and (3) social functioning. These results are reported in K. A. Phillips, "Quality of Life in Body Dysmorphic Disorder," *Journal of Nervous and Mental Disease,* 188 (2000): 170–175.

163 *a recent article in a major news magazine:* J. Stein, "A Man and His Colorist," *Time,* July 19, 1999, 78.

164 *More than 200,000 men receive hair transplants:* See http://cosmeticsurgery-online.com.

166 *Magnum Extension System:* See online http://www.sexmall.com/magnum/printorder.htm.

166 *Extender Penis Enlargement Pump:* See online http://www.skyhorn.com/406/kaplan.html.

166 *Some critics maintain it's an unsafe procedure:* C. Kalb, "Our quest to be perfect," *Newsweek,* August 9, 1999, 52–59.

166 *Although the diagram on page 155 suggests:* Phillips and Diaz, "Gender Differences in Body Dysmorphic Disorder."

167 *patients come to us specifically complaining:* "Gynecomastia" literally means "woman" (from the Greek *gyne*) and "breast" (from the Greek *mastos*).

168 *one out of every six men:* Garner, "Body Image Survey."

169 *men with a more ordinary:* D. I. Perrett et al., "Effects of Sexual Dimorphism on Facial Attractiveness," *Nature* 394 (1998): 884.

169 *Studies have found that as many as one-third:* For studies in cosmetic surgery settings, see D. B. Sarwer et al., "Body Image Concerns of Reconstructive Surgery Patients: An Underrecognized Problem," *Annals of Plastic Surgery* 40 (1998): 403–407. See also D. B. Sarwer et al., "Body Image Dissatisfaction and Body Dysmorphic Disorder in 100 Cosmetic Surgery Patients," *Plastic and Reconstructive Surgery* 101 (1998): 1644–1649. See also Ishigooka et al., "Demographic Features of Patients Seeking Cosmetic Surgery." For studies in dermatology settings, see K. A. Phillips et al., "Prevalence of Body Dysmorphic Disorder in Dermatology Patients," *Journal of the American Academy of Dermatology,* 2000; 42: 436–41.

170 *But countless men, especially those:* J. A. Cotterill and W. J. Cunliffe, "Suicide in Dermatological Patients," *British Journal of Dermatology* 137 (1997): 246–250. See also K. A. Phillips, S. L. McElroy, and J. R. Lion, "Body Dysmorphic Disorder in Cosmetic Surgery Patients (letter), *Plastic and Reconstructive Surgery* 90 (1992): 333–334.

170 *The good news is that most people:* Phillips, *The Broken Mirror.*

170 *the class of medications:* E. Hollander et al., "Clomipramine vs. Desipramine Crossover Trial in Body Dysmorphic Disorder: Selective Efficacy of Serotonin Reuptake Inhibitors in Imagined Ugliness," *Archives of General Psychiatry,* 56(1999): 1033–1039. K. A. Phillips, M. M. Dwight, and S. McElroy, "Efficacy and Safety of Fluvoxamine in Body Dysmorphic Disorder," *Journal of Clinical Psychiatry* 59 (1998): 165–171; Phillips et al., "Body Dysmorphic Disorder: 30 Cases of Imagined Ugliness"; E. Hollander et al., "Fluvoxamine

Treatment of Body Dysmorphic Disorder" (letter), *Journal of Clinical Psychopharmacology* 14 (1994): 75–77; E. Hollander et al., "Treatment of Body-Dysmorphic Disorder with Serotonin Reuptake Blockers," *American Journal of Psychiatry* 146 (1989): 768–770; G. Perugi et al., "Fluvoxamine in the Treatment of Body Dysmorphic Disorder (Dysmorphophobia)," *International Clinical Psychopharmacology* 11 (1996): 247–254.

170   *The other treatment that appears effective:* F. A. Neziroglu and J. A. Yaryura-Tobias, "Exposure, Response Prevention, and Cognitive Therapy in the Treatment of Body Dysmorphic Disorder," *Behavior Therapy* 24 (1993): 431–438; J. C. Rosen, J. Reiter, and P. Orosan, "Cognitive-Behavioral Body Image Therapy for Body Dysmorphic Disorder," *Journal of Consulting and Clinical Psychology* 63 (1995): 263–269; D. Veale et al., "Body Dysmorphic Disorder: A Cognitive Behavioural Model and Pilot Randomized Controlled Trial," *Behaviour Research and Therapeutics* 34 (1996): 717–729; S. Wilhelm et al., "Cognitive Behavior Group Therapy for Body Dysmorphic Disorder: A Case Series," *Behaviour Research and Therapy* 37 (1999): 71–75.

171   *We started Pete on paxil:* The SSRIs currently available in the United States are fluvoxamine (Luvox), fluoxetine (Prozac), paroxetine (Paxil), sertraline (Zoloft), and citalopram (Celexa). Clomipramine (Anafranil), known as an SRI, is very similar to these other medications and also appears effective for BDD.

Chapter 8   Boys at Risk

173   *These are a few quotes from among hundreds on the Internet:* These messages have been posted on http://www.musclenet.com/teenage.htm and on http://www.musclenet.com/steroid.htm.

174   *Previous studies by comparison:* G. H. Cohane and H. G. Pope, Jr., "Body Image in Boys: A Review of the Literature," *International Journal of Eating Disorders,* in press.

176   *Psychologists like William Pollack and Michael Gurian:* W. S. Pollack, *Real Boys: Rescuing Our Sons from the Myths of Boyhood* (New York: Random House, 1998); M. Gurian, *A Fine Young Man: What Parents, Mentors, and Educators Can Do to Shape Adolescent Boys into Exceptional Men* (New York: Jeremy P. Tarcher/Putnam, 1998); M. Gurian, *From Boys to Men: All About Adolescence and You* (New York: Jeremy P. Tarcher, 1999); M. Gurian, *Understanding Guys: A Guide for Teenage Girls* (New York: Price Stern Sloan 1999); M. Gurian, *The Wonder of Boys: What Parents, Mentors, and Educators Can Do to Shape Boys into Exceptional Men* (New York: Putnam, 1996); M. Gurian, *Mothers, Sons, and Lovers: How a Man's Relationship with His Mother Affects the Rest of His Life* (New York: Random House, 1994); M. Gurian, *The Prince and the King: Healing the Father-Son Wound: A Guided Journey of Initiation* (New York: Putnam's Sons, 1992).

176   *In a recent study by researcher Dan Moore:* D. C. Moore, "Body Image and Eating Behavior in Adolescent Boys," *American Journal of Diseases of Children* 144 (1990): 475–479.

177   *in one study done more than thirty years ago:* R. L. Huenemann et al., "A Longitudinal Study of Gross Body Composition and Body Conformation and

Their Association with Food and Activity in a Teenage Population," *American Journal of Clinical Nutrition* 18 (1966): 325–338.

177 *Additional studies from the 1960s:* J. R. Staffieri, "A Study of Social Stereotype of Body Image in Children," *Journal of Personality and Social Psychology* 7 (1967): 101–104; J. Dwyer and J. Mayer, "Psychological Effects of Variations in Physical Appearance During Adolescence," *Adolescence* 3 (1968): 353–380.

177 *In another large study done in 1991:* M. E. Collins, "Body Figure Perceptions and Preferences Among Preadolescent Children," *International Journal of Eating Disorders* 10 (1991): 199–208.

177 *an unusually large study:* R. M. Page and O. Allen, "Adolescent Perceptions of Body Weight and Weight Satisfaction," *Perceptual and Motor Skills* 81 (1995): 81–82.

177 *Another study of 6,500 adolescents:* R. Levinson, B. Powell, and L. C. Steelman, "Social Location, Significant Others, and Body Image Among Adolescents," *Social Psychology Quarterly* 49 (1986): 330–337.

178 *(though not all):* M. Rauste-von Wright, "Body Image Satisfaction in Adolescent Girls and Boys: A Longitudinal Study," *Journal of Youth and Adolescence* 18 (1989): 71–83.

178 *Lori Folk and her colleagues:* L. Folk, J. Pedersen, and S. Cullari, "Body Satisfaction and Self-concept of Third and Sixth Grade Students," *Perceptual and Motor Skills* 76 (1993): 547–553.

178 *Dan Moore has speculated:* Moore, "Body Image and Eating Behavior in Adolescent Boys."

178 *one study found that a majority:* A. M. Gustafson-Larson and R. D. Terry, "Weight-Related Behaviors and Concerns of Fourth-Grade Children," *Journal of the American Dietetic Association* 92 (1992): 818–822.

178 *And in a community study:* J. J. Sternlieb and L. Munan, "A Survey of Health Problems, Practices, and Needs of Youth," *Pediatrics* 49 (1972): 177–186.

178 *Another community-based study:* W. Feldman et al., "Health Concerns and Health Related Behaviours of Adolescents," *Canadian Medical Association Journal* 134 (1986): 489–493.

178 *A survey from the early 1970s:* J. J. Sternlieb and L. Munan, "A Survey of Health Problems, Practices, and Needs of Youth," *Pediatrics* 49 (1972): 177.

178 *one done in the 1980s yielded:* Moore, "Body Image and Eating Behavior in Adolescent Boys."

179 *Folk and her colleagues found:* Folk, Pedersen, and Cullari, "Body Satisfaction and Self-concept of Third and Sixth Grade Students."

179 *Other studies have come out with the same news:* R. M. Lerner et al., "Self-concept, Self-esteem, and Body Attitudes Among Japanese Male and Female Adolescents," *Child Development* 51 (1980): 847–855; M. A. Padin, R. M. Lerner, and A. Spiro, "Stability of Body Attitudes and Self-Esteem in Late Adolescence," *Adolescence* 16 (1981): 371–384.

179 *One study found that:* P. Kenealy et al., "The Importance of the Individual in the 'Causal' Relationship Between Attractiveness and Self-Esteem," *Journal of Community and Applied Social Psychology* 1 (1991): 45–56.

179   *Another study found that boys:* J. Rierdan, E. Koff, and M. L. Stubbs, "Gen-
       der, Depression, and Body Image in Early Adolescence," *Journal of Early Ado-
       lescence* 8 (1988): 109–117.

179   *Researcher Dan Blyth and colleagues:* D. A. Blyth et al., "The Effects of Phys-
       ical Development in Self-Image and Satisfaction with Body Image for Early
       Adolescent Males," *Research in the Community and Mental Health* 2 (1981):
       43–73.

179   *late-maturing boys are less satisfied:* P. D. Duncan et al., "The Function of Pu-
       bertal Timing on Body Image, School Behavior, and Deviance," *Journal of
       Youth and Adolescence* 14 (1985): 227–235; A. C. Petersen, and L. Crockett,
       "Pubertal Timing and Grade Effects on Adjustment," *Journal of Youth and
       Adolescence* 14 (1985): 191–206; Rauste-von Wright, "Body Image Satisfac-
       tion in Adolescent Girls and Boys."

179   *According to one study, feeling good:* S. Harter, "Self and Identity Develop-
       ment," in S. S. Feldman et al., *At the Threshold: The Developing Adolescent*
       (Cambridge: Harvard University Press, 1990), 352–387.

183   *One study of boys as young:* K. Rolland, D. Farnill, and R. A. Griffiths, "Body
       Figure Perceptions and Eating Attitudes Among Australian Schoolchildren
       Aged 8 to 12 Years," *International Journal of Eating Disorders* 2 (1997):
       273–278.

183   *Another found that* 36 percent: M. J. Maloney et al., "Dieting Behaviors and
       Eating Attitudes in Children," *Pediatrics* 84 (1989): 482–489.

183   *And a recent study by Susan Paxton:* S. J. Paxton et al., "Body Image Satis-
       faction, Dieting Beliefs, and Weight Loss Behaviors in Adolescent Girls and
       Boys," *Journal of Youth and Adolescence* 20 (1991): 361–379.

184   *restricted food intake at a young age:* I. Nylander, "The Feeling of Being Fat
       and Dieting in a School Population," *Acta Medica Scandinavica* 214 (1971):
       17–26.

184   *It may also retard growth:* D. Davis et al., "Diet and Retarded Growth,"
       British Medical Journal 1 (1978): 539–542; M. Pugliese et al., "Fear of Obe-
       sity," *New England Journal of Medicine* 309 (1983): 512–518; Gustafson-
       Larson and Terry, "Weight-Related Behaviors and Concerns of Fourth-Grade
       Children."

184   *And dieting during childhood:* I. Nylander, "The Feeling of Being Fat and
       Dieting in a School Population."

184   *In fact, eating disorders in males:* D. J. Carlat, C. A. Camango, and D. B. Her-
       zog, "Eating Disorder in Males: A Report on 135 Patients," *American Journal
       of Psychiatry* 154 (1997): 1127–1132.

184   *Wrestlers are a group of boys:* M. P. Enns, A. Drewnowski, and J. A. Grinker,
       "Body Composition, Body Size Estimation, and Attitudes Towards Eating in
       Male College Athletes," *Psychosomatic Medicine* 49 (1987): 56–64.

184   *although boys who participate:* D. R. Black and M. E. Burckes-Miller, "Male
       and Female College Athletes: Use of Anorexia Nervosa and Bulimia Nervosa
       Weight Loss Methods," *Research Quarterly for Exercise and Sport* 59 (1988):
       252–256.

185   *Charles Tipton and his colleagues:* C. M. Tipton, T. K. Tcheng, and W. D. Paul, "Evaluation of the Hall Method for Determining Minimum Wrestling Weights," *Journal of the Iowa Medical Society* 59 (1969): 571–574.

185   *A more recent study by researchers:* S. Steen and K. D. Brownell, "Patterns of Weight Loss and Regimen in Wrestlers: Has the Tradition Changed?" *Medicine and Science in Sports and Exercise* 22 (1990): 762–768.

185   *These practices can cause:* K. D. Brownell, S. N. Steen, and J. H. Wilmore, "Weight Regulation Practices in Athletes: Analysis of Metabolic and Health Effects," *Medicine and Science in Sports and Exercise* 19 (1987): 546–556; M. E. Houston et al., "The Effect of Rapid Weight Loss on Physiological Function in Wrestlers," *Physician and Sportsmedicine* 3 (1984): 583–593; L. M. Hursh," "Food and Water Restriction in the Wrestler," *JAMA* 241 (1979): 915–916; P. M. Ribisl, "Rapid Weight Reduction in Wrestling," *American Journal of Sports Medicine* 3 (1975): 55–57; S. N. Steen et al., "Metabolic Effects of Repeated Weight Loss and Regain in Adolescent Wrestlers," *JAMA* 260 (1988): 47–50; R. H. Strauss, R. R. Lanese, and W. B. Malarky, "Weight Loss in Amateur Wrestlers and Its Effects on Serum Testosterone Levels," *JAMA* 254 (1985): 3337–3338; C. M. Tipton, "Physiologic Problems Associated with the 'Making of Weight,' " *American Journal of Sports Medicine* 8 (1980): 449–450.

185   *In late 1997, many people were shocked:* See http://thepost.baker.ohiou.edu/archives/011598/wrestlers.html, http://seattle.divein.student.com/article /michiganwrestler, http://espn.sportszone.com/gen/features/weight/Friday.html.

186   *the National Collegiate Athletic Association:* See http://seattle.divein.student.com/article/wrestlingrules and http://205.227.50.68/news/19980119/active/3503n04.html.

186   *the previously mentioned study:* Steen and Brownell, "Patterns of Weight Loss and Regimen in Wrestlers."

186   *Patric Charest has stated that:* http://seattle.divein.student.com/article/wrestlingdeath.

186   *Even Mike Moyer, the chair:* http://www.dailyemerald.com/archive/v100/2/990115/wrestlers.html

186   *A 1998 survey by the National Federation:* http://www.nfhs.org/1998–ten_most_popular_boys_programs.htm

187   *In the study by M. Elizabeth Collins:* Collins, "Body Figure Perceptions and Preferences Among Preadolescent Children."

188   *protein powders and bars:* See, for example, S. Nissen et al., "Effect of Leucine Metabolite Beta-Hydroxy-Beta-Methylbutyrate on Muscle Metabolism During Resistance Exercise Training," *Journal of Applied Physiology* 81 (1996): 2095–2104.

188   *creatine:* P. D. Balsom, K. Söderlund, and B. Ekblom, "Creatine in Humans with Special Reference to Creatine Supplementation," *Sports Medicine* 18 (1994): 268–280; M. S. Juhn and M. Tarnopolsky, "Oral Creatine Supplementation and Athletic Performance: A Critical Review," *Clinical Journal of Sports Medicine* 8 (1998): 286–297; M. S. Juhn and M. Tarnopolsky, "Poten-

tial Side Effects of Oral Creatine Supplementation: A Critical Review," *Clinical Journal of Sports Medicine* 8 (1998): 298–304.

188 *supplements containing ephedrine:* Food and Drug Administration, *Dietary Supplements Containing Ephedrine Alkaloids;* A. J. Gruber, H. G. Pope, Jr., "Ephedrine Abuse Among 36 Female Weightlifters," *American Journal of Addictions* 7 (1998): 256–261.

188 *adrenal hormones such as DHEA:* Life Plus Products, *Product Information Sheet no. 8009: Endocryn DHEA* (Batesville, Ark., 1997); A. J. Morales et al, "Effects of Replacement Dose of Dehydroepiandrosterone in Men and Women of Advancing Age," *Journal of Clinical Endocrinology and Metabolism* 78 (1994): 1360–1367; O. M. Wolkowitz et al., "Dehydroepiandrosterone (DHEA) Treatment of Depression," *Biological Psychiatry* 41 (1997): 311–318; D. S. King et al., "Effect of Oral Androstenedione on Serum Testosterone and Adaptations to Resistance Training in Young Men: A Randomized Controlled Trial," *JAMA* 281 (1999): 2020–2028; C. E. Yesalis, "Medical, Legal, and Societal Implications of Androstenedione Use," *JAMA* 281 (1999): 2043–2044.

191 *Football players, wrestlers, and boys:* J. Radakovich, P. Broderick, and G. Pickell, "Rate of Anabolic Steriod Use Among Students in Junior High School," *Journal of the American Board of Family Practice* 6 (1993): 341–345; M. S. Bahrke, C. E. Yesalis, and K. J. Brower, "Anabolic-Androgenic Steroid Abuse and Performance-Enhancing Drugs Among Adolescents," *Child and Adolescent Psychiatric Clinics of North America* 7 (1998): 821–838.

191 *many boys use these drugs:* Bahrke et al., "Anabolic-Androgenic Steroid Abuse and Performance-Enhancing Drugs Among Adolescents."

191 *decreasing boys' height:* "Creatine and Androstenedione: Two 'Dietary Supplements,'" *Medical Letter on Drugs and Therapeutics* 40 (1998): 105–106.

193 *During one study, we carefully interviewed:* R. S. Albertini and K. A. Phillips, "33 Cases of Body Dysmorphic Disorder in Children and Adolescents," *Journal of the American Academy of Child and Adolescent Psychiatry* 38 (1999): 453–459.

198 *boys who used steroids:* D. Elliot and L. Goldberg. "Intervention and Prevention of Steroid Use in Adolescents," *American Journal of Sports Medicine* 24 (1996): 546–547.

Chapter 9 Dealing with the Adonis Complex: Women's Voices

209 *a study that we did in collaboration:* P. Y. L. Choi, H. G. Pope, Jr., "Violence Towards Women and Illicit Androgenic-Anabolic Steroid Use," *Annals of Clinical Psychiatry* 6 (1994): 21–25.

210 *In March 1991, a British women's magazine:* Take a Break magazine, March 2, 1991.

Chapter 10 Straights and Gays: Not So Different After All

213 *Studies of men in eating disorder clinics:* D. J. Carlat and C. A. Camargo, Jr., "Review of Bulimia Nervosa in Males," *American Journal of Psychiatry* 148

(1991): 831–843; Carlat, Camargo, and. Herzog, "Eating Disorders in Males: A Report on 135 Patients."

213 *But in our two studies:* Olivardia et al., "Eating Disorders in College Men"; Mangweth et al., "Eating Disorders in Austrian Men: An Intracultural and Cross-Cultural Comparison Study," *Psychotherapy Psychosomatics* 66 (1997): 214–221; R. Olivardia and H. G. Pope, Jr., "Eating Disorders in Men: Prevalence, Recognition, and Treatment," *Directions in Psychiatry* 17 (1997): 41–51.

214 *For example, one study of Yale University:* L. R. Silberstein et al., "Men and Their Bodies: A Comparison of Homosexual and Heterosexual Men," *Psychosomatic Medicine* 51 (1989): 337–346.

214 *gay men are more dissatisfied:* M. D. Siever, "Sexual Orientation and Gender as Factors in Socioculturally Acquired Vulnerability to Body Dissatisfaction and Eating Disorders," *Journal of Consulting and Clinical Psychology* 62 (1994): 252–260; S. E. Beren et al., "The Influence of Sexual Orientation on Body Dissatisfaction in Adult Men and Women," *International Journal of Eating Disorders* 20 (1996): 135–141; D. B. Herzog, K. L. Newman, and M. Warshaw, "Body Dissatisfaction in Homosexual and Heterosexual Males," *Journal of Nervous and Mental Disease* 179 (1991): 356–359.

215 *examined attitudes toward body image:* A. Hausmann et al., "Body Image in Gay Men as Assessed by the 'Somatomorphic Matrix,'" presented at the World Congress of Psychiatry, Hamburg, Germany, August 10, 1999.

215 *Although another study using figure drawings:* Silberstein et al., "Men and Their Bodies."

215 *One standard theory is that:* Siever, "Sexual Orientation and Gender as Factors in Socioculturally Acquired Vulnerability to Body Dissatisfaction and Eating Disorders."

215 *For example, gay activist:* M. Signorile, *Life Outside: The Signorile Report on Gay Men: Sex, Drugs, Muscles, and the Passages of Life* (New York: Harper-Collins, 1997).

216 *twenty years ago, a study of body image:* R. E. Prytula, C. D. Wellford, and B. G. DeMonbreun, "Body Self-Image and Homosexuality," *Journal of Clinical Psychology* 35 (1979): 567–572.

217 *and body appearance is more important:* Silberstein et al., "Men and Their Bodies"; Siever, "Sexual Orientation and Gender as Factors in Socioculturally Acquired Vulnerability to Body Dissatisfaction and Eating Disorders."

218 *The AIDS epidemic has particularly heightened:* M. Signorile, *Life Outside.*

218 *Anabolic steroids, especially testosterone injections:* See J. G. Rabkin, R. Rabkin, and G. Wagner, "Testosterone Replacement Therapy in HIV Illness," *General Hospital Psychiatry* 17 (1995): 37–42; S. Grinspoon et al., "Effects of Androgen Administration in Men with the AIDS Wasting Syndrome: A Randomized, Double-Blind, Placebo-Controlled Trial," *Annals of Internal Medicine* 129 (1998): 18–26; A. Strawford et al., "Resistance Exercise and Supraphysiologic Androgen Therapy in Eugonadal Men with HIV-Related Weight Loss: A Randomized Controlled Trial," *JAMA* 281 (1999): 1282–1290.

222 *Some writers have seemed to imply:* Klein, *Little Big Men.*

Chapter 11 Rx for the Adonis Complex: A Guide for Men and Their Loved Ones

226 *Ordinary activities to improve:* K. Dion, E. Berscheid, and E. Walster, "What Is Beautiful Is Good," *Journal of Personality and Social Psychology* 24 (1972): 285–290; E. Berscheid, and E. H. Walster, *Interpersonal Attraction* (Reading, Mass.: Addison-Wesley, 1978).

232 *Cognitive-behavioral therapy, or CBT:* See C. G. Fairburn, "A Cognitive Behavioral Approach to the Management of Bulimia," *Psychological Medicine* 11 (1981): 707–711; W. S. Agras et al., "Nonpharmacological Treatments of Bulimia Nervosa," *Journal of Clinical Psychiatry* 52(Suppl) (1991): 29–33; C. G. Fairburn, M. D. Marcus, and G. T. Wilson, "Cognitive Behavior Therapy for Binge Eating and Bulimia Nervosa: A Comprehensive Treatment Manual," in C. G. Fairburn and G. T. Wilson, eds., *Binge Eating: Nature, Assessment, and Treatment* (New York: Academic Press, 1993); and C. G. Fairburn, *Overcoming Binge Eating* (New York: Guilford Press, 1995).

232 *preliminary data suggest that:* F. Neziroglu et al., "Effect of Cognitive-Behavior Therapy on Persons with BDD and Comorbid Axis II Diagnoses," *Behavior Therapy* 27 (1996): 67–77. J. C. Rosen, J. Reiter, and P. Orosan, "Cognitive/ Behavioral Body Image Therapy for Body Dysmorphic Disorder," *Journal of Consulting and Clinical Psychology* 63 (1995): 263–269.

232 *The basic premise behind CBT:* For reviews, see A. T. Beck, *Cognitive Therapy and the Emotional Disorders* (New York: Meridien, 1976); L. W. Craighead et al., *Cognitive and Behavioral Interventions: An Empirical Approach to Mental Health Problems* (New York: Allyn & Bacon, 1994).

234 *exposure plus response prevention treatment (EPRP):* H. Leitenberg et al., "Exposure Plus Response Prevention Treatment of Bulimia Nervosa," *Journal of Consulting and Clinical Psychology* 56 (1988): 535–541. W. S. Agras et al., "Cognitive-Behavioral and Response Prevention Treatment for Bulimia Nervosa," *Journal of Consulting and Clinical Psychology* 57 (1985): 215–221. J. C. Rosen and H. Leitenberg, "Exposure Plus Response Prevention Treatment of Bulimia Nervosa," in D. M. Garner and P. E. Garfinkel, eds., *Handbook of Therapies for Anorexia Nervosa and Bulimia* (New York: Guilford Press, 1985), 193–209.

235 *certain antidepressant medications:* For reviews, see J. I. Hudson et al., "Pharmacologic Therapy of Bulimia Nervosa"; and K. A. Phillips, "Pharmacologic Treatment of Body Dysmorphic Disorder: A Review of Empirical Data and a Proposed Treatment Algorithm," *Psychiatric Clinics of North America*, 2000; 7: 59–82.

236 *treatment is not always so simple:* Some of these practical issues are discussed in H. G. Pope, Jr., and J. I. Hudson, "Pharmacologic Treatment of Bulimia Nervosa: Research Findings and Practical Suggestions," *Psychiatric Annals* 19 (1989): 483–487; and H. G. Pope, Jr., "Update on the Treatment of Bipolar Depression," *Currents in Affective Illness* 8 (1994): 5–13.

237 *whether or not you are depressed:* J. I. Hudson and H. G. Pope, Jr., "Affective Spectrum Disorder: Does Antidepressant Response Identify a Family of Disorders with a Common Pathophysiology?" *American Journal of Psychiatry* 147 (1990): 552–564; Hudson et al., "Pharmacologic Therapy of Bulimia

Nervosa"; and Phillips, "Pharmacologic Treatment of Body Dysmorphic Disorder."

238 *the function of the brain actually becomes:* L. R. Baxter et al., "Caudate Glucose Metabolic Rate Changes with Both Drug and Behavior Therapy for Obsessive-Compulsive Disorder," *Archives of General Psychiatry* 49 (1992): 681–689.

240 *89 percent of the men in one survey:* Garner, "Body Image Survey."

Index